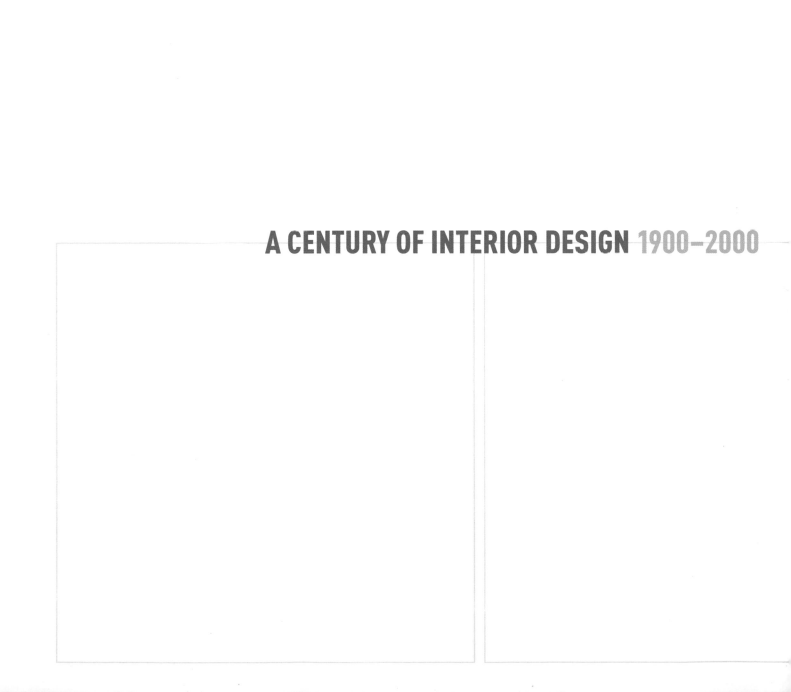

A CENTURY OF INTERIOR DESIGN 1900–2000

A CENTURY OF INTERIOR DESIGN

1900–2000

A TIMETABLE OF THE DESIGN, THE DESIGNERS, THE PRODUCTS, AND THE PROFESSION

BY STANLEY ABERCROMBIE

RIZZOLI
NEW YORK

ACKNOWLEDG- MENTS

Assembling the following chronology has been a process greatly dependent on previous work by others. The primary sources of information have been back issues of *Interiors* magazine (going back, under various titles, to the beginning of the century) and *Interior Design* magazine (going back to its founding in 1932); for access to these back issues, I am grateful to the Avery Architectural Library at Columbia University. I am also grateful for the help of Mayer Rus of *House and Garden* and of Pernille Pedersen of *Interior Design*. Special thanks go to photographer extraordinaire Peter Paige of Upper Saddle River, New Jersey, and to the Hedrich-Blessing photography studio in Chicago. Erica Stoller and her staff at ESTO Photographics, Marmaroneck, New York, have also been very helpful. Other published sources that have been particularly useful include:

Banham, Joanna, ed. *Encyclopedia of Interior Design*. London and Chicago: Fitzroy Dearborn, 1997.
Byars, Mel. *The Design Encyclopedia*. New York: John Wiley & Sons, 1994.
Calloway, Stephen. *Twentieth-Century Decoration*. New York: Rizzoli, 1988.
Ferebee, Ann. *A History of Design from the Victorian Era to the Present*. New York: Van Nostrand Reinhold, 1970.
Grun, Bernard. *The Timetables of History*. New York: Simon & Schuster, 1975.
Gueft, Olga. "The Past as Prologue: ASID from 1931 to 1981, and the Profession Now." In *ASID Professional Practice Manual*, ed. Jo Ann Asher Thompson. New York: Whitney Library of Design, 1992.
Julier, Guy. *The Thames and Hudson Encyclopaedia of Twentieth Century Design and Designers*. London and New York: Thames and Hudson, 1993.
Luckhurst, Kenneth W. *The Story of Exhibitions*. London and New York: The Studio Publications, 1951.
Massey, Anne. *Interior Design of the Twentieth Century*. New York and London: Thames & Hudson, 1990.
Neumann, Claudia. *Design Directory Italy*. New York: Rizzoli, 1999.
Ochoa, George, and Melinda Corey. *The Timeline Book of the Arts*. New York: Ballantine, 1995.
Pevsner, Nikolaus. *Industrial Art in England*. London: Cambridge University Press, 1937.
Pile, John. *The Dictionary of Twentieth-Century Design*. New York: Facts on File, 1990.
Polster, Bernd. *Design Directory Scandinavia*. New York: Rizzoli, 1999.
Sharp, Dennis. *Twentieth-Century Architecture: A Visual History*. New York: Facts on File, 1991.
Sparke, Penny. *An Introduction to Design and Culture in the Twentieth Century*. London: Unwin Hyman, 1986.
Tate, Allen, and C. Ray Smith. *Interior Design in the Twentieth Century*. New York: Harper & Row, 1986.

The author is also grateful to editor Christopher Steighner of Rizzoli; to literary agent Alison Bond; and to graphic designers Paul Carlile, Paul McKevitt, and Alessia Usai of Subtitle.

First published in the United States of America in 2003
by Rizzoli International Publications, Inc.
300 Park Avenue South
New York, NY 10010
www.rizzoliusa.com

2003 2004 2005 2006 2007/ 10 9 8 7 6 5 4 3 2 1

Library of Congress Control Number: 2002115807

Printed in China

Designed by Subtitle

Marcel Breuer's cantilevered
"Cesca" chair from 1928;
Frontispiece: Eliel Saarinen's
interior for the Cranbrook
Academy of Art from 1930

The twentieth century has been a time of unprecedented and unexpected change, particularly in technical and scientific fields. We expect less change in artistic fields, which we often think of as less progressive, less cumulative, and more concerned with enduring values. Yet interior design in 2000 is different from interior design in 1900 to a revolutionary degree.

Aesthetically, interior design entered the century obsessed with past traditions and intrigued by a few current novelties such as the Arts and Crafts movement and the Art Nouveau style, both popular since the 1890s. A quarter century later, interior design—like its tomboy big sister, architecture—was beginning to be transformed by the tenets of modernism, a style that considered itself more than a style: a moral imperative, an instrument of social reform, and a more appropriate way of responding to a newly mechanized world. As the century ended, the moral fervor of modernism had cooled, the charms of tradition had persevered, and no single expression was dominant. Modernism and tradition coexisted and even blended in a way that would earlier have been unthinkable.

PREFACE: A CENTURY SUMMA-RIZED

The profession of interior design changed even more. Near the beginning of the century, as our chronology notes, Elsie de Wolfe could declare herself a professional simply by having some cards engraved, announcing her availability as a designer; there were no standards—and few opportunities—for training of any sort. By the end of the century, there would be professional schools and standards for their accreditation, there would be standardized testing of professional knowledge, there would be state requirements for designer certification, and there would be professional organizations (unfortunately, not a single unified organization) with their own standards for membership.

The practice of interior design changed most of all. For de Wolfe it was largely a matter of exercising taste and talent while being mindful of a few practicalities. Today it is still a matter of taste and talent—interior design remains our most personal, most intimately experienced art form—but it is much more as well. The interior designer at the end of the twentieth century is necessarily a businessperson as well as an artist, and also the master of expert knowledge in building codes, fire and safety codes, environmental issues, ergonomics, space planning, accessibility, and more. Interior design has become a major factor in office and factory productivity, in retail sales, and in hospitality facility profit. It has even become a matter of life and death, acknowledged now to directly affect the health, safety, and welfare of its users.

The following chronology attempts to tell the story of interior design's most eventful century in an incremental manner, by listing some of the steps along the way. The author acknowledges at the outset that the listing here is incomplete; this is the sort of book, after all, that can never be fully finished. Many of the people, projects, and events that a reader most admires may have been omitted. And events of equal importance may be given unequal attention, depending on the amount of competition occurring in any specific year. Some assigning of dates may also be questioned; it is rare that a design proceeds from concept to completion within a single year, and some interiors have been mentioned in the year of their design, others in the year of their occupancy or manufacture. Acknowledging that there is some dispute about when our current century and millennium began, we have tried to please both factions by including both the year 1900 and the year 2000.

Although personal judgments about what has been most interesting have inescapably guided the selections here, an attempt has been made to deny dominance to any particular program. This view of twentieth-century design is not, I hope, another advertisement for modernism, the century's dominant style, and its antecedents. While modernism is, admittedly, my own enthusiasm and is certainly well represented, it is accompanied by many other styles. Indeed, what has been most striking to me in assembling these citations and images is the multiplicity of viewpoints prevailing through the century. The design of the hundred years just past has not been as uniform or consistent as we are sometimes told.

Striking, too, as already noted, are the differences between the design of the century's first years and that of its last. Despite this survey's omissions, it is hoped that enough has been included to suggest the dramatic—though gradual—transformation that has been the reality of interior design in the twentieth century.

Stanley Abercrombie

THE START OF THE CENTURY

As the century opens, two styles born in the 1890s continue to flourish, the flirtatious Art Nouveau and the sober Arts and Crafts. These will not outlast World War I, but in 1901 Frank Lloyd Wright lectures on a topic that will dominate design thinking for the whole century; in "The Art and Craft of the Machine," he speculates on technology's proper expression in the arts. He demonstrates his ideas in the 1904 Larkin building in Buffalo, giving it an early example of mechanically powered ventilation and air treatment and an architectural expression that distinguishes between services and spaces to be served. The 1903 founding of the Wiener Werkstätte in Vienna institutionalizes a more geometric version of Art Nouveau and predates the Art Deco style, but the 1907 founding of the Deutscher Werkbund in Munich prefigures something of more importance, the Bauhaus, which will be established a dozen years later. A small but significant step on the road toward greater professionalism comes in 1905 when Elsie de Wolfe has business cards printed announcing her availability as an interior designer, thus implying that interior design is indeed a business. She takes another step in 1909 when she opens a newly designed New York townhouse to the press, setting the precedent for the decorator show house; the publicity, incidentally, will enable de Wolfe to sell the townhouse for what she calls "an encouraging profit."

Lobby of Antoni Gaudi's Casa Calvet, Barcelona, 1904

ARCHITECTURE

Belgian architect Victor Horta finishes the Hôtel Solvay and a house for Baron van Eetvelde, both in Brussels, both in the Art Nouveau style. The Gare d'Orsay railroad terminal opens in Paris; it will be transformed into a museum by Gae Aulenti in 1987. Also in Paris, Hector Guimard, having recently completed his Castel Béranger, begins work on his series of Métro entrances, bringing Art Nouveau to the masses.

Belgian designer, painter, and architect Henry Van de Velde begins the interiors of the Folkwang Museum in Hagen, Germany. Antoni Gaudí begins the design of the Park Güell, Barcelona, a project that will last until 1914. In Newport, Rhode Island, Ogden Codman, Jr., designs the Villa Rosa and its interiors. McKim, Mead, & White complete the University Club and its interiors in New York.

BOOKS

Hermann Muthesius, superintendent of the Prussian Board of Trade for Schools of Arts and Crafts and attached to the German embassy in London, writes *The Arts and Crafts Movement in England*.

CULTURE AT LARGE

Sir Arthur Evans, excavating in Crete, discovers remains of the Minoan Palace of Knossos. Oscar Wilde and John Ruskin die. Sigmund Freud publishes *The Interpretation of Dreams*. Giacomo Puccini's *Tosca* premieres in Rome. L. Frank Baum writes *The Wizard of Oz*, and Beatrix Potter creates Peter Rabbit.

DESIGNERS AND INSTALLATIONS

C. F. A. Voysey designs interiors for his own house, the Orchard, Chorleywood, Hertfordshire. Joseph Maria Olbrich designs interiors and furniture for his own house at Darmstadt. Ernesto Basile, a key exponent of the Italian Art Nouveau, *Stile floreale*, completes the Grand Hotel Villa Igeia, Palermo, Sicily. Milanese designer Carlo Bugatti supplies furniture for the palace of the Khedive in Istanbul. Richard Norman Shaw designs first-class interiors for the steamship *Oceanic*.

Hendrik Petrus Berlage designs interiors and furnishings for Villa Parkwijk in Amsterdam, and he and others open Het Binnenhuis, a studio and shop for furniture and crafts, also in Amsterdam. In Paris, René Guilleré and other designers conceive the Société des Artistes Décorateurs to foster high standards in the design and production of decorative arts.

Paris exposition glorifies Art Nouveau

The *Paris Exposition Universelle* is the apotheosis of the Art Nouveau style; for the exposition, the Grand Palais and Petit Palais are built, Richard Riemerschmid designs a "Room for an Art Collector," Bruno Paul designs a "Hunting Room," Bernhard Pankok designs a room for the German section, Hector Guimard's designs for Sèvres porcelain are shown, Émile Gallé receives top awards for his glassware and furniture designs, designer Carlo Bugatti receives a Silver Medal, Siegfried Bing shows six "rooms beautiful," Frédéric-Henri

Sauvage designs a pavilion for the dancer Loie Fuller, and many of the 39 million visitors travel on a moving sidewalk (*trottoir roulant*). The *Wiener Sezession* (Vienna Secession) exhibition shows the work of Josef Hoffmann, Henry Van de Velde, C. R. Ashbee, and Charles Rennie Mackintosh. Mackintosh marries Margaret Macdonald, who will be his constant collaborator. The Wallace Collection opens in London.

Louis Majorelle designs a walnut armchair with tooled leather upholstery in the Art Nouveau style. Louis Comfort Tiffany designs a mosaic mural and a glass dome for the Chicago Public Library, as well as the "Dragonfly" electric lamp with a colored glass shade. A mahogany armchair designed by Richard Riemerschmid for his Paris exposition room will be manufactured by Dunbar beginning in 1950. Achille Brunschwig establishes a tapestry-weaving mill in Aubusson, France, which will evolve into the Brunschwig & Fils fabric company.

The Commonwealth of Australia is created.

As the century opens, the United States has only one serious magazine devoted to interior design, *The Upholsterer*, founded in 1888; it will later become *Interiors*. One earlier magazine, *Decorator and Furnisher*, founded in 1882, had ceased publication in 1898. The architecture magazines *Architectural Forum* and *Architectural Record* had both been founded in the last decade of the nineteenth century, as had *House Beautiful* and the English magazine *Country Life*.

Radon is discovered, and Max Planck formulates the "quantum theory" of indivisible units of energy. The century of steam ends, and the century of electricity begins.

1900

From left to right:

H. P. Berlage: Villa Parkwijk, Amsterdam

Miss Cranston's Ingram Street Tea Room, Glasgow, by Charles Rennie Mackintosh

Fruitwood marquetry vitrine by Émile Gallé

The library of McKim, Mead, & White's University Club, New York

Frank Lloyd Wright lectures at Hull House, Chicago; his subject is "The Art and Craft of the Machine." Peter Behrens designs a house for himself in Darmstadt, Germany. Edwin Lutyens designs Homewood, a house for his mother-in-law, at Knebworth, Hertfordshire. Josef Hoffmann designs a house and interiors for painter and decorative artist Koloman Moser in Vienna; Moser himself designs the furnishings.

Hermann Muthesius writes *Baillie Scott: London* on the architecture and interior design of M. H. Baillie Scott. Another English designer, C. R. Ashbee, writes *An Endeavor towards the Teaching of John Ruskin and William Morris*; an edition of 350 copies is printed with woodcuts by George Thompson. Edith Wharton and Ogden Codman, Jr.'s 1897 *The Decoration of Houses* is reprinted.

Pablo Picasso begins his "blue period." Charles Munch paints *Girls on the Bridge*. Giuseppe Verdi dies. Ragtime jazz is heard.

The Victorian era ends: "Get this tomb cleaned up!"

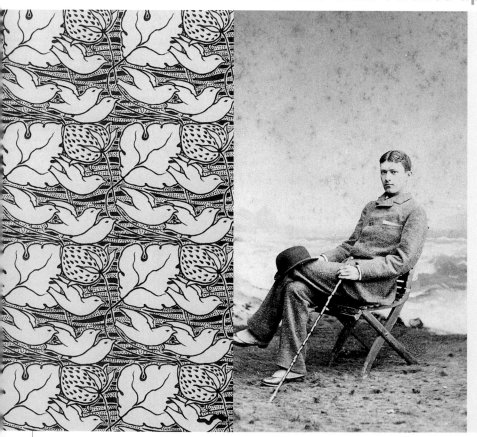

Victor Horta designs the À l'Innovation department store in Brussels. Paris architect Frédéric-Henri Sauvage, having recently completed the rue Royale shop for the House of Jansen decorating studio, completes the Villa Majorelle in Nancy. T. E. Corbett designs the General Committee Room for Lloyd's Register of Shipping, London. Henry Van de Velde designs Hoby's barbershop in Berlin. Carlo Bugatti designs an interior for Cyril Flowers, the first Lord Battersea, in London. After the death of his mother Queen Victoria, Edward VII asks London decorator Sir Charles Carrick Allom to refurbish Buckingham Palace, saying "Get this tomb cleaned up!"

At the Buffalo *Pan-American Exposition*, gold medals go to furniture designer Gustav Stickley and ceramicist William Grueby.

Antoni Gaudí designs an armchair for his Casa Calvet in Barcelona. Josef Hoffmann designs a desk lamp for Woka. Elbert Hubbard's Roycroft company in East Aurora, New York, begins its manufacture of Arts and Crafts furniture. The J. Stroheim fabric company, founded in 1865, changes its name to Stroheim & Romann and moves to new quarters on East 19th Street in New York, near the stores of B. Altman and W. & J. Sloane.

President William McKinley, visiting the Buffalo exposition, is assassinated, and Theodore Roosevelt becomes president.

House and Garden begins publication, with Wilson Eyre as its first editor. *Connoisseur* is also begun. Gustav Stickley's *The Craftsman* begins publication, supporting the American Arts and Crafts movement. In Vienna, *Das Interieur* is founded; for fifteen years it will publish interiors and decorative art in the Art Nouveau style.

Ransome Olds begins the mass production of automobiles; Guglielmo Marconi invents the radio. The safety razor and instant coffee become available.

1901

From left to right:

C. F. A. Voysey's "Merle" wallpaper design

Ogden Codman, Jr.

Charles Rennie Mackintosh's high-backed chair for Windyhill, Kilmacolm, stained oak with rush seat

The Paneled Room, Ogden Codman, Jr., house, Lincoln, Massachusetts

Liqueur glass with a gold band designed by Peter Behrens

ARCHITECTURE

Frank Lloyd Wright designs the Ward Willits house in Highland Park, Illinois. Gustav Stickley designs his own house in Syracuse, New York. Edwin Lutyens designs Deanery Garden, Berkshire, a house for Edward Hudson, the founder of *Country Life* magazine. Babb, Cook, & Willard design a New York mansion for Andrew Carnegie; it will become the Cooper-Hewitt Museum in 1976.

BOOKS

Carl Larsson's *At the Larssons* shows idyllic pictures of residential interiors in Sweden.

CULTURE AT LARGE

Horn & Hardart introduce the Automat. Joseph Conrad writes *Heart of Darkness*; in 1979 it will be the model for Francis Ford Coppola's Vietnam War film *Apocalypse Now*. President Theodore Roosevelt reinforces his reputation for adventurousness by riding in an automobile.

DESIGNERS AND INSTALLATIONS

Hector Guimard's Humbert de Romans concert hall in Paris has an interior with elaborate Art Nouveau cast-iron work. Ernesto Basile begins a long series of additions and renovations for the Palazzo Montecitorio (now the Parliament building) in Rome. In contrast to the flourishes of Art Nouveau, groups such as the Dresden Workshops for Arts and Crafts are returning to the ideals of William Morris and C. R. Ashbee to promote a simple, utilitarian style. Arthur Joseph Gaskin, formerly with Morris's Kelmscott Press, becomes principal of the Birmingham (England) School of Design. Josef Hoffmann designs interiors for the Max Biach house, Vienna. Henry Van de Velde, working in Berlin, moves to Weimar, where he will establish a new School for Arts and Crafts.

EXHIBITIONS

Turin's International Exposition of Decorative Arts marks the peak of accomplishment in the *Stile floreale* movement, Italy's version of the Art Nouveau movement; Louis Comfort Tiffany wins the fair's grand prize for his lily-cluster glass lamp; and Ernesto Basile's furniture for the Ducrot Company is displayed under the name Basile-Ducrot. Peter Behrens contributes the cryptlike *Hamburger Vestibühl*, said to be inspired by Nietzsche's *Also Sprach Zarathustra*; Victor Horta designs the Belgian Pavilion; and Charles Rennie Mackintosh designs the Scottish section. The star of the exposition, however, is Carlo Bugatti, who

has his own distinct style; he shows four rooms, including the "Camera del Bovolo" ("Snail Room"), eccentrically furnished with his own furniture designs and finished in wood veneers, pewter, and red- and gold-painted vellum; Bugatti's son Ettore will later become known as a designer of racing cars. A Budapest exhibition of British decorative art shows work by M. H. Baillie Scott and Charles Rennie Mackintosh. *Architecture and Design of the New Style* is seen in Moscow; it also includes a room setting by Mackintosh.

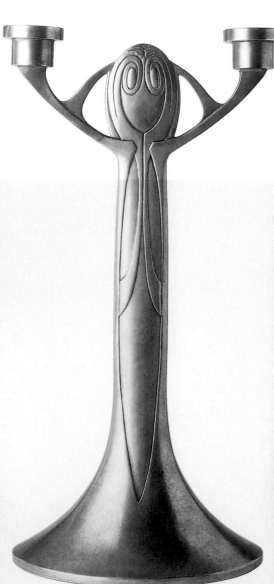

Otto Wagner designs bent-wood armchairs for the monumental banking hall of his Austrian Postal Savings Bank in Vienna. In Germany, Richard Riemerschmid, whose earlier furniture has been in the neo-Gothic style, designs some plainer pieces for the Dresden Workshops, which had been founded by his brother-in-law, Karl Schmidt. In Venice, painter, etcher, and photographer Mariano Fortuny invents a system of naturalistically diffused lighting based on reflecting light from a fabric dome; his lamp design will be reproduced by Écart International beginning in 1979. Another lighting design of the year is a ceiling fixture by English designer W. A. S. Benson.

Charles P. Limbert establishes the Holland Dutch Arts and Crafts furniture company in Holland, Michigan; its designs are inspired by those of Charles Rennie Mackintosh.

The Boer War is ended, and an Anglo-Japanese alliance is formed.

In Italy, *Il Leonardo* and *Il Regno* are founded to promote Futurist art and design.

The American Section of the International Association for Testing Materials, founded in 1898, is reorganized as the American Society for Testing Materials (ASTM); Dr. Charles Dudley is its first president.

The Aswan dam is opened. The ionosphere is discovered.

1902

McKim, Mead, & White lead "American Renaissance"

From left to right:

Pewter candlestick by Joseph Maria Olbrich

McKim, Mead, & White's banking hall for the Bowery Bank, New York

Furniture display at the W. & J. Sloane store, New York

Deanery Garden, Berkshire, by Edwin Lutyens

ARCHITECTURE

Antoni Gaudí's Sagrada Familia cathedral is begun in Barcelona; at the century's end, it will remain unfinished. The Stock Exchange (Beurs) in Amsterdam is designed by Hendrik Petrus Berlage, including its interiors and furniture. Auguste Perret designs a reinforced-concrete apartment block at 25b rue Franklin, Paris. Cass Gilbert's competition-winning design for the Minnesota State Capitol is built, and his U.S. Custom House at the tip of Manhattan is under construction. McKim, Mead, & White begin the design of ten buildings for Columbia University, New York, and add office wings to the White House. Paul Philippe Cret designs the Pan-American Union Building in Washington, D.C. Frank Lloyd Wright designs the Dana house, in Springfield, Illinois. Eliel Saarinen, with Herman Gesellius and Armas Lindgren, designs his own housing complex, Hvittrask, near Helsinki.

BOOKS

Textile and wallpaper designer Candace Thurber Wheeler writes *Principles of Home Decoration with Practical Examples*; even closets and basements, she says, should "share in the thought which makes the genuinely beautiful home and the genuinely perfect life." Thomas Arthur Strange writes *An Historical Guide to French Interiors, Furniture, and Decoration.*

CULTURE AT LARGE

Henry James writes *The Ambassadors*; Giuseppe Verdi's *Ernani* is the first opera to be recorded.

DESIGNERS AND INSTALLATIONS

McKim, Mead, & White redesign the interiors of the public rooms of the White House in an opulent Federal style. Edith Wharton and architect Ogden Codman, Jr., design interiors for Wharton's New York house on Park Avenue. The Dresden Workshops designs interiors for the Saxon State Assembly Building in Dresden; they include furniture by Richard Riemerschmid. Edwin Lutyens designs interiors for Little Thakeham, Sussex. Ernesto Basile designs interiors of the Villino Basile, Palermo.

Mackintosh gives Art Nouveau a personal tweak

Victor Horta designs buildings and interiors for the Max Hallet house, Brussels, and for the Grand Bazaar department store, Frankfurt. *The Wiener Werkstätte*, the commercial arm of the Vienna *Sezession* movement, is founded by Josef Hoffmann, Kolomon ("Kolo") Moser, and others and is supported by architect Otto Wagner and painter Gustav Klimt; other branches will be formed in Munich, Dresden, and elsewhere, and the organization will be active until disbanded in 1932.

For the Vienna *Hagenbund* exhibition, Joseph Urban designs room settings and furniture, including mahogany chairs inlaid with silver and others inlaid with mother-of-pearl and with aluminum legs. For the Venice International Exhibition, Ernesto Basile designs the Naples and Sicily Pavilion. The *École de Nancy* exhibition in Paris shows the work of Louis Majorelle, Émile Gallé, the Daum brothers, and others.

Henry Van de Velde designs an upholstered side chair for the Nietzsche Archives in Weimar. Frederick Carder, having emigrated to the United States from England in 1900, founds Steuben Glass in Corning, New York.

Vladimir I. Lenin heads the first Soviet government.

The magazine *Art Amateur: Devoted to Art in the Household*, established in 1879, ceases publication. The Austrian Art Nouveau journal *Ver sacrum*, begun in 1898, also ceases. *Burlington Magazine* is founded in England.

The Wright brothers fly. Bertrand Russell publishes his *Principles of Mathematics*.

1903

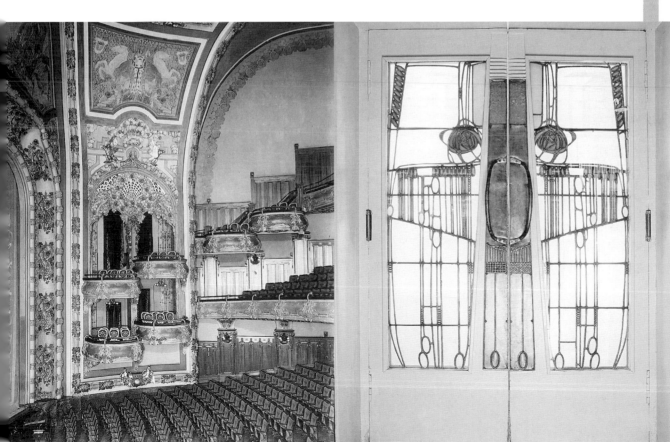

From left to right:

The State Dining Room of the White House, Washington, D.C., as redesigned by McKim, Mead, & White for President William McKinley

Cutlery and dinner plate designed by Henry Van de Velde

Ogden Codman, Jr., parlor for the future novelist Edith Wharton at 884 Park Avenue, New York

Frank Lloyd Wright's "light screen" for a window of the Dana house, Springfield, Illinois

New Amsterdam Theater, New York, by Herts & Tallant

Doors to the Salon de Luxe, Willow Tea Rooms, Glasgow, by Charles Rennie Mackintosh

Frank Lloyd Wright's Larkin Administration Building is finished in Buffalo, New York, its interior among the first to have a rudimentary air-conditioning system; its Wright-designed metal furniture is manufactured by Van Dorn Iron Works of Cleveland. Otto Wagner designs St. Leopold's church in Vienna with stained-glass windows by Koloman Moser. Louis Sullivan's Schlesinger-Meyer department store opens on State Street in Chicago; it will later become Carson, Pirie, Scott.

Percy Macquoid begins writing *A History of English Furniture*; the first volume is *The Age of Oak, 1500–1660*. Hermann Muthesius begins to explain English design to his fellow Germans in his three-volume *Das englische Haus*; the complete work will be revised by Dennis Sharp and published in 1979 as *The English House*. Arts and Crafts poet and philosopher Charles Keeler writes *The Simple House*. Edith Wharton writes *Italian Villas and Their Gardens*; it is illustrated by Maxfield Parrish.

Henry James writes *The Golden Bowl*; Giacomo Puccini's *Madama Butterfly* opens in Milan; Auguste Rodin models *The Thinker*; on the stage are James M. Barrie's *Peter Pan* and Anton Chekhov's *The Cherry Orchard*.

Frank Lloyd Wright devises air-conditioning

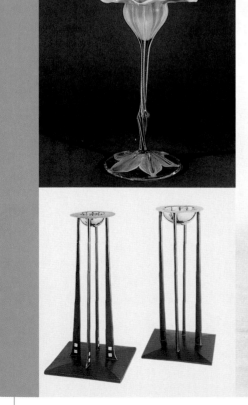

DESIGNERS AND INSTALLATIONS

Charles Rennie Mackintosh and Margaret Macdonald Mackintosh design interiors and furniture for the Willow Tea Rooms in Glasgow and for nearby Hill House. Carlo Bugatti moves from Milan to Paris; although his furniture will continue to be produced by De Vecchi of Milan, he will now devote himself to painting and designs in silver. John Paul Cooper becomes head of the metalwork department of the Birmingham School of Design. French glass designer Émile Gallé dies at fifty-eight, but the work of his studio will continue until 1931. Silversmith Georg Jensen opens a shop in Copenhagen. In Paris, Siegfried Bing sells his shop/studio Le Salon de l'Art Nouveau.

EXHIBITIONS

The Louisiana Purchase International Exhibition is held in St. Louis, its displays including a music room designed by Bernhard Pankok. Tiffany exhibits its Favrile glass and Charles Rohlfs and Gustav Stickley their Arts and Crafts furniture; Joseph Urban wins a gold medal for his interiors of the Austrian Pavilion; over 150 examples of "horseless carriages" are displayed, a dirigible is flown, and wireless telegraphy is demonstrated. For an exhibition in Düsseldorf, Peter Behrens designs the Jungbrunnen restaurant.

FURNITURE AND FURNISHINGS

Frank Lloyd Wright designs a side chair with a dominant back splat and uses it in both the Larkin building and in his own house in Oak Park, Illinois.

GOVERNMENT EVENTS

Theodore Roosevelt is elected U.S. president.

MAGAZINES

Art Interchange: A Household Journal, established in 1878, ceases publication. *Heating and Ventilating* magazine is founded.

TECHNICAL AND SCIENTIFIC ADVANCES

The photoelectric cell is developed. The cylindrical phonograph record is replaced by the flat disk. Trowbridge and Livingston's St. Regis Hotel, New York, provides individual temperature controls in each guest room.

1904

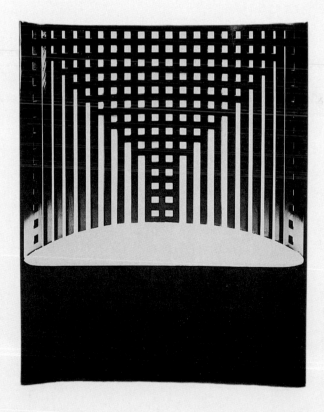

From left to right:

Floriform Favrile glass vase by Louis Comfort Tiffany

Charles Rennie Mackintosh's ebonized wood and silver candlesticks for Hill House near Glasgow

Painted steel chair with an oak seat by Frank Lloyd Wright for the Larkin Administration Building, Buffalo, New York

Cover by A. Cossard for the magazine *Art et décoration*

Slant-back chair designed by Frank Lloyd Wright for his own house in Oak Park, Illinois

Curved-back chair designed by Charles Rennie Mackintosh for the Willow Tea Rooms, Glasgow, Scotland

Four villas designed by Josef Hoffmann are built in a suburb of Vienna, and his Purkersdorf Sanitorium is finished, also near Vienna. In Buckinghamshire, C. F. A. Voysey designs Burke house, Hollymount—the house, its interiors, and its furniture—and also Broadleys in the Lake District.

Percy Macquoid writes volume two of his history of English furniture, *The Age of Walnut, 1660–1720*. Swedish artist Carl Larsson shows further domestic interior scenes in his *Rural Legacy*. Walter Crane writes *Ideals in Art*.

Edith Wharton writes *The House of Mirth*. Franz Lehár's *The Merry Widow* and Richard Strauss's *Salomé* are produced. Jean Galatoire opens a restaurant in New Orleans. Pablo Picasso, arrived in Paris, begins his "pink period," and Henri Matisse paints *Luxe, Calme et Volupté*.

In New York, Elsie de Wolfe, recently retired from the theater, has business cards engraved; they show a wolf bearing a rose in its mouth, and they announce to potential clients de Wolfe's availability as a designer; some will later interpret this as the first step in the foundation of the interior design profession. Her cards at the ready, de Wolfe begins the design of interiors for the Colony Club, a New York club for women in a building designed by Stanford White at Madison Avenue and 30th Street; she will install trelliswork in some rooms for an indoor/outdoor effect. She also buys the Villa Trianon at Versailles, a house she will spend the next forty-five years decorating for herself. In London, Sir

Edwin Lutyens designs interiors for the offices of *Country Life* magazine. In Berlin, Josef Hoffmann and Koloman Moser design interiors and furniture for the Stoneborough apartment, and Peter Behrens designs the world's first corporate identity program for the German electric conglomerate AEG. In Oyster Bay, New York, Louis Comfort Tiffany is at work on the interiors and windows of his country estate, Laurelton Hall; it will be destroyed in 1957.

Elsie de Wolfe a self-proclaimed interior designer

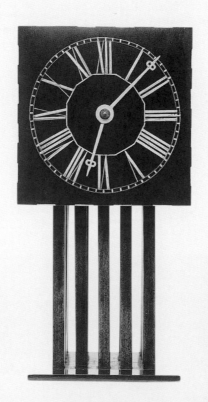

For an exhibition at Letchworth, England, M. H. Baillie Scott designs a pair of cottages.

Josef Hoffmann designs the "Sitzmachine" and "Egg Rocking" chairs. In Dresden, Richard Riemerschmid designs a range of machine-made furniture in pine and smoked oak with black iron fittings. In Zeeland, Michigan, the Star Furniture Co. is founded, its best-seller being the "Princess" dresser; in 1909 it will change its name to Michigan Star, and in 1923 it will be renamed the Herman Miller Furniture Co. Edwin Lutyens designs a set of twenty-one chairs for the boardroom of *Country Life* magazine.

Workers' uprisings begin in Russia.

The English magazine *Cabinet-Maker and Art Furnisher*, founded in 1881, ceases publication. *Form* is founded in Sweden.

Albert Einstein formulates the photon theory of light and the Special Theory of Relativity. Viscose rayon yarn is commercially manufactured. Safety glass is patented.

1905

From left to right:

Thirteen-branch candelabrum designed by Bruno Paul

Josef Hoffmann's armchair design for his Purkersdorf Sanatorium, near Vienna

Clock for a house in Glasgow by Charles Rennie Mackintosh, ebonized oak and sycamore with ivory inlay

Elsie de Wolfe in the New York townhouse she shared with Elisaberth Marbury from 1887 to 1911

Nesting tables attributed to Josef Hoffmann and made by Jacob & Josef Kohn, Vienna

Unity Temple, Oak Park, Illinois, is designed by Frank Lloyd Wright. The first phase of Otto Wagner's steel- and glass-roofed Post Office Savings Bank, Vienna, is completed, although other parts will not be finished until 1912. The Kunstgewerbeschule in Weimar is designed by Henry Van de Velde; upon its completion in 1908, he will be named head of the school.

C. R. Ashbee's *A Book of Cottages and Little Houses* is published in London. Percy Macquoid writes *The Age of Mahogany, 1720–1770*. M. H. Baillie Scott publishes his own designs in *Houses and Gardens*.

Theodore Dreiser's *Sister Carrie* is published, as is O. Henry's short story collection *The Four Million*, referring to the current population of the city of New York. Marie Curie becomes the first female professor at the Sorbonne, and Alla Nazimova makes her U.S. acting debut in Henrik Ibsen's *Hedda Gabler*. George M. Cohan presents *Forty-five Minutes from Broadway*.

Loos, Hoffmann, and Wright manipulate geometry

DESIGNERS AND INSTALLATIONS

McKim, Mead, & White design the interiors of J. Pierpont Morgan's private library building in New York. In London, Mewès and Davis design the dining room of the Ritz Hotel in Louis XVI style. In Berlin, Josef Hoffmann and Koloman Moser design the J. & J. Kohn shop for a manufacturer of bentwood furniture. Peter Behrens designs a concert hall in Dresden and interiors for the Klein carpet shop in Hagen, Germany. Also in Berlin, Hermann Muthesius designs his own house, its interiors, and its furniture. In Paris, there is a major sale of Siegfried Bing's Oriental art collection, adding to the fame of his connoisseurship.

EXHIBITIONS

At the International Exposition of Decorative Arts in Turin, the Premio Reale goes to Italian cabinetmaker and interior designer Eugenio Quarti. At the Dresden Exhibition, a highlight is the model "Saxon House," designed by Wilhelm Kreis with interiors by Kreis and Fritz Schumacher.

FURNITURE AND FURNISHINGS

Josef Hoffmann's bentwood side chair with a column of seven wood balls dividing the back is manufactured by J. & J. Kohn, Vienna. In Venice, Mariano Fortuny turns his attention to fabric and fashion design; his most famous fashion creation will be the "Delphos" dress of finely pleated silk; his fabric will use natural dyes and new printing processes to reproduce Italian Renaissance designs. The interior design and furniture manufacturing firm of Herter Brothers, established in 1865, is dissolved.

GOVERNMENT EVENTS

On "Bloody Sunday," a demonstration in St. Petersburg is crushed by Russian police.

MAGAZINES

The Studio Year Book of Decorative Art is founded in London and will continue to be published through 1932.

TECHNICAL AND SCIENTIFIC ADVANCES

Willis Havilland Carrier, the father of air-conditioning, patents dew-point control.

1906

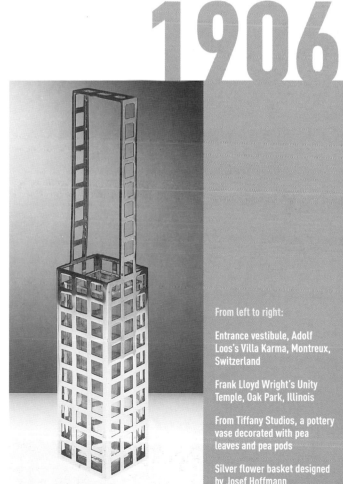

From left to right:

Entrance vestibule, Adolf Loos's Villa Karma, Montreux, Switzerland

Frank Lloyd Wright's Unity Temple, Oak Park, Illinois

From Tiffany Studios, a pottery vase decorated with pea leaves and pea pods

Silver flower basket designed by Josef Hoffmann

Antoni Gaudí designs the Casa Battló in Barcelona. McKim, Mead, & White design The Orchard, a house for James L. Breese in Southampton, New York. New York's Plaza Hotel is finished to the designs of Henry J. Hardenbergh. Charles Sumner Greene and Henry Mather Greene design the Robert R. Blacker house in Pasadena, California, including its interiors and much of its furniture. In Paris, La Samaritaine department store opens to the design of Frantz Jourdain.

John Hudson Elder-Duncan writes *The House Beautiful and Useful*.

Pablo Picasso paints *Les Demoiselles d'Avignon*, and Gustav Klimt paints *The Kiss*. Joseph Conrad writes *The Secret Agent*. Maria Montessori founds a school for infants. In Philadephia, the second Sunday in May is designated Mother's Day.

Deutscher Werkbund founded

DESIGNERS AND INSTALLATIONS

Peter Behrens is appointed design director of the Berlin-based electrical combine AEG, for which he will design products, industrial buildings, graphics, workers' housing, and more. In Vienna, Josef Hoffmann designs interiors for the Fledermaus cabaret-theater; its chair and table designs are manufactured by Thonet. Eugenio Quarti's interiors for the Grand Hotel at San Pellegrino Terme are completed. Murray's Roman Gardens, on New York's West 42nd Street, is designed by Henry Erkins with a blend of Egyptian, Pompeiian, and eighteenth-century French motifs. Candace Wheeler, at eighty, dissolves Associated Artists, her textile and wallpaper company, the successor to the decorating firm of the same name in which she had been a partner with Louis Comfort Tiffany and which had closed in 1883. The Deutscher Werkbund is founded in Munich by Peter Behrens, Hermann Muthesius, Richard Riemerschmid, Heinrich Tessenow, and others "to raise the standard of manufactured products by the joint efforts of art, industry, and craftsmanship." Its first president is Theodor Fischer, and important members will include Walter Gropius, Bruno Taut, Henry Van de Velde, Hermann Obrist, Hans Poelzig, and Mies van der Rohe. Upon his father's death, twenty-eight-year-old Èmile-Jacques Ruhlmann takes over the family business, a painting and contracting firm dealing with architects and designers.

EXHIBITIONS

The first exhibition of Cubist paintings is held in Paris. An exhibition of Austro-Hungarian design is seen in London.

FURNITURE AND FURNISHINGS

C. F. A. Voysey designs an oak armchair with a leather-upholstered seat for the Essex and Suffolk Equitable Insurance Co. Gustav Stickley begins his Craftsmans Farms project in Morris Plains, New Jersey. In England, the Dryad furniture company is founded by Harry Peach.

GOVERNMENT EVENTS

Siam becomes an independent country and will later be known as Thailand. The emperor of Korea abdicates, and the country becomes a protectorate of Japan.

TECHNICAL AND SCIENTIFIC ADVANCES

L. H. Baekeland invents a plastic he calls Bakelite; it will be sold commercially the following year. Henry Ford mass-produces the Model T.

1907

From left to right:

East Room, the Morgan Library, New York, by McKim, Mead, & White

Entrance hall, the residence of John Innes Kane, New York, by McKim, Mead, & White

"Isabelle," a wool crewel embroidery on linen, is a popular introduction from F. Schumacher.

An apartment interior, Antoni Gaudí's Casa Batlló, Barcelona. The furniture is also by Gaudí.

AEG Turbine Factory, Berlin, is designed by Peter Behrens. Frank Lloyd Wright's Robie house, Chicago, is built. The Gamble house, Pasadena, California, is designed by Greene & Greene. The Singer building, New York, is designed by Ernest Flagg; at 612 feet, it will be the tallest building in the world for a year—until it is superseded by the 700-foot Metropolitan Life Tower by Napoleon LeBrun & Sons. The Singer will be demolished in 1967.

Percy Macquoid writes *The Age of Satinwood, 1770–1820*, the fourth and last volume of *A History of English Furniture*. C. R. Ashbee writes *Craftsmanship in Competitive Industry*.

Isadora Duncan dances; Gertrude Stein writes *Three Lives*; E. M. Forster writes *A Room with a View*. The one-reel *Dr. Jekyll and Mr. Hyde* is the first horror film.

Edwin Lutyens is at work on the interiors of his recently completed house, Folly Farm, Sulhampstead, Berkshire. Bruno Paul designs interiors for the North German Lloyd oceanliners *George Washington* and *Prinz Friedrich Wilhelm*. M. H. Baillie Scott begins the design of the house, interiors, and furniture of Waldbühl at Uzwil, Switzerland; it will later become a museum. Otto Wagner designs interiors of the Lupus Hospital, Vienna. Rutan & Russell of Pittsburgh design a house in Sewickley Heights for Mrs. Benjamin Franklin Jones. German architect Adolf Loos publishes his essay "Ornament and Crime."

Loos equates "Ornament and Crime"

For the *Franco-British Exhibition* in London, a "White City" is constructed.

Craftsman-style furniture is popular, and Gustav Stickley its chief proponent; other designers in the style are Stickley's two brothers, Leopold and George; Elbert Hubbard; and George Niedecken. In Pittsburgh, Thomas Armstrong begins to produce linoleum (a nineteenth-century invention) in many patterns and colors. Danish artisan F. C. V. Rambusch begins the manufacture of lighting fixtures in New York; his company will become a leading producer of reproductions of historical metal objects.

The Union of South Africa is established.

House and Garden focuses on a new building need in "Housing the Automobile" and shows a new building method in "A Cement Block House."

Frank Alvah Parsons is appointed president of the New York School of Art, founded in 1896 as the Chase School by artist William Merritt Chase. The next year it will be renamed the New York School of Fine and Applied Art, and in 1941 it will be renamed in honor of Parsons.

In Italy, the Olivetti company is founded.

1908

From left to right:

The living room of Frank Lloyd Wright's May house, Grand Rapids, Michigan

Charles Rennie Mackintosh's gridded table of ebonized pine with mother-of-pearl inlay for Hill House

Folly Farm, Berkshire, by Sir Edwin Lutyens

Table of corrugated cardboard, laminated wood, and bent solid wood designed in Germany by Hans Günther Reinstein

ARCHITECTURE

Charles Rennie
Mackintosh's Glasgow
School of Art, begun in
1897, is completed, as is
Edwin Lutyens's Nashdom
at Taplow, Buckingham-
shire. The Metropolitan Life
Insurance tower, New York,
is built to the design of
Napoleon Le Brun & Sons.
Charles Follen McKim dies.

The decorator show house instituted

Filippo Marinetti publishes the "Futurist Manifesto." Sergey Diaghilev's Ballets Russes appears in Paris. Richard Strauss writes *Elektra*. Sigmund Freud lectures on psychoanalysis in the United States.

Elsie de Wolfe, assisted by architect Ogden Codman, Jr., designs a townhouse on East 71st Street in Manhattan and invites the press and some members of the public to see it; thus the decorator show house is born. Ogden Codman Jr. is designing a house in Washington, D.C., for his cousin Martha Codman. C. R. Ashbee designs the Villa San Giorgio and its interiors in Taormina, Sicily. Bruno Paul designs interiors for the oceanliner *Kronprinzessin Cecelie*. "The House of the Seven Chimneys" is built for Charles Henry Davis in South Yarmouth, Massachusetts, with furnishings chosen by Francis H. Bigelow of Cambridge.

The Danish National Exhibition is opened in Aarhus.

Hector Guimard designs interiors and furniture for his own house on the avenue Mozart, Paris. The Murphy Door and Bed Company of San Francisco introduces the "concealed bed."

The Anglo-Persian Oil Company is founded. Women are admitted to German universities. The first collective farm or *kibbutz* is founded in Palestine.

Explorer Robert Peary reaches the North Pole. General Electric introduces the electric toaster.

1909

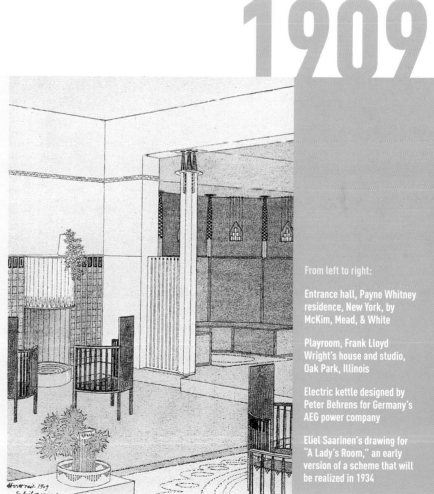

From left to right:

Entrance hall, Payne Whitney residence, New York, by McKim, Mead, & White

Playroom, Frank Lloyd Wright's house and studio, Oak Park, Illinois

Electric kettle designed by Peter Behrens for Germany's AEG power company

Eliel Saarinen's drawing for "A Lady's Room," an early version of a scheme that will be realized in 1934

THE TEENS

Art Nouveau has a final curvaceous fling with what is known as the Ballet style, inspired by Sergey Diaghilev's Ballets Russes with its sets by Léon Bakst, its choreography by Michel Fokine, its music by Igor Stravinsky and Maurice Ravel, and its dancers Vaslav Nijinsky and Anna Pavlova. And Art Nouveau's cousin, the Wiener Werkstätte, has its most thorough and luxurious expression in Josef Hoffmann's Palais Stoclet. A decorating department is established in Wanamaker's in Philadelphia, beginning what will be an important and mutually beneficial relationship between large department stores and design; through the first three quarters of the century, such stores will be the public's chief source of design information. In the middle of the decade, educator Frank Alvah Parsons, for whom the Parsons School of Design will be named, writes *Interior Decoration: Its Principles and Practice*. "The first error to combat in this field," he writes, "is the one through which the object bequeathed by a relative is confused with the relative himself. Because one's uncle possessed . . . a mahogany table ugly in line, bad in proportion, and disagreeable in colour, is no reason why [it] should be perpetuated in each generation until the family line is extinct." Elsie de Wolfe takes another step toward professionalism: hired to design rooms for the Frick mansion in New York, she demands a fee of ten percent of the cost. Perhaps the most telling indication of a change in the interior design field is the 1916 change of a magazine's title: what has been *The Upholsterer* becomes *The Upholsterer and Interior Decorator*; it will eventually become *Interiors*. Not everyone has a clear idea of the field, of course. In 1917, Rose Cumming arrives in New York from Australia at age forty. Frank Crowninshield, the editor of *Vanity Fair*, suggests she become a decorator. "What is that?" she is said to have asked.

Émile Gallé's glass-painting studio, Nancy, France, 1913

ARCHITECTURE

Antoni Gaudí completes the Casa Milá, Barcelona. McKim, Mead, & White design New York's Pennsylvania Station, based in part on the Baths of Caracalla; it will stand until 1963. Also in New York, the Ritz-Carlton hotel is built to designs by Warren & Wetmore. For part of this year, young architects Le Corbusier, Walter Gropius, and Mies van der Rohe are all working side by side in the Berlin office of Peter Behrens.

BOOKS

Alexander Speltz's 1904 *Styles of Ornament from Prehistoric Times to the Middle of the XIX Century* is translated from the German and published in America. Carl Larsson's *Towards the Sun* is published in Sweden. In Berlin, Ernst Wasmuth publishes *The Buildings and Projects of Frank Lloyd Wright*.

CULTURE AT LARGE

E. M. Forster writes *Howard's End*. Victor Herbert writes *Naughty Marietta*. Elizabeth Arden opens her first beauty salon in New York. In San Francisco on Christmas Eve, 250,000 fans attend a free open-air concert by opera diva Luisa Tetrazzini. The tango is popular in the United States and Europe. Burberry introduces the trenchcoat in England, and Michelin introduces the road map in France.

DESIGNERS AND INSTALLATIONS

EXHIBITIONS

FURNITURE AND FURNISHINGS

GOVERNMENT EVENTS

MAGAZINES

TECHNICAL AND SCIENTIFIC ADVANCES

Edwin Lutyens begins the design of interiors and furniture of his Castle Drogo, Devonshire, work that will continue until 1932. Mariano Fortuny, who will become famous for his fabrics, designs sets for *Tristan und Isolde* at Milan's La Scala.

At the International Exposition in Brussels, Bruno Paul and his young protégé Karl Emanuel Martin (Kem) Weber design the German section, and Richard Riemerschmid designs interiors and furnishings for three rooms. Alfred Stieglitz's 291 Gallery in New York shows work by John Marin, Gaston Lachaise, Joseph Stella, and others. Roger Fry's post-Impressionist exhibition in London shows work by Paul Cézanne, Henri Matisse, and Vincent van Gogh. Eugène Vallin, a designer of the École de Nancy group, designs rooms for the Salon d'Automne in Nancy. The first European exhibition of Frank Lloyd Wright's work is seen in Berlin.

Joseph Hoffmann designs the leather-upholstered "Kubus" armchair. Eileen Gray produces her first lacquered furniture designs, including screens and small tables. Richard Riemerschmid designs a range of standardized furniture elements. The English furniture company Heal's is established by Ambrose Heal. Newly wed, Èmile-Jacques Ruhlmann designs furniture for his own apartment in Paris.

France executes Mata Hari for spying. The Union of South Africa becomes part of the British Empire.

Arts and Decoration magazine is founded, edited by painter Guy Pène du Bois, and will be published until 1942.

Marie Curie isolates radium. In Paris, inventor Léon Ernest Gaumont demonstrates the first talking pictures. The industrial production of plywood begins. The Grand Palais in Paris is lighted by the first neon lamps. Westinghouse applies Bakelite to heavy canvas to produce an early version of plastic laminate.

1910

Gaudí tweaks Art Nouveau his own way

From left to right:

McKim, Mead, & White's Pennsylvania Station, New York

Walter Gropius's chair design for the Fagus factory, as reproduced later by Tecta

Armchair designed by Josef Hoffmann for his Villa Ast, Vienna

Entrance gate, Antoni Gaudí's Casa Milá, Barcelona

Oval dining room, Ritz-Carlton Hotel, New York, by Warren & Wetmore

The vaulted attic of Antoni Gaudí's Casa Milá, Barcelona. This space will later be converted into apartments.

Walter Gropius and Adolf Meyer pioneer the glass curtain wall in their Fagus factory, Alfeld, Germany. Bernard Maybeck completes the First Chuch of Christ, Scientist, in Berkeley, California. Frank Lloyd Wright builds his home and studio Taliesin in Spring Green, Wisconsin; there will be major remodelings in 1914 and 1925. Carrère and Hastings's New York Public Library is completed.

"Efficiency expert" Frederick Winslow Taylor begins a trend that will revolutionize office design with his book *Principles of Scientific Management*. Edward J. Duveen writes *Colour in the Home, with Notes on Architecture, Sculpture, Painting, and upon Decoration and Good Taste*.

Professor Hiram Bingham of Yale discovers the ruins of Machu Picchu in the mountains of Peru. The *Mona Lisa* is stolen from the Louvre, but will be recovered in 1913. Sculptor Jacob Epstein designs the tomb of Oscar Wilde in Paris. Richard Straus composes *Der Rosenkavalier*; Irving Berlin composes "Alexander's Ragtime Band"; Henri Matisse paints *The Red Studio*; and Edith Wharton's writes *Ethan Frome*. Crisco cooking oil and the Oreo cookie are introduced.

Office productivity examined

DESIGNERS
AND INSTALLATIONS

EXHIBITIONS

FURNITURE
AND FURNISHINGS

GOVERNMENT EVENTS

TECHNICAL AND
SCIENTIFIC ADVANCES

Josef Hoffman's Palais Stoclet and its interiors are completed in Brussels in what will be called a "Rectilinear Art Nouveau" style; its furnishings and appointments are all from the Wiener Werkstätte. The "Pompeiian Bath" at the Royal Automobile Club, London, is completed to the designs of Charles Mewès and Arthur Davis. For King George V, Sir Charles Carrick Allom redecorates rooms in Buckingham Palace and Windsor Castle. Architect, interior designer, and stage designer Joseph Urban, at thirty-nine, moves from his native Vienna to New York, where he will direct the local branch of the Wiener Werkstätte and design more than fifty sets for the Metropolitan Opera. Louis Comfort Tiffany designs a glass curtain for the Palacio de Bellas Artes in Mexico City; it will still be in use at the end of the century. In France, the term *ensembliers* is adopted for those who design entire interiors and select all their components.

An exhibition of Cubist art is seen in Paris. The *House and Home* exhibition is seen in London.

Paris couturier Paul Poiret establishes the École Martine, an art school for young women, and the Atelier Martine for the design of interiors and decorative furnishings, including textiles, wallpapers, and carpets, some of which will be sold in London through Marcel Boulestin's shop, Décoration Moderne. Gerrit Rietveld opens a furniture company in Utrecht. German designer Bernhard Pankok designs a chair of tubular aluminum for use in the Zeppelin airship.

Turkey and Italy are at war. The Russian premier is assassinated. In China, the Manchu dynasty, in power since 1644, falls, a republic is proclaimed, and the wearing of pigtails is banned.

Lord Rutherford publishes his theory that the atom contains a central nucleus. Charles Kettering invents the self-starter for automobiles, and Elmer Sperry invents the gyrocompass.

1911

From left to right:

Entrance hall, New York Public Library, by Carrère and Hastings

Elbert Hubbard's Roycrofters chair. The word *Roycroft* is carved into the top rail.

Frank Lloyd Wright in his studio

Bernard Maybeck's First Church of Christ, Scientist, Berkeley, California

From Tiffany Studios, a "Trumpet Creeper" leaded glass and bronze table lamp

Edwin Lutyens begins work on the Viceroy's House (later Rashtrapati Bhavan) in New Delhi; it will not be completed until 1931, and Lutyens will produce over a thousand drawings for the furniture alone. The German embassy, in St. Petersburg, is built to designs of Peter Behrens, with Ludwig Mies van der Rohe as project designer. A new Paris store for the Galeries Lafayette is finished to designs by Ferdinand Chanut. Horace Trumbauer designs the James B. Duke house in New York, later the home of New York University's Institute of Fine Arts.

Herbert Cescinsky's three-volume *English Furniture of the Eighteenth Century* is completed. E. W. Gregory writes *The Art and Craft of Homemaking*. Mary H. Northend writes *American Homes and Their Furnishings in Colonial Times*.

CULTURE AT LARGE	DESIGNERS AND INSTALLATIONS	EXHIBITIONS	FURNITURE AND FURNISHINGS	GOVERNMENT EVENTS	TECHNICAL AND SCIENTIFIC ADVANCES
Marcel Proust finishes the first draft of what will become *Remembrance of Things Past*. The SS *Titanic* hits an iceberg and sinks on her maiden voyage.	Ogden Codman, Jr., designs interiors for his own New York townhouse; like his villa on the Riviera, the house is given an "Old French" look. Codman also adds the East Wing to McKim, Mead, & White's 1893 Metropolitan Club in New York. Louis Comfort Tiffany designs the "Peacock" and "Cockatoo" glass panels for the Joseph DeLamar residence, New York. In Paris, the decorating firm of Jallot designs interiors of a house for Charles Stern. French designer René Prou designs the council room of the Comptoir d'Escompte in Paris and the apartment of the French ambassador in Paraguay. Richard Riemerschmid is named the director of the Kunstgewerbeschule, Munich.	The exhibition *Modern German Applied Arts* is shown at the Newark Museum, Newark, New Jersey. At the Salon d'Automne, Paris, architect and painter Louis Süe and painter André Mare, later to be partners in a design firm, collaborate on the "Maison Cubiste" with painters Roger de la Fresnaye, Raymond Duchamp-Villon, and Jacques Villon.	Walter Gropius's "furniture for a gentleman's study" is shown in the first yearbook of the German *Werkbund*. Raoul Dufy, who will become known as a painter, joins the Paris firm Bianchini et Ferier as a fabric designer, a position he will hold until 1930. A firm called Metal Office Furniture is founded in Grand Rapids, Michigan, by engineer Peter M. Wege and others; it will later change its name to Steelcase, and by 1993 it will be the largest furniture manufacturer in the world.	Arizona and New Mexico are admitted as U.S. states. New Delhi replaces Calcutta as the capital of India.	Stainless steel, invented in the nineteenth century, is perfected. Cellophane is manufactured. Pyrex is developed by Corning Glass Works. Cadillac introduces the self-starter, ending the hand-cranking of automobiles.

1912

Stainless steel perfected, but sharkskin preferred

From left to right:

Commode designed by Paul Iribe of mahogany faced with blue-green sharkskin inlaid with strips of ebony. The top is of black marble.

Aeolian Hall, New York, by Warren & Wetmore

Grand foyer of the SS *France*

Carved and painted armchair by James Rorimer of Rorimer-Brooks Studios, Cleveland. The back splat is carved with two dolphins.

Stair detail, Les Galeries Lafayette, Paris, by Ferdinand Chanut. The stair will be destroyed in 1974.

ARCHITECTURE

Grand Central Station, by Reed & Stem and Warren & Wetmore, opens in New York. At 792 feet, New York's Woolworth Building—the "Cathedral of Commerce"—by Cass Gilbert, will be the world's tallest until 1930.

BOOKS

Christine Frederick writes *The New Housekeeping: Efficiency Studies in Home Management*, suggesting that electricity can be the house's "modern servant." Candace Wheeler's 1903 *Principles of Home Decoration* is reprinted. Elsie de Wolfe publishes her book *The House in Good Taste*, based on previously published articles ghost-written for her by Ruby Ross Wood.

CULTURE AT LARGE

Igor Stravinsky's *Rite of Spring*, starring Vaslav Nijinsky, causes riots at its Paris premiere. Vladimir Tatlin makes abstract structures of wood, metal, and glass, establishing Russian Constructivism, which will be an aesthetic force into the mid-'20s. The fox-trot is the new popular dance. Victor Herbert writes the operetta *Sweethearts*.

DESIGNERS AND INSTALLATIONS

At Wanamaker's department store in Philadelphia, Nancy McClelland establishes a decorating department, "Au Quatrième." The Omega Workshops are founded by artist and critic Roger Fry and his Bloomsbury friends Vanessa Bell and Duncan Grant; one of the group's first commissions is a room in London's *Ideal Home* exhibition, and between now and 1919 it will also produce designs for furniture, fabrics, and carpets. In Paris, René Guilleré establishes the Primavera decorating studio in Les Printemps department store. In Vienna, Adolf Loos designs the Knitze shop.

EXHIBITIONS

Gustav Stickley converts a New York building into showrooms, offices, and a restaurant. Elsie de Wolfe is hired by Henry Clay Frick to design the private family rooms on the second floor of his New York house by Carrère & Hastings; Sir Charles Carrick Allom is hired for the first-floor public rooms. The house will later become the Frick Collection.

Rooms furnished by Walter Gropius win a gold medal at the World's Fair in Ghent, which also features a house by Henry Van de Velde. The Armory show in New York introduces Cubism, post-Impressionism, and Marcel Duchamp's *Nude Descending a Staircase* to the United States. For the *Salon d'Automne* in Paris, Robert Mallet-Stevens designs a music room and Jacques-Émile Ruhlmann designs a dining room. Also in Paris, the Salon des Artistes Décorateurs includes work by Eileen Gray.

FURNITURE AND FURNISHINGS

Francis Jourdain, son of architect Frantz Jourdain, designs furniture for his own apartment in Paris.

GOVERNMENT EVENTS

War in the Balkans continues. Suffragettes stage demonstrations in London. The Sixteenth Amendment to the U.S. Constitution legalizes income tax.

TECHNICAL AND SCIENTIFIC ADVANCES

Henry Ford introduces the first moving assembly line, at Highland Park, Michigan. Cellulose acetate is industrially produced. Niels Bohr shows that changes in electrons' orbits within the atom can produce energy. The newly formed Formica Company manufactures plastic laminate.

1913

Department stores offer decorating services

From left to right:

Grand Central Terminal, New York, by Reed & Stem, Warren & Wetmore

Upholstered armchair by Josef Hoffmann for Moritz Gallia, Vienna

Mantel clock of white oak designed by Gustav Stickley

Elsie de Wolfe's New York dining room, as shown in her book *The House in Good Taste*

Eliel Saarinen designs the Railway Terminus in Helsinki. Frank Lloyd Wright designs the Midway Gardens in Chicago. Henry Van de Velde designs the Werkbund Theater in Cologne.

Ruby Ross Wood and Rayne Adams write *The Honest House*. Frances Lenygon, a designer who will be active in restoration work, writes *Furniture in England from 1660 to 1770*.

Henri Matisse paints *The Red Studio*. James Joyce writes *Dubliners*. Edgar Rice Burroughs writes *Tarzan of the Apes*. Charlie Chaplin and Marie Dressler appear in Mack Sennett's film *Tillie's Punctured Romance*. Marcel Duchamp produces ready-made art.

Ernesto Basile designs both the building and interiors of the Municipal Palace, Reggio Calabria, Italy. The Omega Workshops designs the Cadena Café in London's Westbourne Grove. Robert Mallet-Stevens designs interiors for Le Roses Rouges, Mme. Paquin's house in Deauville, France. Charles Rennie Mackintosh and his wife move from Dublin to London and will later move to the south of France.

Arts and Crafts movement on its last legs

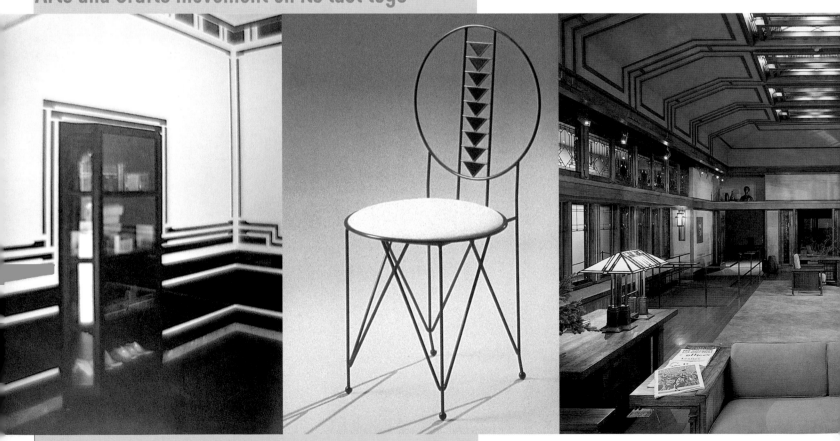

The exhibition *British Arts and Crafts* is seen in Paris. At the *Deutsche Werkbund-Ausstellung* exhibition in Cologne, Josef Hoffmann designs the Austrian exhibition pavilion, Henry Van de Velde designs a model theater, Walter Gropius designs a model factory, Bruno Taut designs the Glass Industries Pavilion, Hermann Muthesius designs the pavilion for the Hamburg-Amerika steamship line, and the Transport Hall shows a railway dining-car interior by August Endell.

Walter Gropius designs steel furniture for the German battleship *von Hindenburg*; it is also shown at the Werkbund Exhibition in Cologne. Frank Lloyd Wright designs the furniture for his own Midway Gardens; it will later be manufactured by Cassina. Kaare Klint designs a chair for the Faaborg Museum, Denmark.

Archduke Ferdinand, the heir to the Austrian throne, is assassinated, and World War I begins in Europe. Mahatma Gandhi becomes leader of the Indian National Congress.

Good Furniture magazine is founded. With the advent of war, several magazines cease publication, including the American *Art Amateur*, founded in 1879, the German *Jugend*, founded in 1896, the German *Dekorative Kunst*, founded in 1897, and the French *L'Art Décoratif*, founded in 1898.

The Decorators Club is founded in New York; it will still be meeting at the end of the century. The American Society for Testing Materials publishes its first standards for the textile industry. The American Institute of Graphic Arts is founded.

The Panama Canal opens. Red and geen traffic lights are introduced in Cleveland, Ohio. English astronomer Arthur Eddington suggests that spiral nebulae are distant galaxies. The brassiere is patented.

1914

From left to right:

Interior of Walter Gropius's compleated Faguswerk factory, Alfeld, Germany

Metal-based chair designed by Wright for Midway Gardens, Chicago

Living room of Frank Lloyd Wright's Francis W. Little house, Wayzata, Minnesota, as reconstructed at the Metropolitan Museum of Art, New York

Serving table from a dining room suite by Leopold and George Stickley (brothers of Gustav Stickley)

Wood-framed chair designed by Wright for Midway Gardens

ARCHITECTURE

Frank Lloyd Wright designs the Imperial Hotel in Tokyo; it will be completed in 1922. From now until his death in 1926, Antoni Gaudí devotes himself completely to his principal work, the church of Sagrada Familia in Barcelona.

BOOKS

Interior Decoration: Its Principles and Practice is written by Frank Alvah Parsons.

CULTURE AT LARGE

Lillian Gish stars in D. W. Griffith's *The Birth of a Nation*. Virginia Woolf writes her first novel, *The Voyage Out*. The Dada movement is founded. Margaret Sanger is jailed for writing the first book on birth control, *Family Limitation*.

DESIGNERS AND INSTALLATIONS

Louis Comfort Tiffany designs "Dream Garden," a large mosaic based on a painting by Maxfield Parrish, for the Curtis Publishing Co. building in Philadelphia. Elsie de Wolfe designs sets for the musical comedy *Nobody's Home*. Albert Munsell develops a systematic description of color.

San Francisco's *Panama-Pacific International Exhibition* celebrates the opening of the Panama Canal and the rebuilding of San Francisco after the earthquake and fire of 1906; Bernard Maybeck's Palace of Fine Arts is built; Kem Weber, who had been sent from Berlin to San Francisco to design the German section, is unable to return because of the war.

Charles Rennie Mackintosh is designing textiles for Seftons and for William Foxton, work that will continue through the early 1920s.

German submarines torpedo the *Lusitania* and attack Le Havre. The German blockade of England begins.

The Craftsman ceases publication as Gustav Stickley's furniture empire collapses. In Paris, Amédée Ozenfant explains the principles of Purism in his new magazine *L'Élan*. In New York, Dadaism is supported by the publication *291*.

The Design and Industries Association (DIA) is founded in England; modeled in part on the Deutscher Werkbund, its aim is to improve the design of goods on the market.

Einstein presents his General Theory of Relativity. In the first transcontinental telephone call, Alexander Graham Bell in New York talks to Dr. Thomas A. Watson in San Francisco. Henry Ford develops a farm tractor and produces his millionth car. Maytag introduces a gas-powered washing machine.

1915

Frank Alvah Parsons codifies design principles

PROJECTIVE ORNAMENT
by
Claude Bragdon

ROCHESTER·N·Y
THE MANAS PRESS
·1915·

From left to right:

Entrance hall designed by Ogden Codman, Jr., for a Fifth Avenue residence, New York, later the home of the National Academy of Design. The stair and floor are marble, the walls of plaster imitating marble. The sculpture is *Diana* by Anna Hyatt Huntington.

Antoni Gaudí

Title page, Claude Bragdon's *Projective Ornament*

A reproduction chair (called the "St. Cloud" model) by Palmer & Eubury. Its Aubusson tapestry upholstery is by F. Schumacher.

Irving Gill designs the Dodge house in Los Angeles. In Miami, Vizcaya is finished for James Deering of the International Harvester company; the Italianate house is by F. Burrall Hoffman, Jr., and its interiors by Paul Chalfin.

Sherrill Whiton publishes his first "Home Study Catalogues in the Decorative Arts"; they will later be combined in book form. Hazel Adler writes *The New Interior*. D'Arcy Wentworth Thompson writes *On Growth and Form*; an enlarged version will be published in 1942 and an abridged one in 1961. Alfred D. F. Hamlin writes *A History of Ornament: Ancient and Medieval*.

Tristan Tzara, Hans Arp, Marcel Duchamp, and others pursue Dadaist art. Carl Jung completes *The Psychology of the Unconscious*. Franz Kafka writes *Metamorphosis*. In New York, Margaret Sanger opens the country's first birth control clinic; judged a "public nuisance," she is given thirty days in jail. Nathan's Hot Dogs opens at Coney Island. Gabrielle "Coco" Chanel opens her fashion house in Paris. T. S. Eliot writes "The Love Song of J. Alfred Prufrock"; Edna St. Vincent Millay writes *Renascence*; Ezra Pound's first three *Cantos* are published. Sergey Prokofiev composes his *Classical Symphony*.

Mrs. Edgar de Wolfe (Elsie's sister-in-law) is commissioned to redesign the public rooms of the Hotel del Monte in California. Henry Erkins designs the Persian Roof Garden of the New York Theater. The W. P. Nelson Co. redesigns the banquet hall of the Chicago Athletic Club. Vanessa Bell moves to Charleston, a farmhouse near Lewes in East Sussex, and, with Duncan Grant, begins to develop a colorful and informal style of interior decoration. Designer Syrie Barnardo marries playwright Somerset Maugham; the marriage will last twelve years. Unitt & Wickes designs interiors of the Broadhurst and Morosco theaters, both in New York.

In Moscow, the Café Pittoresque is designed by Aleksandr Rodchenko, Georgii Yakulov, and Vladimir Tatlin. Rose Cumming, just arrived in New York from Australia, designs her own house on East 53rd Street, filling it with mirrors, black candles, and silver wallpaper.

Mackintosh's last design commissio

The Union of Youth exhibits its design in Moscow. Duchamp submits a urinal (titled *Fountain*) to the first exhibit of the Society of Independents in New York. The *Home Exhibition of the Swedish Society of Arts and Crafts* is held in Stockholm, showing a living room and kitchen designed by Gunnar Asplund.

Charles Rennie Mackintosh designs furniture for the Lowke house in Northampton, England; although he will live until 1928, it will be one of his last commissions. Gerrit Rietveld designs his "Red Blue" chair. Wallace Nutting, a proponent of the Colonial Revival, begins manufacturing furniture; he will also be known for his writings about antiques. Marshall Burns Lloyd patents a system for using twisted paper as a substitute for wicker; his company, Lloyd Loom, will become part of Heywood-Wakefield in 1921.

The United States enters World War I. Air attacks begin in England, and bread is rationed there. Revolution begins in Russia. The Balfour Declaration expresses British support for a Jewish homeland.

The Upholsterer changes its name to *Upholsterer and Interior Decorator.* Theo van Doesburg founds the Dutch magazine *De Stijl*; its subtitle can be translated as "Monthly Journal of the Expressive Professions"; it will be published in Leiden until 1932, and it will give its name to a design movement involving Piet Mondrian, J. J. P. Oud, Georges Vantongerloo, Gerrit Rietveld, and others. Dadaism is espoused by *391*, published in Barcelona as a tribute to *291*, which has just ceased publication in New York.

In Berkeley, California, Kem Weber establishes a course for modern interior decorating at the California School of Arts and Crafts. The Carpet Club changes its name to the Carpet Association of America. The Commercial Travelers' Association of the Upholstery and Allied Trades holds its first annual meeting. The Association of Interior Decorators is formed in New York. Frank Alvah Parsons addresses the first annual convention of the Allied Furnishing Industries at New York's Hotel Astor in Times Square.

Sir Arthur Eddington studies the physical properties of stars. U.S. Gypsum puts Sheetrock wallboard on the market.

America's first design association

1916–17

From left to right:

Gerrit Rietveld's "Red Blue" chair

Steelcase's first desk line, the "601 Series"

Charles Rennie Mackintosh's guest bedroom design for 78 Derngate, Northampton

Mackintosh's chair for the Dug Out, Willow Tea Rooms, Glasgow

Paul Chaffin's interior design for James Deering's Vizcaya, Miami

Gunnar Asplund designs the Villa Snellman at Djursholm, near Stockholm. Hendik Petrus Berlage begins the design of a building and interiors for the Municipal Museum (Gemeentemuseum), The Hague; it will take a decade to complete. Edwin Lutyens designs the Cenotaph, London.

Frank Alvah Parsons writes *The Art of Home Furnishing and Decoration*. Parsons's protégé William Odom writes the two-volume *History of Italian Furniture*, which will be reissued in 1966. Amédée Ozenfant and Charles-Édouard Jeanneret (Le Corbusier) write the manifesto of Purism, *Après le cubisme*. Swedish art historian and critic Gregor Paulsson writes *More Beautiful Things for Everyday Use*.

James Joyce's *Ulysses*, being published in installments in *The Little Review*, is burned by the U.S. Post Office. Willa Cather writes *My Ántonia*, and Kasimir Malevich paints *White on White*. Playwright W. Somerset Maugham publishes *The Moon and Sixpence*. "Swanee" is George Gershwin's first hit song. American jazz arrives in Europe.

J. J. Petit redesigns the roof garden of New York's Waldorf-Astoria Hotel, presently at Fifth Avenue and 34th Street. In Madrid, painter and designer Sonia Delaunay opens Casa Sonia, a small studio and shop selling cushions, lampshades, and accessories. In Havana, Tiffany Studios designs interiors for the newly constructed Presidential Palace. Frances Elkins buys an 1830 adobe house, Casa Amesti, in Monterey, California, has additions designed by her brother, architect David Adler, and furnishes it in eclectic taste; its interior will be an influential trendsetter, and the house will eventually become a Historic Trust landmark. Austrian designer Koloman Moser dies at sixty-seven. John J. Morrow decorates the Somerset Hills Country Club in Bernardsville, New Jersey. Hans Poelzig

remodels the Grosses Schauspielhaus in Berlin. The W. E. Browne Decorating Co. opens in Atlanta. The design firm of Thedlow Inc. opens in New York. The Omega Workshops closes in London. Kem Weber opens his design studio in Santa Barbara, California. In Paris, architect and painter Louis Süe and painter André Mare form the interior design studio Compagnie des Arts Français, popularly known as Süe et Mare. Eileen Gray designs interiors and furniture for the Paris apartment of Mme. Mathieu Lévy (the model known professionally as Suzanne Talbot). The Russian artists' group Proun (Project for the Affirmation of the New) is founded by architect El Lissitsky as "an intermediate between painting and architecture"; it will be active until 1922. The Bauhaus is founded in

Weimar, Germany, by Walter Gropius; first faculty members include the painters Lyonel Feininger and Johannes Itten and the sculptor Gerhard Marcks; others to come are Paul Klee, Vassily Kandinsky, Josef Albers, Marcel Breuer, László Moholy-Nagy, and Ludwig Mies van der Rohe. The school, in Gropius's words, will aim "to collect all artistic creativity into a unity, to reunite all artistic disciplines into a new architecture."

French photographer, painter, and designer Jacques-Henri Lartigue designs a table with a spherical base. Émile-Jacques Ruhlmann and Pierre Laurent found the Établissements Ruhlmann et Laurent to produce furniture designs. Jean Dunand begins making lacquered furniture and screens for Pierre Legrain, Émile-Jacques Ruhlmann, Eugène Printz, and other designers.

World War I ends; Woodrow Wilson presents his Fourteen Points peace plan to Congress; Nicholas II, the last tsar of Russia, is assassinated. The Eighteenth Amendment to the U.S. Constitution makes prohibition federal law. The League of Nations is convened in Paris.

The journal *Wendingen* is begun by the Amsterdam art society Architectura et Amicitia.

As will later be reported by the U.S. Census Bureau, 1919 furniture sales in the United States were $574 million, up from $266 million in 1914.

Astronomer Harlow Shapley measures the size of the Milky Way. Acetate rayon, more stain- and crease-resistant than viscose rayon, is developed in England. Observations of a total eclipse of the sun confirm Einstein's Theory of Relativity. The first regular radio broadcasts begin in the United States and England.

1918–19

Bauhaus founded

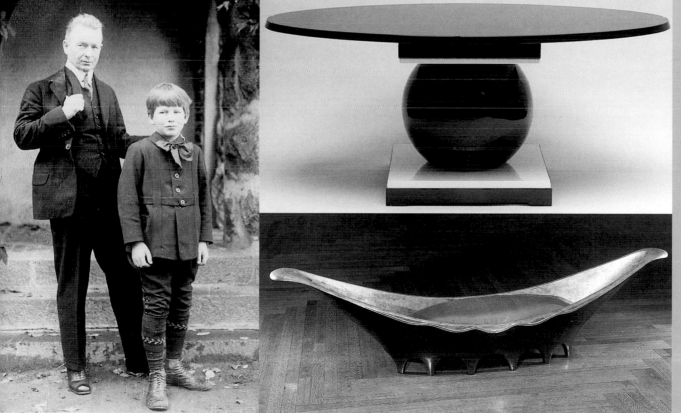

From left to right:

Eliel Saarinen's three-legged chair of oak with leather upholstery

Elsie de Wolfe's interiors for her own Villa Trianon at Versailles, a continuing design project for more than four decades

Two generations of design: Eliel Saarinen and his son Eero

Table designed by Jacques Henri Lartique, as reproduced by Écart and available through Pucci International

Eileen Gray's "Piroque" daybed of lacquered wood and silver leaf

THE '20s

The recently founded Bauhaus grows steadily in size and prestige, establishing a new artistic marriage of craft and technology, but through the decade it moves gradually toward an emphasis on the latter. Another expression of the modern spirit is the 1922 founding of the Paris decorating firm Dominique by André Domin and Marcel Genevrière; its motto is Délivré du cauchemar de l'ancien—"Delivery from the nightmare of the ancient." Still another is the 1923 publication of Le Corbusier's *Vers une architecture (Toward a New Architecture)*, illustrated with photographs of grain silos, airplanes, ships, racing cars, and the Parthenon. "The Plan," Le Corbusier writes, "proceeds from within to without; the exterior is the result of an interior. The elements of architecture are light and shade, walls and space." But in the middle of the decade, most eyes are on a more decorative, less functional style, Art Deco. Paris's highly influential *Exposition Internationale des Arts Décoratifs et Industriels Modernes*, which opens in 1924, represents the peak of the style. Highlights of the exposition include Émile-Jacques Ruhlmann's Salon d'un Collectionneur, Süe et Mare's Musée d'Art Contemporain, Sonia Delaunay's Boutique Simultanée, Robert Mallet-Stevens's Une Ambassade française, Victor Horta's Belgian Pavilion, Josef Hoffmann's Austrian Pavilion, the Primavera design studio pavilion by Henri Sauvage, seven room designs by La Maîtrise, and Pierre Patout's monumental gate at the Porte de la Concorde. Couturier Paul Poiret shows his collection on three barges decorated by painter Raoul Dufy and named Amours, Délices, and Orgues. Even at the Paris exposition, however, there are hints of the growing strength of modernism, such as the USSR Pavilion by Konstantin Melnikov, a greenhouse by Peter Behrens, and the Pavilion de l'Esprit Nouveau by Le Corbusier (born Charles-Édouard Jeanneret-Gris).

Marcel Breuer's 1925 "Wassily" chair of leather and tubular steel. The woman in the mask may be Walter Gropius's wife Ise.

Vladimir Tatlin builds a model of his spiral tower honoring the Soviets' Third International; if built, it would be thirteen hundred feet high. Frank Lloyd Wright designs the Hollyhock House in Los Angeles. Victor Horta begins five years of work on the Palais des Beaux-Arts, Brussels.

Christine Frederick writes *Household Engineering: Scientific Management in the Home*. A. J. Stratton writes *The English Interior*. R. R. Phillips edits *The Modern English Interior*.

Sidonie-Gabrielle Colette writes *Chéri*. Carl Jung publishes *Psychological Types*. "Coco" Chanel designs her first chemise dress. Agatha Christie writes the first Hercule Poirot mystery, *The Mysterious Affair at Styles*. Babe Ruth, in his first year with the New York Yankees, hits fifty-four home runs. The Baby Ruth candy bar is named for the daughter of President Grover Cleveland.

In London, Lady Diana Cooper redesigns a Bloomsbury house for her own use; it includes a large bathroom with walls painted in imitation of a Chinese wallpaper from her family house, Belvoir Castle in Leicestershire. Ogden Codman, Jr., closes his New York office and moves to France, where he will live until his death in 1951. German artist Winold Reiss designs the Crillon restaurant in New York; he will redesign it in another location in 1927.

Christine Frederick applies science to the household

EXHIBITIONS

The *Ideal Home Exhibition* is seen at London's Olympia exhibition center. At the *Salon d'Automne* in Paris, Lucie Renaudot designs "A Room in a Country House" and "A Room for a Young Girl."

FURNITURE AND FURNISHINGS

Gerrit Rietveld designs a hanging lamp of neon strips; in 1923, Walter Gropius will duplicate it for his own office at the Bauhaus. Italian-born Lucian Ercolani establishes the British furniture company Ercol; it will specialize in simple, solid wood furniture, particularly updated versions of traditional Windsor chairs. Armand-Albert Rateau opens a shop in Paris, specializing in objects in metal and lacquer.

GOVERNMENT EVENTS

The Nineteenth Amendment to the U.S. Constitution gives women the vote.

MAGAZINES

In France, architect Le Corbusier, painter Amédée Ozenfant, and poet Paul Dermée found a periodical called *L'Esprit Nouveau*; the next year it will publish the principal manifesto of the Purist movement, "Le Purisme," stating that art should "induce a sensation of mathematical order," and it will introduce to France the ideas of Adolf Loos, Theo van Doesburg, and Filippo Marinetti. In the United States, *Pencil Points* is founded; it will later become *Progressive Architecture*.

PROGRESS IN THE PROFESSION

Lilly Reich is the first woman member of the board of directors of the Deutscher Werkbund.

TECHNICAL AND SCIENTIFIC ADVANCES

The first bathroom fixtures in color are introduced, as is the electric hair dryer.

1920

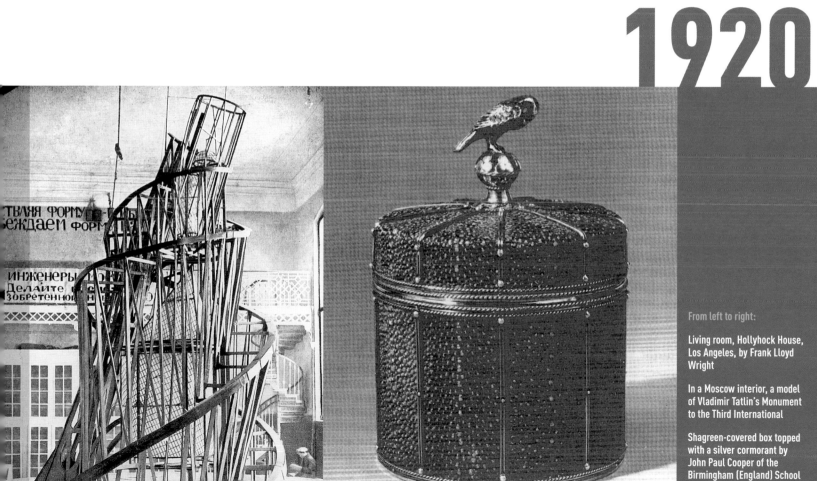

From left to right:

Living room, Hollyhock House, Los Angeles, by Frank Lloyd Wright

In a Moscow interior, a model of Vladimir Tatlin's Monument to the Third International

Shagreen-covered box topped with a silver cormorant by John Paul Cooper of the Birmingham (England) School of Design

Eric Mendelsohn's expressionistic Einstein Tower is built in Potsdam, and Simon Rodilla's more vernacular tower is built in the Watts section of Los Angeles. Ludwig Mies van der Rohe's skyscraper project for the Friedrichstrasse, Berlin, is not built. Walter Gropius reverts to a rustic style in his Berlin log house for lumber merchant Adolf Sommerfeld. Rudolph Schindler designs the Schindler-Chace house in Los Angeles.

John Gloag writes *Simple Furnishing and Arrangement*. Robert Wemyss Symonds writes *The Present State of Old English Furniture*, the first of a series of books that will establish widely respected criteria for furniture collectors. Poet Paul Valéry writes the text for *Architecture*, a portfolio of interior design by Süe et Mare. Wilhelm von Bode's *Italian Renaissance Furniture* is published in English. Arthur Byne and his wife, Mildred Stapley Byne, begin the publication of their three-volume *Spanish Interiors and Furniture*; the Bynes will write a dozen books on Spanish interiors and, from their base in Madrid, will send Spanish antiques to American architect Julia Morgan for her client William Randolph Hearst.

Edith Wharton wins the Pulitzer Prize for her 1920 novel *The Age of Innocence*; Georges Braque paints *Still Life with Guitar*; Sergey Prokofiev composes *The Love for Three Oranges*.

Vienna-born architect and designer Joseph Urban, in the United States for a decade, establishes the Wiener Werkstätte of America in New York, but it will not prosper. Betty Joel opens a showroom on Sloane Street in London; her commissions will include interiors of the Savoy hotel and residences for Winston Churchill and Lord Mountbatten; she will be active as a designer until 1937. New York's Ambassador Hotel, at Park Avenue and 52nd Street, opens with interiors by Joseph L. Emanuel of L. & E. Emanuel, San Francisco; all the hotel's appointments are from the contract division of John Wanamaker's New York store. Watterson Lowe

Metropolitan Museum recognizes industrial design

designs the interiors of the Great Neck, New York, house of actor, dramatist, and director George M. Cohan. Rapp & Rapp design the Tivoli Theater in Chicago, its foyer a replica of the Chapelle Royale at Versailles. Sonia Delaunay designs the interiors and furnishings of a Paris house for herself and her husband, Robert.

Richard Bach curates the first of a series of industrial design exhibitions at the Metropolitan Museum of Art, New York.

Mariano Fortuny opens a textile factory on the Giudecca in Venice for the production of printed cottons, some of them employing metallic pigments; although Fortuny will die in 1949, his factory will still be in operation at the end of the century. The Alessi tableware company is founded in Milan. Gunnar Asplund designs furniture for the Stockholm city hall. Kem Weber, now in Los Angeles, becomes art director for the Barker Brothers furniture company. For the Paris apartment of fashion designer Jeanne Lanvin, Armand-Albert Rateau's interiors include bronze furniture in the Pompeian style; Rateau will later design Lanvin's fashion house and its distinctive spherical perfume flacon.

The Viennese journal *Kunst und Kunsthandwerk*, published since 1898, folds. In Milan and Rome, *Architettura e arti decorative* is founded; in 1928 it will become *Casabella*.

The New York School of Fine and Applied Art, later to be renamed the Parsons School of Design, opens its Paris branch on the Place des Vosges.

Albert Einstein wins the Nobel Prize for his discovery of the photoelectric effect.

1921

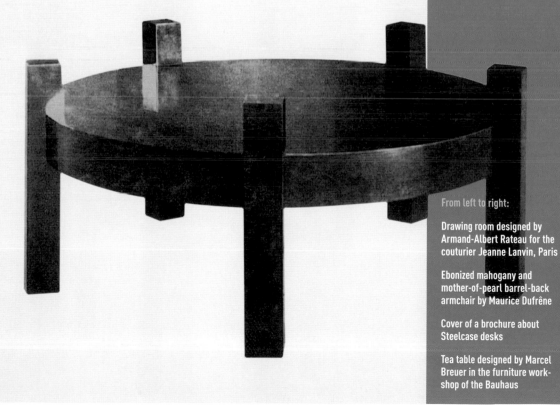

From left to right:

Drawing room designed by Armand-Albert Rateau for the couturier Jeanne Lanvin, Paris

Ebonized mahogany and mother-of-pearl barrel-back armchair by Maurice Dufrêne

Cover of a brochure about Steelcase desks

Tea table designed by Marcel Breuer in the furniture workshop of the Bauhaus

ARCHITECTURE

The Imperial Hotel by Frank Lloyd Wright is completed in Tokyo. Hood & Howells win a competition for the design of the Chicago Tribune Tower; it will be completed in 1924; second prize in the competition goes to Eliel Saarinen. Bertram Grosvenor Goodhue designs the Nebraska state capitol.

BOOKS

W. R. Lethaby writes *Form in Civilization*. John Gloag writes *Simple Schemes for Decoration*. Edward Stratton Holloway writes *The Practical Book of Furnishing the Small House and Apartment*, naming two American designers working in the "modern, non-period" style: Pieter Meyer and Edward Aschermann, both of New York. Louis Sullivan produces a portfolio of ornament drawings, *A System of Architectural Ornament According with a Philosophy of Man's Powers*.

CULTURE AT LARGE

James Joyce's complete *Ulysses* is published in Paris and is burned again by the U.S. Post Office; *The Waste Land* is written by T. S. Eliot, and *Tales of the Jazz Age* by F. Scott Fitzgerald. Emily Post writes a book on etiquette.

DESIGNERS AND INSTALLATIONS

Nancy McClelland leaves "Au Quatrième" at Wanamaker's in Philadelphia and opens her own design firm in New York. Syrie Maugham opens her own shop and design studio, Syrie Ltd., in London; her clients will include Noel Coward, Tallulah Bankhead, Mary Pickford, and the Duke and Duchess of Windsor. Eileen Gray opens the Galerie Jean Désert in Paris; it shows her furniture, lacquerware, and carpets. At the Paris department store Galeries Lafayette, Jacques Adnet becomes head of the decorating studio La Maîtrise; his brother Jean will later become director of the store's window displays. Jules Leleu opens a shop in Paris, offering furniture veneered in shagreen; he will later open a branch in New York. Also in Paris, André Domin and Marcel Genevrière found the decorating firm Dominique on rue du Faubourg Saint-Honoré; it will have clients in Cuba and the Netherlands as well as France. In the Paris suburb of Neuilly, Sonia Delaunay designs the bookstore Au Sans Pareil. In Chicago, Albert Pick & Co. designs the New Montrose Hotel. William D. McCann designs San Francisco's 3,500-seat Granada Theater, and Gunnar Asplund designs the interiors of the Scandia theater in Stockholm. Rorimer-Brooks Studios of Cleveland designs the Kansas City Club. For Barker Brothers, Kem Weber designs the Modes and Manor shop in Los Angeles. The tomb of Egypt's eighteenth-dynasty king Tutankhamun ("King Tut") is discovered by British Egyptologists Howard Carter and George Herbert (Lord Carnarvon), and the treasures in it will result in a popular passion for Egyptian Revival design; an early and lavish example is Grauman's Egyptian Theater in Hollywood, designed by Meyer & Holler.

King Tut prompts an Egyptian Revival

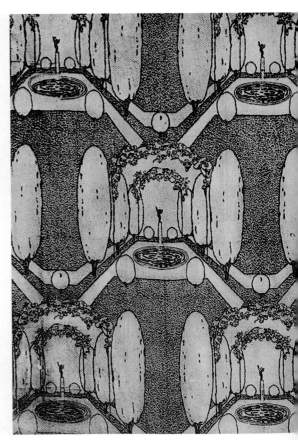

A Duncan Phyfe exhibition at the Metropolitan Museum of Art, New York, includes over one hundred examples of furniture from his workshop. The work of the Deutscher Werkbund is shown at the Newark Museum.

In his Bauhaus workshop, Marcel Breuer designs an armchair with an oak frame supporting a seat and back of stretched fabric. Kaare Klint begins the design of a furniture collection for the Thorvaldsens Museum, Copenhagen.

In Italy, Benito Mussolini becomes dictator. In Russia, the Union of Soviet Socialist Republics is formed, and Joseph Stalin becomes secretary of the Communist Party Central Committee.

Better Homes and Gardens is founded.

Peter Behrens is appointed director of architecture at the Vienna Academy.

The self-winding wrist-watch is invented.

1922

From left to right:

Amboyna root mirror by Jacques Leleu

Gilt-bronze clock by André Mare for Süe & Mare

Marcel Breuer chair design with an oak frame and orange herringbone wool fabric

Printed silk fabric by Émile-Jacques Ruhlmann

Dining room, Imperial Hotel, Tokyo, by Frank Lloyd Wright

ARCHITECTURE

Le Corbusier designs the La Roche–Jeanneret houses in Paris.

BOOKS

Süe et Mare present their own work in *Rythme de l'architecture*. Phyllis Ackerman writes *Wallpaper: Its History, Design, and Use*. Le Corbusier writes *Vers une architecture (Toward a New Architecture)*. *The History of Ornament: Renaissance and Modern* by Alfred D. F. Hamlin, *Old English Walnut and Lacquer Furniture* by Robert Wemyss Symonds, and *History and Crafts* by Gordon Russell are published.

Le Corbusier: "A grea

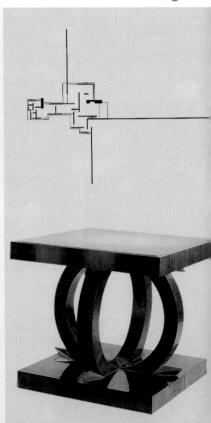

The first supermarket opens in San Francisco. William Butler Yeats wins the Nobel Prize for literature.

Europe is becoming fascinated with African and Oceanic design motifs. Walker & Gillette design interiors of the ship SS *Leviathan*. John Eberson designs the Majestic in Houston, the first of his many "atmospheric" movie theaters with lighting giving the illusion of the outdoors. Pierre Chareau designs a Paris apartment for couturier and art collector Jacques Doucet, who had commissioned furniture by Eileen Gray beginning in 1914, including her 1919 folding screen, *Le Destin*, and who had bought Pablo Picasso's *Demoiselles d'Avignon* in 1920; the apartment will be published in *Art et décoration* the following year. Candace Wheeler dies at ninety-six.

The International Silk Exposition is held at the Grand Central Palace, New York. Marcel Breuer designs furniture for the "Haus-am-Horn" at the Bauhaus exhibition in Weimar. In Paris, the work of the De Stijl group is shown at the Galerie Léonce Rosenberg and the first Salon des Arts Ménagers is held. The Biennale exhibition is instituted in Monza, Italy; it will later become the Triennale and move to Milan.

Josef Albers, who has just begun teaching at the Bauhaus, designs a vitrine of clear and obscure glasses held in chrome frames. Also at the Bauhaus, Wilhelm Wagenfeld designs the "MT8" glass-shaded table lamp. Pierre Legrain designs a curved seat clearly based on an Ashanti stool for the Salon des Artistes Décorateurs, Paris. Gerrit Rietveld designs his "Berlin" chair and table. Jean Prouvé opens a studio in Nancy and designs the first of his metal furniture.

Martial law is declared in Oklahoma to protect against Ku Klux Klan attacks.

The hot-strip rolling of steel is perfected by John B. Tytus.

poch has begun. There exists a new spirit."

1923

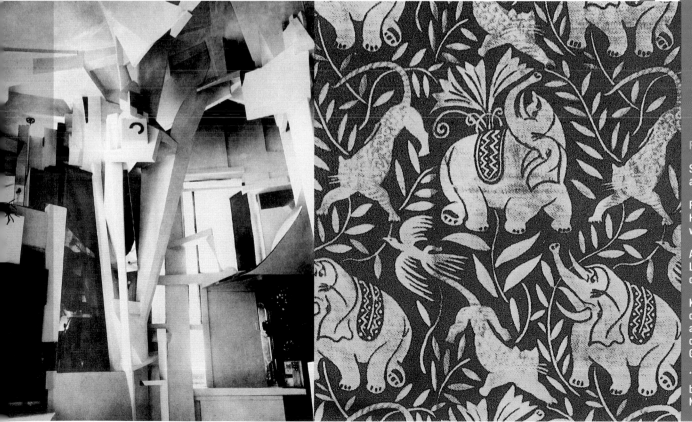

From left to right:

Screen of lacquered wood and aluminum by Eileen Gray

Plan for the Brick Country House project by Ludwig Mies van der Rohe

A gueridon designed by Pierre Legrain of rosewood on ebony, oak, and silver paint

Kurt Schwitters begins the construction of his interior assemblage Merzbau; it will continue until he leaves Germany in 1936.

"La Jungle" brocade designed by Raoul Dufy for L'Atelier Martine

ARCHITECTURE

Louis Sullivan dies. "He knew the truths of architecture," his disciple Frank Lloyd Wright writes in *Architectural Record*, "as I believe no one before him knew them. And profoundly he realized them." Wright designs the Ennis house (later known as the Ennis-Brown house) in Los Angeles, using textured concrete block. Auguste Perret designs the concrete church of Notre Dame du Raincy at Le Raincy, France. Raymond Hood designs the American Radiator Building in New York. Gerrit Rietveld, with Truus Schröeder-Schräder, designs the Schröder house in Utrecht, defining the De Stijl movement.

BOOKS

The American Institute of Architects Press publishes Louis Sullivan's *The Autobiography of an Idea*. Nancy McClelland's *Historic Wallpapers*, Lewis Mumford's *Sticks and Stones: A Study of American Architecture and Civilization*, Geoffrey Scott's *The Architecture of Humanism: A Study in the History of Taste*, and Ethyl Davis Seal's *Furnishing the Little House* are published. Jean Badovici produces both *Intérieurs de Süe et Mare*, and *Harmonies: Intérieurs de Ruhlmann*.

CULTURE AT LARGE

George Gershwin composes *Rhapsody in Blue*. E. M. Forster's *A Passage to India* is published. The first Surrealist manifesto is printed.

DESIGNERS AND INSTALLATIONS

Pierre Chareau opens a Paris shop (La Boutique) for the sale of his furniture designs. The House of Jansen designs interiors for the Villa Carne d'Or in Cannes. Serge Chermayeff is chief designer, until 1927, for the London decorating firm E. Williams Ltd. Robert Mallet-Stevens designs the Château de Gibet, Mézy, France, and its interiors for couturier Paul Poiret. Filmmaker Marcel L'Herbier hires Robert Mallet-Stevens, Pierre Chareau, and Fernand Léger to design sets for his film *L'Inhumaine*. Vanessa Bell and Duncan Grant begin the decoration of Monks House for Bell's sister Virginia Woolf and her husband, Leonard.

EXHIBITIONS

Marcel Breuer's wood armchair with a stretched fabric seat and back is shown at the Summer Exhibition of the Bauhaus. The British Empire Exhibition is held at Wembley.

Art Deco at its zenith in France

FURNITURE AND FURNISHINGS

Gerrit Rietveld designs a lamp of chrome-plated and painted metal. Poul Henningsen designs the "PH" lamp series for Louis Poulsen; Mies van der Rohe will use it in his 1930 Tugendhat house, and it will still be in production at the end of the century. Kaare Klint establishes a school of furniture design at the Royal Academy School of Architecture in Copenhagen, and Estrid Ericson opens the Svenskt Tenn furniture store in Stockholm. Michel Dufet designs the first Cubist wallpapers. For his father's house in Phoenix, Arizona, Warren McArthur designs what may be the first furniture of tubular metal; in Germany, brothers Heinz and Bodo Rasch also design chairs of tubular steel that will be produced by L. C. Arnold. Stanislav V'Soske, Polish-born textile designer and manufacturer, designs and weaves the first hand-tufted rugs in the United States; his company will later employ Stuart Davis, George Nelson, and Michael Graves as rug designers.

GOVERNMENT EVENTS

Vladimir I. Lenin dies. Greece is proclaimed a republic.

MAGAZINES

An entire issue of the Dutch journal *Wendingen* is devoted to the work of Eileen Gray.

PROGRESS IN THE PROFESSION

Sherrill Whiton's New York School of Interior Design is chartered by the New York State Board of Regents, becoming one of the country's first accredited interior design schools. Eleanor McMillen, who will become Mrs. Archibald Brown in 1934, opens McMillen Inc., which she calls "the first professional full-service interior decorating firm in America."

TECHNICAL AND SCIENTIFIC ADVANCES

Clarence Birdseye freezes food for retail sale. William Mason presses discarded wood chips into Masonite. The Celanese Corporation introduces acetate fibers.

1924

From left to right:

Gerrit Rietveld's Schröder house, Utrecht, the Netherlands

Mahogany, amboyna, and ebony chest of drawers by Maurice Dufrêne

Stools designed by Pierre Chareau, as reproduced by Écart and available through Pucci International

Eleanor McMillen, the future Eleanor Brown

Living room, Frank Lloyd Wright's Ennis house, Los Angeles

Walter Gropius moves the Bauhaus from Weimar to Dessau and into a new complex of buildings of his own design. Frank Lloyd Wright redesigns Taliesin, his home, studio, and school at Spring Green, Wisconsin, after a disastrous fire.

Le Corbusier's *L'Art Décoratif d'aujourd'hui (The Decorative Art of Today)* states that "Modern decorative art is not decorated." Also published in Paris are the *Encyclopédie des arts décoratifs et industriels modernes* and *La Ferronnerie Moderne*. Roberto Papini's *Le Arti d'Oggi* is published in Rome and Milan.

The first Guggenheim Fellowship is awarded to composer Aaron Copland. Harold Lloyd's *The Freshman* and Charlie Chaplin's *The Gold Rush* are on the screen. F. Scott Fitzgerald writes *The Great Gatsby*, and Virginia Woolf writes *Mrs. Dalloway*. *The New Yorker* magazine begins publication. Harold S. Vanderbilt, aboard the SS *Finland*, invents contract bridge. Flappers dance the Charleston.

Stage designer Erté designs his own apartment in Paris, as does architect and designer Ernö Goldfinger. Also in Paris, Robert Mallet-Stevens designs an Alfa Romeo automobile showroom. In New York, Elsie Cobb Wilson designs interiors for both the Fifth Avenue house and the Long Island house of her sister Mrs. Cornelius N. Bliss. Dorothy Draper opens a design firm in New York; called the Architectural Clearing House, it will soon change its name to Dorothy Draper & Company; the firm's first successes will be a series of apartment building lobbies in the Art Deco style. Le Corbusier designs a studio-house for sculptor Jacques Lipschitz in Boulogne-sur-Seine, France, with furniture designs by Pierre Chareau. Brazilian-born painter and designer Ivan Da Silva-Bruhns opens a shop on rue de l'Odeon, Paris; he will become best known for his rug designs. Syrie Maugham of London opens an outlet in Chicago in partnership with Elizabeth Arden. Basil Ionides redesigns his weekend retreat in Essex in the Arts and Crafts style. Süe et Mare designs the d'Orsay perfume shop in Paris and an octagonal flacon for its perfume. Marcel Breuer designs interiors for the Masters' Houses at the Bauhaus, Dessau.

Breuer bends steel tubing into furniture

EXHIBITIONS

The Metropolitan Museum of Art, New York, opens its American Wing. Paris's *Exposition Internationale des Arts Décoratifs et Industriels Modernes*, which gives its imprimatur and will later give its name to the Art Deco style, is in full swing.

FURNITURE AND FURNISHINGS

In the Bauhaus workshops, Josef Albers designs glass and metal tableware, and Marcel Breuer produces tubular-steel-frame tables and chairs; one of the Breuer designs will later be marketed under the name "Wassily" after Breuer's Bauhaus colleague, painter Wassily Kandinsky. Erik Gunnar Asplund designs the "Senna" lounge chair; it will be revived by Cassina in the 1980s. For Thonet, Josef Hoffmann designs the "Prague" chair of steam-bent elm. Le Corbusier designs his "Casiers Standard" group of modular storage units. *Vogue* magazine publishes the batiks of textile designer Marion Dorn. Eugenio Quarti designs furniture for the Grand Hotel, Pellegrino, Italy. Adelgunde "Gunta" Stözl, the first weaver at the Bauhaus, opens her own studio in Switzerland; she will head the Bauhaus weaving studio from 1927 to 1931. Pierre de Maria designs a folding screen of lacquer and pewter. Édouard-Wilfrid Busquet designs the "Anglepoise" lamp; he will patent it in 1927, and it will become one of the most useful lighting designs of the century; George Carwardine will produce a popular version for Herbert Terry in 1934, and it will inspire Jacob Jacobsen's 1937 "Luxo" lamp. Captain Roger E. Brunschwig opens a Brunschwig & Fils showroom in New York.

GOVERNMENT EVENTS

Hitler reorganizes the Nazi Party and publishes volume one of *Mein Kampf*. John Scopes, defended by Clarence Darrow against prosecutor William Jennings Bryan, is tried for teaching the theory of evolution.

MAGAZINES

Architectural Digest is founded in the United States, and *Apollo* in England. The Paris-based *L'Ésprit Nouveau* ceases publication. The Dutch magazine *Wendingen* devotes seven special issues to the work of Frank Lloyd Wright.

TECHNICAL AND SCIENTIFIC ADVANCES

Cosmic rays are discovered in the upper atmosphere. Heisenberg and Bohr develop quantum mechanics. Professor A. O. Rankine predicts the advent of talking pictures.

1925

From left to right:

Breuer's nesting tables on tubular-steel frames

Steel fan table designed by Pierre Chareau, as reproduced by Écart and available through Pucci International

Console of wrought iron, marble, and tole by Süe et Mare.

Rudolph Schindler designs the Lovell beach house in Newport Beach, California. Eliel Saarinen, now in the United States, designs the Cranbrook Academy of Art in Bloomfield Hills, Michigan. In Paris, Robert Mallet-Stevens designs several houses on what will later be named rue Mallet-Stevens. Le Corbusier publishes the "Five Points of a New Architecture." Antoni Gaudí is hit by a trolley car in Barcelona and dies three days later.

British designer and color theorist Basil Ionides presents his ideas in *Colour and Interior Decoration*, illustrated with the watercolors of W. B. E. Ranken. The U.S. Department of Agriculture publishes Bulletin 66, *The Identification of Furniture Woods*. Nancy McClelland writes *The Practical Book of Decorative Wall Treatments*.

In Hollywood, Rudolph Valentino finishes *The Son of the Sheik* and dies; John Barrymore stars as *Don Juan*. Gertrude Ederle swims the English Channel in record time.

Elsie de Wolfe, at sixty-one, marries Sir Charles Mendl, the British press attaché in Paris, becoming Lady Mendl. In Paris, Adolf Loos designs a house for Dadaist poet Tristan Tzara, Ernö Goldfinger designs an apartment interior and furniture for paint manufacturer M. Coutrot, Émile Jacques Ruhlmann designs interiors for the chamber of commerce, Pierre Legrain designs a house for couturier Jacques Doucet, Robert Mallet-Stevens designs sets for the film *Le Vertige*, and the House of Jansen is designing a salon for "Coco" Chanel on the rue Faubourg St.-Honoré. In London, painter and theater designer Rex Whistler decorates the refreshment room of the Tate Gallery. In Cologne, Richard Riemerschmid is named director of the Werkschule. In Strasbourg, Theo van Doesburg, with Hans Arp and Sophie Tauber-Arp,

Art Deco invades the U.S.

EXHIBITIONS

FURNITURE
AND FURNISHINGS

HONORS AND AWARDS

MAGAZINES

TECHNICAL AND
SCIENTIFIC ADVANCES

begins the renovation of Café L'Aubette and an adjacent cinema. Painter Piet Mondrian is commissioned to design an interior for a Dresden art collector; his design will not be executed, but the Pace Gallery, New York, will construct it in 1970. In Madrid, Armand-Albert Rateau designs a bathroom with gold lacquered walls for the Duchess of Alba. Kem Weber designs interiors and furniture for the Mayfair Hotel, Los Angeles. Eric Mendelsohn designs the Universum Cinema in Berlin. The Rationalist movement is launched in Italy by Giuseppe Terragni and others.

The Art Deco movement arrives in the United States, with selected designs from the previous year's exhibition in Paris being shown at New York's Metropolitan Museum of Art. The Royal Academy, London, presents a John Singer Sargent memorial exhibition.

In the auditorium of the Bauhaus building, the first large-scale installation of tubular-steel furniture; it is designed by Marcel Breuer with a cantilevered fold-down seat; the auditorium lighting design is by László Moholy-Nagy. T. H. Robsjohn-Gibbings designs a modern version of the Greek klismos chair. Eileen Gray designs the "Transat" chair and the "Satellite" mirror. French designer and cabinetmaker Louis Majorelle dies at sixty-seven.

Pierre Chareau is awarded the medal of the French Legion of Honor.

Cahiers d'art and *Art et industrie* begin publication in Paris. Danish designer Poul Henningsen edits the journal *Kritisk Revi*.

Assembly-line production is in use for the manufacture of electric lamps.

1926

From left to right:

Marcel Breuer's dining room design for László Moholy-Nagy's house at the Bauhaus. The furniture is by Breuer, the painting by Moholy-Nagy, and the ceiling lighting fixture by Walter Gropius.

Modern reconstruction, based on vase paintings, of an ancient Greek klismos chair. This 1926 version by T. H. Robsjohn-Gibbings has a frame of walnut and a seat of leather thongs.

Eileen Gray's "Satellite" mirror as reproduced by Écart and available through Pucci International

The "Bloch" daybed design by Émile-Jacques Ruhlmann

Eileen Gray's "Transat" chair as reproduced by Écart and available through Pucci International

R. Buckminster Fuller designs an industrialized "Dymaxion" house of aluminum suspended from a central mast. Le Corbsuier designs the Villa Stein at Garches, France, for Gertrude Stein's brother Leo. Giuseppe Terragni designs the Novocomum apartment block in Como, Italy. Joseph Urban and Thomas W. Lamb design the Ziegfeld Theater, New York.

Nancy McClelland's *The Young Decorator*, Edwin Avery Park's *New Backgrounds for a New Age*, Frances Lenygon's *Decoration in England from 1660 to 1770*, and Shirley P. Wainwright's *Modern Plywood* are published.

The Jazz Singer, starring Al Jolson, is the first "talkie," and Virginia Woolf writes *To the Lighthouse*. The musical *Good News* is on Broadway, and in the cast is young William Pahlmann, earning money for his studies at the Parsons School of Design.

In London, Syrie (Mrs. W. Somerset) Maugham creates a sensation by redecorating her King's Road drawing room *all in white*. But she also designs the Villa Elisa at Le Touquet, France, in peach and beige. The *Île-de-France*, the largest oceanliner of its time, is launched, with a lounge by Étienne Kohlmann, a lecture room by Jules Leleu, a children's playroom by Michel Dufet, and other interiors by Émile-Jacques Ruhlmann, René Prou, Pierre Patout, Jacques Adnet, Maurice Dufrêne, and Süe et Mare; the ship establishes the luxurious *style paquebot*. Also being designed by Süe et Mare are a villa at Saint-Cloud for comedienne Jane Renouard, and an apartment in Paris and country house in Ustaritz for couturier Jean Patou. Ernö Goldfinger designs a Paris apartment for the husband of Helena Rubenstein, and

Syrie Maugham's all-white room; the fluorescent lamp

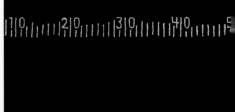

EXHIBITIONS

FURNITURE
AND FURNISHINGS

GOVERNMENT EVENTS

TECHNICAL AND
SCIENTIFIC ADVANCES

the following year he will design a London apartment for Rubenstein herself and glass furniture for her showroom. John Eberson designs the Avalon Theater, Chicago, in Moorish style, and Meyer & Holler design a Grauman's Theater, Hollywood, in Chinese style. Donald Deskey designs the interiors and furniture for the New York apartment of Adam Gimbel, the president of Saks, with cork walls, linoleum floors, a copper ceiling, and chairs covered in pigskin. Also in New York, Elsie de Wolfe designs a residence for Condé Nast. In London, Kenneth Anns designs interiors for the Park Lane Hotel with an Art Deco ironwork mural and furniture painted silver. At Roquebrune, on the French coast, Eileen Gray designs a villa for herself; she calls it "E-1027."

The Deutscher Werkbund's *Die Wohnung* exhibition is staged in Stuttgart. Also in Stuttgart, the *Weissenhof Seidlung* housing exhibition is held, its participants including Ludwig Mies van der Rohe, Josef Frank, Peter Behrens, Le Corbusier, J. J. P. Oud, and Walter Gropius; the units are furnished in part with tubular-steel furniture by Oud, Marcel Breuer, and Mart Stam. Ludwig Mies van der Rohe, in collaboration with Lilly Reich, also designs the "Velvet and Silk Café" for the *Mode der Dame* exhibition in Berlin.

The Metropolitan Museum of Art, New York, presents exhibitions of Swedish and Danish decorative arts, and an exhibition at the Museum of Applied Arts in Copenhagen will become an annual event. The first Finnish Furniture Exhibition is held in Helsinki. Also in New York, Macy's shows *New Art*, including a room of Paul Frankl's "skyscraper furniture" with stepped outlines.

Marcel Breuer, Mart Stam, and Ludwig Mies van der Rohe are all designing cantilevered chairs of tubular steel. A cylindrical table lamp by Wolfgang Tümpel is manufactured by Goldschmidt und Schwabe, Berlin. Eileen Gray designs an adjustable-height table of glass and steel; the design will be reproduced by Stendig in 1978. The furniture company Cassina is founded in Meda, Italy, by brothers Umberto and Cesare Cassina. Walter von Nessen and his wife, Greta, establish Nessen Studios for the design and manufacture of lighting; one of its earliest products, a swing-arm lamp, will be its most popular. For the Green Room of the White House, Tiffany Studios designs an Aubusson rug with the U.S. seal in the center.

The German economy collapses. The Parliament House opens in Canberra, Australia.

Albert W. Hall perfects the fluorescent lamp. Lindbergh makes the first transatlantic flight. In the first U.S. demonstration of television, images of Secretary of Commerce Herbert Hoover are sent from Washington to New York. Werner Heisenberg formulates the Uncertainty Principle. In Germany, Otto Röhm develops acrylic plastics. The Hotel Statler in Boston is the first hotel with radio reception. Formica learns how to imitate wood grain.

1927

From left to right:

Marcel Breuer's dining room for theater director Erwin Piscator, Berlin. The chair is a Breuer design of 1926.

Paul Frankl's "Skyscraper" bookcase of maple with Bakelite plastic

Eileen Gray's "Centimetre" rug designed c. 1927 as reproduced by Écart and available through Pucci International

The Velvet and Silk Café, Berlin, by Ludwig Mies van der Rohe and Lilly Reich. The hangings were in black, orange, and red velvet and black, silver, gold, and lemon yellow silk.

Ludwig Mies van der Rohe's "MR10" side chair of nickel-plated tubular steel and cane

ARCHITECTURE

The Congrès Internationaux d'Architecture Moderne (CIAM) is founded in Geneva, its founding members including Le Corbusier and Walter Gropius. Gropius resigns from the Bauhaus and is replaced by Hannes Meyer. Alvar Aalto designs the Sanomat newspaper plant in Turku, Finland. Edwin Lutyens designs the British embassy and its interiors in Washington, D.C. Ludwig Mies van der Rohe designs the Tugendhat house in Brno, Czechoslovakia. Eliel Saarinen designs the president's house at Cranbrook Academy, Bloomfield Hills, Michigan, with his own interiors and furniture and with textiles by his wife, Loja. Horace Trumbauer designs the Philadelphia Museum of Art. Gunnar Asplund designs the Municipal Library, Stockholm.

BOOKS

New Dimensions: The Decorative Arts of Today in Words and Pictures is written by Paul T. Frankl; it is dedicated to "great American architect and creative artist Frank Lloyd Wright" and shows work by Wright, André Lurçat, Robert Mallet-Stevens, Jean Dunand, Paul Poiret, René Herbst, Bruno Paul, Frankl himself, and others. Heinz Rasch edits *Der Stuhl* (*The Chair*). László Moholy-Nagy writes *The New Vision*. Amédée Ozenfant writes *Art*, which will be published in English in 1931 as *Foundations of Modern Art*.

CULTURE AT LARGE

Virginia Woolf writes *Orlando*; Arturo Toscanini becomes conductor of the New York Philharmonic.

DESIGNERS AND INSTALLATIONS

Ruby Ross Wood is commissioned for the interiors of Swan House, the Inman house in Atlanta; its architect is Philip Trammell Schutze; the house will later be given, with furnishings intact, to the Atlanta Historical Society. Eleanor McMillen designs an apartment for herself in New York. Süe et Mare designs interiors for the liner *Île-de-France* and names Jacques Adnet its director of design. Paul Follot and Serge Chermayeff are made codirectors of the Modern Art Department of Waring & Gillow, a British furniture company with a branch in Paris; they present an exhibition of sixty modern room settings. Hans Poelzig designs the Babylon Cinema in Berlin. Josef Hoffmann designs the Graben Café in Vienna. Robert Mallet-Stevens designs a casino and its interiors at Saint-Jean-de-Luz, France, and, with Claude Lévy, Paris offices for the journal *Semaine à Paris*. Pierre Patout designs the Robert Bély department store in Paris. Cedric Gibbons puts Art Deco interiors on the screen with sets for *Our Dancing Daughters*; he will do the same for *Our Modern Maidens* the following year and *Our Blushing Brides* the year after. Charles Rennie Mackintosh dies in London at age sixty.

EXHIBITIONS

Eugène Printz's gray metal chandelier "Couronne Lumineuse" is shown at the Salon d'Automne, Paris. The Art Deco style and other current trends reach a popular American audience with exhibitions at New York department stores: an *Exposition of Art and Industry* is at Macy's, including room settings by Josef Hoffmann, Bruno Paul, and Gio Ponti; *The Livable House Transformed* is at Abraham & Straus, Brooklyn; and an *Exposition of Modern French Decorative Arts* is at Lord & Taylor.

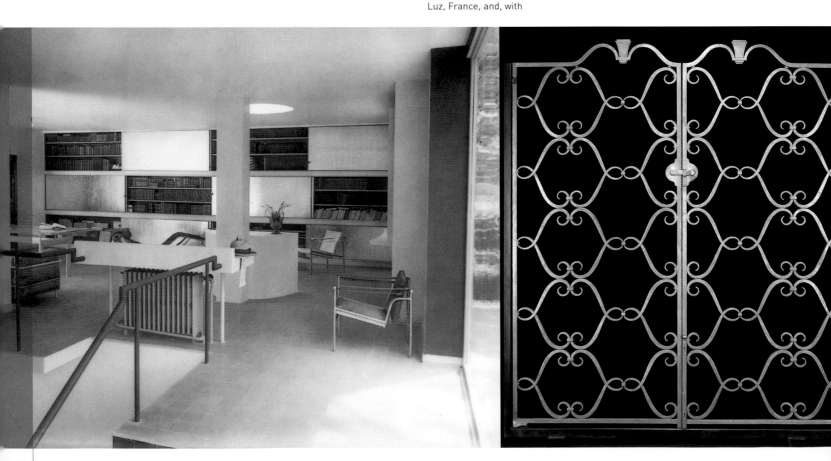

FURNITURE AND FURNISHINGS

The "Cesca" cantilevered chair and a lounge chair made from a continuous length of tubular steel are designed by Marcel Breuer, and a chaise longue, the "LC1" sling chair, and the "Grand Confort" armchairs are all designed by Le Corbusier, Pierre Jeanneret-Gris, and Charlotte Perriand; all these designs are manufactured by Thonet. Eyre de Lanux designs a table of sandblasted glass resting on glass blocks. Austrian architect Bruno Weil, also known as "Béwé," designs the "B282" table and the "B250" office storage unit.

Edwin Lutyens designs the "Pall Mall" chair for the Crane Bennet Co., London. Kem Weber designs lamps for the Brilliant Glass Co. and the "Bentlock" furniture line for Higgins Manufacturing. Donald Deskey designs an aluminum-based table for the Ypsilanti Reed Furniture Co.

GOVERNMENT EVENTS

In England, the age of women's voting rights is reduced from thirty to twenty-one.

MAGAZINES

In Italy, architect and designer Gio Ponti founds *Domus* magazine, and *Casabella* also begins publication. In Germany, the periodical *Bauhaus* begins publication; eight issues will be produced.

PROGRESS IN THE PROFESSION

The American Union of Decorative Artists and Craftsmen (AUDAC) is formed by Kem Weber, Donald Deskey, Frederick Kiesler, and other designers to promote decorative art and artists. The American Designers' Gallery is also formed with the same purpose and some of the same members; its headquarters is the studio of designer Paul Frankl, and its initial exhibition is in the Chase National Bank building, New York.

TECHNICAL AND SCIENTIFIC ADVANCES

Chemist Waldo Semon, working for the B. F. Goodrich Co., develops vinyl. Alexander Fleming discovers penicillin. Scotch tape is marketed by 3-M.

1928

Breuer's "Cesca" chair; Ponti's *Domus*; B. F. Goodrich's vinyl

From left to right:

Library, Le Corbusier's Villa Church, Ville d'Avray, France. The chair at right is the "LC1" sling by Le Corbusier, Pierre Jeanneret-Gris, and Charlotte Perriand

Pair of wrought-iron gates attributed to Raymond Subes

Breuer's cantilevered steel lounge chair with rattan seat

Breuer's cantilevered "Cesca" chair

A glass-topped table by Marcel Breuer for Thonet

ARCHITECTURE

Ludwig Mies van der Rohe designs the German Pavilion and its furniture for the Barcelona Exhibition. Le Corbusier designs the Villa Savoie at Poissy, near Paris. In New York, Hood & Howells design the Daily News Building. At Roquebrune on the French Riviera, Eileen Gray finishes her House E-1027. In Copenhagen, Arne Jacobsen designs a "House of the Future" for the Danish Building Exhibition. In Los Angeles, Richard Neutra designs the Lovell "Health House." In Washington, D.C., Paul Philippe Cret designs the Folger Shakespeare Library. In Phoenix, the Arizona Biltmore is designed by Albert Chase McArthur with consultation from his former teacher, Frank Lloyd Wright; it will be restored in 1981.

BOOKS

The New Interior Decoration by Raymond Mortimer and Dorothy Todd shows the latest in English interiors, including work by Vanessa Bell and Duncan Grant; it will be reprinted in 1977. *Répertoire du goût modern* is published in Paris, as is Sonia Delaunay's *Tapis et tissus*. Robert Wemyss Symonds writes *English Furniture from Charles II to George II*. Henry Dreyfuss writes *Industrial Design: A Pictorial Accounting*.

CULTURE AT LARGE

The Sound and the Fury by William Faulkner and *A Room of One's Own* by Virginia Woolf are published. The Nobel Prize for literature goes to Thomas Mann. Martha Graham founds a dance group. In Hollywood, the first Oscars are awarded to Janet Gaynor, Emil Jannings, and the film *Wings*. On October 24, "Black Monday," Wall Street crashes, which will lead to the Great Depression.

DESIGNERS AND INSTALLATIONS

In Los Angeles, Bullock's Wilshire, a department store epitomizing the Art Deco style, opens; its interior designer is Jock Peters. Kem Weber, in similar style but on a smaller scale, designs the Sommer and Kaufmann shoe store in San Francisco. The gallery/shop Vincon opens in Barcelona. In Wiesbaden, Germany, Marcel Breuer designs an apartment interior for the Harnishmacher family and an office for Mr. Harnishmacher. Jean-Michel Frank designs an apartment for Templeton Crocker in San Francisco and a salon for the Vicomte and Vicomtesse de Noailles in the Bischoffsheim mansion in Paris; it employs panels of straw marquetry, vellum-covered walls, and shagreen-covered tables.

Also in Paris, Ernö Goldfinger designs the Bugatti showroom on the Champs-Élysées, and Polish-born designer Adrienne Gorska de Montaut designs a two-story apartment for her sister, the painter Tamara de Lempicka, in a building designed by Robert Mallet-Stevens. Le Corbusier, Robert Mallet-Stevens, René Herbst, Eileen Gray, Charlotte Perriand, André Lurçat, and others boycott the traditional Société des Artistes Décorateurs and found the more progressive Union des Artistes Modernes. Gilbert Rohde opens an interior design studio in New York. French designers Evelyn Wyld and Eyre de Lanux open the Décor shop in Cannes. Donald Deskey designs

Miesian essence in Barcelona

FURNITURE AND FURNISHINGS

MAGAZINES

TECHNICAL AND SCIENTIFIC ADVANCES

interiors for the New York apartment of Abby Aldrich Rockefeller. New York's Carlyle Hotel opens with public spaces designed by Dorothy Draper; upstairs, Draper designs an apartment for herself. Also in New York, the interiors of the Chanin Building, in the Art Deco style, are by Jacques Delamarre, including a 52nd-floor suite for Irwin S. Chanin. In London, Trent and Lewis design the Art Deco New Victoria Cinema. In London and other English cities, Wells Coates begins designing interiors and furniture for Cresta Silks shops.

The Museum of Modern Art opens in New York with an exhibition of paintings by Paul Cézanne, Paul Gauguin, Vincent van Gogh, and Georges Seurat. The American Designers' Gallery holds its second exhibition of members' work. The exhibition *Contemporary Glass and Rugs* is shown at the Metropolitan Museum of Art, New York, as is *The Architect and the Industrial Arts: An Exhibition of Contemporary American Design*, this last part of a continuing series and including a conservatory and a man's den designed by Joseph Urban. In London, *Industrial Art for the Slender Purse* is seen at the Victoria & Albert. The first Kölner Möbelmesse furniture exposition is held in Cologne, Germany; in 1903 it will change its name to Internationale Kölner Möbelmesse, and it

will continue throughout the century. In Breslau, Germany, the Home and Work Exhibition Building is designed by Hans Scharoun. In Copenhagen, the Danish Building Exhibition features a *House of the Future* designed by twenty-seven-year-old Arne Jacobsen. At the Barcelona International Exposition a gold medal goes to twenty-two-year-old Alexander Girard. *Modern American Design in Metal* at the Newark Museum shows work by Donald Deskey, Walter von Nessen, Paul Frankl, and others. *Ballets Russes de Diaghelev, 1909–1929* is seen at the Musée des Arts Décoratifs, Paris; another show of the same title will be seen there a decade later.

Ernö Goldfinger designs the *Safari* chair; it will later be produced for photographer Lee Miller. Josef Albers designs a chair of laminated wood and tubular steel. A desk design by Sir Ambrose Heal is in the "Arts and Crafts Survival" style, but also shows the angular influence of Art Deco. Jacques Adnet designs a table lamp manufactured by Lumen Center and later by Pentalux. In Berlin, brothers Wassili and Hans Luckhardt design a cantilevered chair with a plywood seat and back. Scalamandré Silks is established.

Good Furniture changes its name to *Good Furniture and Decoration*. The French journal *Meubles* is founded with architect Pierre Chareau as editor.

The first workable all-electronic television system is demonstrated. French physicist Paul Dirac predicts the existence of antimatter. Frigidaire produces the first residential air conditioner; it is forty-nine inches wide and weighs two hundred pounds.

1929

From left to right:

Dorothy Draper's aubergine-walled sitting room in her apartment at the Hotel Carlyle, New York

Set design by Cedric Gibbons for MGM's *The Kiss*, starring Anders Randolf and Greta Garbo

Ludwig Mies van der Rohe's German Pavilion, Barcelona, furnished with "Barcelona" stools and chairs

Le Corbusier's Villa Savoie, Poissy, France

THE '30s

The Museum of Modern Art, which had opened in New York in 1929, gives early indication of the important role it will play in shaping American taste for modern design. In its third year, its International Style exhibition introduces new trends in European architecture; in its fifth year, its Machine Art exhibition publicizes the simple beauty of industrial products; in its seventh year, it presents the first of a series of exhibitions on the architecture, interiors, and furniture of Ludwig Mies van der Rohe; and in its ninth year, it presents both the work of the Bauhaus and the work of Finnish architect Alvar Aalto. But modernism is accompanied by eclectic traditionalism. Ralph Edward's article "Old Furniture and the Modern Background," published in the magazine *Decoration* in 1937, predicts the eclectic mixture of styles that will be popular throughout the second half of the century. Raymond Mortimer's article "Modern Period Character Mania: The Alternative to Period Style," in *Decoration* the following year, endorses Ralph Edward's prediction of eclecticism from the year before, but emphasizes that "all things that are good of their kind do not necessarily mix. They must have been conceived in the same spirit—have some abstract aesthetic relationship." An eclectic designer new to the New York scene is Mrs. Henry ("Sister") Parish II; "I have a horror of anything matching," she says. What began as *The Upholsterer* magazine and became *Upholsterer and Interior Decorator* now becomes *Interior Decorator* and will later become *Interiors*. In its November 1935 issue Donald Deskey writes, "The modern interior is designed, not decorated."

"House on a Lake for an Artist" designed by Giuseppe Terragni and others for the Milan Triennale, 1933.

ARCHITECTURE

Ludwig Mies van der Rohe completes his Tugendhat house and becomes director of the Bauhaus. New York's Chrysler Building, designed by William Van Alen, is—briefly—the world's tallest. Also in New York, Raymond Hood's Daily News Building is completed, his McGraw-Hill Building is on the boards, and Joseph Urban's New School for Social Research is opened. Konstantin Melnikov designs his own house in Moscow. In Rotterdam, the Van Nelle factory is completed to designs of Van der Vlugt and Brinkman; it is furnished with lighting fixtures and tubular-steel furniture designed by Willem Gispen. The Hilversum Town Hall, designed by Dutch architect Willem Dudok, opens.

BOOKS

Paul Frankl writes *Form and Re-Form: A Practical Handbook of Modern Interiors*. Herbert Hoffmann writes *Modern Interiors in Europe and America*. *Modern American Design* is published by the American Union of Decorative Artists and Craftsmen (AUDAC). Maurice Adams writes *Modern Decorative Art*, J. C. Rogers writes *Modern English Furniture*, and Katherine Morrison Kahle writes *Modern French Decoration*. Photographer and designer Cecil Beaton writes *The Book of Beauty*. Etiquette maven Emily Post writes *The Personality of a House: The Blue Book of Home Design and Decoration*; it includes such chapter headings as "Windows Are the Smiles of a House."

CULTURE AT LARGE

Noel Coward's *Private Lives* is on the stage. On the screen, Greta Garbo stars in *Anna Christie*, and Marlene Dietrich in *The Blue Angel*. A flight from San Francisco to Cheyenne carries the first airline flight attendant.

DESIGNERS AND INSTALLATIONS

Jean-Michel Frank designs the Paris couture house of Schiaparelli and a three-room apartment in a sixteenth-century palace near Rome for Count Cecil and Countess Minie Pecci Blunt; at the century's end, the Blunt rooms will be the only Frank interior still intact. René Herbst designs a Paris apartment for Prince Aga Khan, and Eugène Printz designs one for Princesse de la Tour d'Auvergne. For Robert Mallet-Stevens's house in Neuilly, Pierre Chareau designs a salon; it features an alabaster chandelier Chareau calls "La Religieuse." And in a Paris building by Mallet-Stevens, Louis Sognot and Charlotte Alix design offices for the periodical *La Semaine de Paris*. In London, Ronald Fleming designs an apartment with white and mirrored walls for Gertrude Lawrence; Oliver Percy Bernard designs interiors for the Strand Palace Hotel, using metal-framed furniture from Thonet; and Oswald Milne designs Claridge's Hotel. In New York, Donald Deskey designs an apartment for Helena Rubenstein. In San Francisco, Kem Weber designs the Roos Brothers shoe shop. English interior designer Francis Bacon switches his career to painting. In a suburb of Detroit, Eliel Saarinen's president's house at the Cranbrook Academy of Art is finished; he will occupy the house himself beginning in 1932.

Herman Miller hires modern designer Gilbert Rohde

EXHIBITIONS

AUDAC holds its first exhibition of members' work at Grand Central Palace, New York. In Paris, the Salon des Artistes Décorateurs shows two rooms, one for a woman, one for a man, designed by Marcel Breuer; also at the salon are furniture designs by René Herbst and Robert Mallet-Stevens. For the Stockholm exhibition, Gunnar Asplund designs all the buildings. The Werkbund exhibition in Paris is directed by Walter Gropius. "Modern Age Furniture" is shown at the W. & J. Sloane store in New York. The Biennale in Monza, Italy, becomes the Triennale.

FURNITURE AND FURNISHINGS

Jean Prouvé designs a steel chair, as does Robert Mallet-Stevens. Gilbert Rohde begins designing furniture for Herman Miller, a relationship that will last until Rohde's death in 1944, and also a walnut side chair with vinyl upholstery for Heywood-Wakefield. Edwin Lutyens designs the "New Delhi Circleback" chair for the Viceroy's House. Ruth Reeves designs the "Manhattan" wallpaper line for W. & J. Sloane. French couturier and designer Paul Poiret designs fabrics for Schumacher. Robert Dudley Best designs the "Bestlite" table lamp with a steel arm and spun-aluminum shade. Boris Kroll establishes his textile company. Warren McArthur establishes his namesake furniture company in Rome, New York.

GOVERNMENT EVENTS

The name of Constantinople is changed to Istanbul.

MAGAZINES

L'Architecture d'aujourd'hui begins publication in Paris.

PROGRESS IN THE PROFESSION

Frank Alvah Parsons dies at sixty-two and is succeeded by William Odom as president of the New York School of Fine and Applied Art, later to be renamed for Parsons; Odom will design an apartment for himself in New York's Pierre Hotel. The Society of Industrial Artists is founded in England.

TECHNICAL AND SCIENTIFIC ADVANCES

Acrylic plastics are commercially produced; the planet Pluto is discovered; a practical television broadcast system is developed; photographic flashbulbs are in common use.

1930

From left to right:

Eliel Saarinen's interior for the president's house at the Cranbrook Academy of Art, Bloomfield Hills, Michigan. The textile designs are by his wife, Loja Gesellius Saarinen.

Fire screen designed by Raymond Subes and René Lalique

Cochrane apartment, 856 Fifth Avenue, New York, by Elsie Cobb Wilson

Marcel Breuer's "Room for a Woman" at the Salon des Artistes Décorateurs, Paris

ARCHITECTURE

Le Corbusier's Villa Savoie is finished near Paris, and his apartment for Charles (formerly Carlos) de Beistegui is built in Paris; de Beistegui furnishes it in the newly fashionable Surrealist style. Also in Paris, Pierre Chareau completes the Maison de Verre, begun in 1928; its interiors enjoy full walls of glass, floors of white rubber, and freestanding columns of red-painted steel. In New York, the Empire State Building by Shreve, Lamb, & Harmon is now the world's tallest. André Lurçat designs the École Karl-Marx primary school at Villejuif, near Paris, with murals by his brother Jean Lurçat.

BOOKS

The Annual of American Design 1931, published by the American Union of Decorative Artists and Craftsmen, includes chapters by Paul Frankl, Kem Weber, and Frank Lloyd Wright. Paul Poiret's autobiography is published in London as *My First Fifty Years* and in Philadelphia as *King of Fashion*.

CULTURE AT LARGE

Salvador Dali paints *The Persistence of Memory*. The Sadler's Wells Ballet is founded. The economic depression is at its worst.

DESIGNERS AND INSTALLATIONS

Cecil Beaton buys a house at Ashcombe, Wiltshire, and begins its redecoration in highly Baroque style; he will write about the house in *Ashcombe: The Story of a Fifteen-Year Lease*, to be published in 1949. In London, Wells Coates designs studios for British Broadcasting House and an apartment for actor Charles Laughton. Serge Chermayeff ends his relationship with Waring & Gillow; the next year he will establish the furniture company Plan. Eileen Gray designs the Paris apartment and studio of Romanian architect Jean Badovici. Donald Deskey begins the design of the Radio City Music Hall in New York's Rockefeller Center; it will include murals by Witold Gordon,

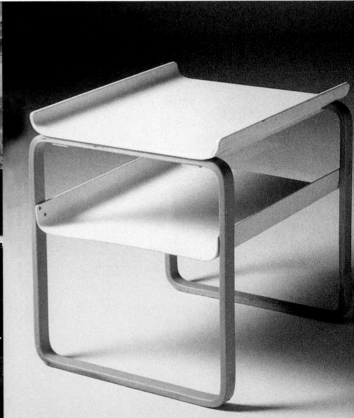

paintings by Stuart Davis, and fabrics by Ruth Reeves, and it will be finished the following year, as will Deskey's apartment for Music Hall impresario Samuel L. "Roxy" Rothafel. Another Art Deco classic, the Paramount theater in Oakland, California, is designed by Timothy L. Pflueger. Frances Elkins designs interiors for the Chicago house of her brother, architect David Adler. Émile-Jacques Ruhlmann and Pierre Patout design interiors for the liner *Atlantique*.

The Berlin Building exposition includes full-size architectural mock-ups by Ludwig Mies van der Rohe and interiors by Lilly Reich, as well as a "Sportsman's House" by Marcel Breuer and a living room by Josef Albers. The American Union of Decorative Artists and Craftsmen (AUDAC) holds its second exhibition of members' work at the Brooklyn Museum, but the organization will soon be dissolved.

Edward Wormley begins designing furniture for Dunbar, an association that will last until 1968. British furniture designer Gerald Summers establishes the firm Makers of Simple Furniture Ltd.; it will close in 1940. The Swiss store Wohnbedarf ("household requirements") is founded in Zürich to sell modern design to the middle class; its founders include Sigfried Giedion, and its designers will include Max Bill, Herbert Bayer, Alvar Aalto, and Marcel Breuer. In London, Elizabeth Peacock and others establish the Guild of Weavers, Spinners, and Dyers.

Interior Architecture and Decoration begins publication and is soon combined with *Good Furniture and Decoration*.

A conference leads to the formation of the American Institute of Interior Decorators (AIID); its first headquarters will be in Chicago, and its first president will be William R. Moore of Chicago, designer of the interiors of that city's Lake Shore Drive Hotel and Belmont Hotel; Moore writes a definition of the profession. In England, the Board of Trade appoints the Committee on Art and Industry, headed by Lord Gorell.

A process for producing neoprene is developed.

1931

From left to right:

A class at what will become the Parsons School of Design, New York

Two-shelf table of laminated wood by Alvar Aalto

Antelopes and gazelles prance on fabric designs by Paul Poiret, produced by F. Schumacher

Donald Deskey's Radio City Music Hall, New York

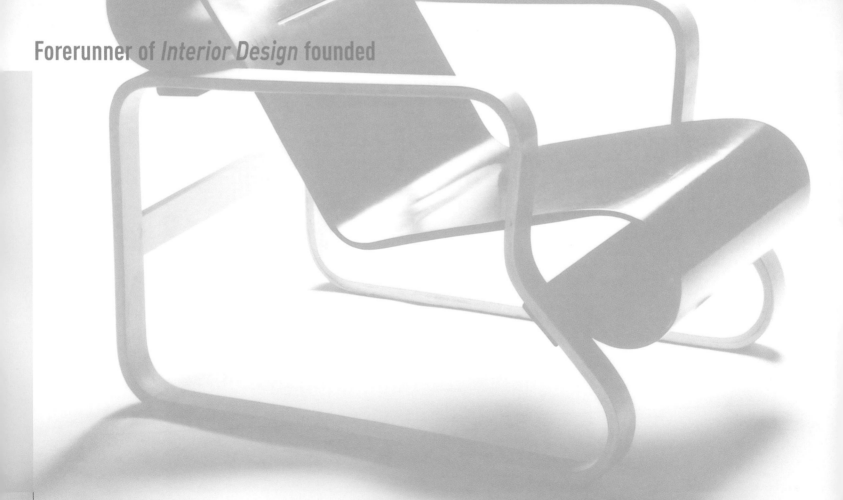

ARCHITECTURE

The Bauhaus, under Ludwig Mies van der Rohe, moves from Dessau to Berlin. Marcel Breuer designs the Harnischmacher house in Wiesbaden, plus its interiors and furniture. Howe & Lescaze design the Philadelphia Savings Fund Society building, including the banking floor interiors; Kurt Versen, recently arrived in the United States from Sweden, outfits it with an early version of fluorescent lighting. Giuseppe Terragni designs the Casa del Fascio in Como, Italy; it will be completed in 1936.

BOOKS

Norman Bel Geddes writes *Horizons*, espousing the sometimes conflicting ideals of technologically based design and streamlined styling. Danish architect and furniture designer Ole Wanscher writes *Furniture Types*. Paul Frankl writes *Machine-Made Leisure*.

CULTURE AT LARGE

With the Depression sweeping the country, 13 million Americans are unemployed. Aldous Huxley writes *Brave New World*. Ernest Herzfeld discovers the ruins of Persepolis in Iran. Jack Benny and Groucho Marx make their radio debuts.

DESIGNERS AND INSTALLATIONS

The Wiener Werkstätte, founded in 1903, is dissolved. Tiffany Studios declares bankruptcy. Raymond McGrath designs Fischer's Restaurant and Long Bar, New Bond Street, London. Also in London, Serge Chermayeff designs interiors for the BBC using furniture from his new company, Plan. Paul Nash designs a bathroom faced with metallic purple-tinted glass and peach-tinted mirror for Edward James as a wedding gift for James's wife, the dancer Tilly Losch. In Paris, Pierre Patout designs an addition to the Galeries Lafayette department store, and a shop/studio is opened by designers Jean-Michel Frank and Adolphe Chanaux. In New York, Alexander Girard opens a design office; he will move it to Detroit in 1937. In Far Hills, New Jersey, Mrs. Henry ("Sister") Parish II opens Mrs. Henry Parish II Inc.; she will open a design studio in New York in 1933. Norman Bel Geddes, best known as a designer for the theater, designs New York offices for the J. Walter Thompson advertising agency, metal bedroom furniture for Simmons, and window displays for the Franklin Simon store. Russel Wright designs a grand piano for Wurlitzer. Cedric Gibbons, best known as a designer for MGM films, designs interiors for himself and his wife, actress Dolores Del Rio. John Eberson designs his only "atmospheric" theater in Europe, the Rex in Paris.

Forerunner of *Interior Design* founded

EXHIBITIONS

The Philadelphia Museum of Art shows *Design for the Machine*; the exhibition design is by Walter Dorwin Teague. Colonial Williamsburg opens. The three-year-old Museum of Modern Art in New York presents its exhibition *The International Style*, prepared by Philip Johnson, Henry-Russell Hitchcock, and Alfred H. Barr.

FURNITURE AND FURNISHINGS

In the Paris branch of the Parsons School of Design, Jean-Michel Frank's studio produces the prototype of the Parsons table; it will remain popular through the rest of the century. Marcel Breuer begins designing furniture in aluminum. Aino Aalto designs glasses and glass pitchers for Karhula. Serge Chermayeff designs steel nesting chairs with canvas seats for the BBC's Broadcasting House, London; they are manufactured by the year-old company Pel (Practical Equipment Ltd.). Alvar Aalto designs the "Scroll" armchair of molded plywood for his Paimio Sanatorium (under construction). Marion Dorn designs rugs for Claridge's Hotel, London.

GOVERNMENT EVENTS

The U.S. Federal Home Loan Bank System is established to stimulate construction.

MAGAZINES

The Decorator's Digest begins publication as an organ of the American Institute of Interior Decorators; it will later become *Interior Design*. The last issue of the Dutch periodical *De Stijl* is a memorial to its founder, Theo van Doesburg, who died in 1931. *Interior Architecture and Decoration & Good Furniture and Decoration* also ceases publication, as does *Wendingen*. *Design in Industry* is launched in England.

PROGRESS IN THE PROFESSION

The Cranbrook Academy of Art opens in Bloomfield Hills, Michigan. The American Institute of Interior Decorators holds its first annual conference at the St. George Hotel, Bermuda; thirty-nine designers attend.

TECHNICAL AND SCIENTIFIC ADVANCES

American inventor Edwin Land develops Polaroid film. British physicist James Chadwick discovers the neutron.

1932

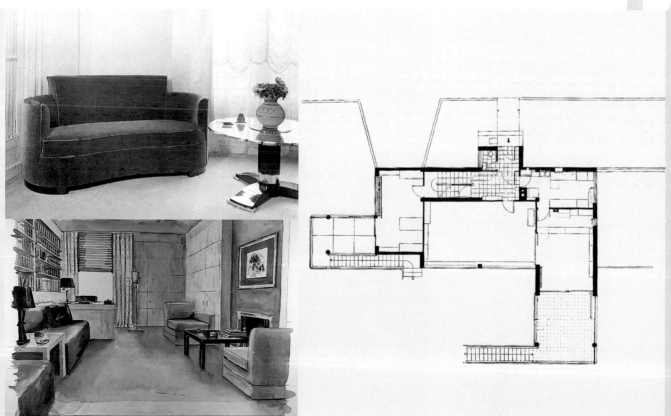

From left to right:

Chair design by Alvar Aalto for the Paimio Sanatorium rests a scroll of plywood on a frame of bent laminated wood.

Upholstered sofa and circular table designed by Jules Leleu

Watercolor sketch of an interior by Eleanor Horst includes two of the new Parsons tables.

Floor plan, Marcel Breuer's Harnischmacher house, Wiesbaden, Germany

ARCHITECTURE

The Hitler regime closes the Bauhaus. Alvar Aalto's Paimio Sanitorium is finished. Le Corbusier completes his Salvation Army building in Paris and is at work on the Centrosoyous project for Moscow.

BOOKS

Wilhelm Ostwald writes *Color Science*, and Derek Patmore writes *Colour Schemes for the Modern Home*.

CULTURE AT LARGE

Fred Astaire and Ginger Rogers are *Flying down to Rio*. Gertrude Stein publishes *The Autobiography of Alice B. Toklas*. Helen Hayes is on Broadway as *Mary of Scotland*, and *King Kong* is on the screen.

DESIGNERS AND INSTALLATIONS

Donald Deskey and Edward Durell Stone begin the design of the Richard H. Mandel house, Mt. Kisco, New York. Emilio Terry designs sets for George Balanchine ballets and *folies* for Charles de Beistegui. Louis Comfort Tiffany dies at age eighty-five, and Émile-Jacques Ruhlmann dies at age fifty-four. New York's Cosmopolitan Club moves to a new location, where its interiors are designed by McMillen Inc. In London, Wells Coates designs interiors for Jack Pritchard and his furniture company Isokon, for which Coates and Marcel Breuer will both design molded-plywood furniture. In Paris, Jean-Michel Frank opens a boutique on the rue du Faubourg-St.-Honoré. In Bel Air, California, T. H. Robsjohn-Gibbings designs interiors of the Casa Encantada for Hilda Weber; it will be finished in 1938. At Hyères, on the French Riviera, the villa of the Vicomte and Vicomtesse de Noailles, begun in 1924, is finally finished; it features architecture and furniture by Robert Mallet-Stevens; interiors and/or furniture by Marcel Breuer, Jean-Michel Frank, Léon David, Eileen Gray, and Édouard-Joseph Bourgeois; paintings by Theo van Doesburg; a suspended bed by Pierre Chareau; sculpture by Alberto Giacometti; and rug designs by Eyre de Lanux. In Indore, India, the Manik Bagh (Garden of Rubies) is completed for the Maharajah of Indore; contributing to its design have been Le Corbusier, Émile-Jacques Ruhlmann, René Lalique, Bruno Da Silva Bruhns, Jean Puiforcat, René Herbst, and Eileen Gray. In Oxfordshire, Ronald Tree and his wife, Nancy (the future Nancy Lancaster), buy Ditchley Park and redecorate it with the help of Stéphane Boudin of the House of Jansen.

EXHIBITIONS

The exhibition *British Industrial Art in Relation to the Home* is held at Dorland Hall, London; for it, Serge Chermayeff designs a weekend house, and Oliver Hill designs a boudoir with a glass floor, mirrored walls, and a glass chaise longue; the exhibition will travel to Manchester and other sites. Also seen in London is an exhibition of work by Alvar Aalto. The *Century of Progress* exhibition opens in Chicago and serves as a showcase of Art Deco and modern design; architects of the fair include Joseph Urban, Raymond Hood, and Paul Cret, and exhibits include R. Buckminster Fuller's

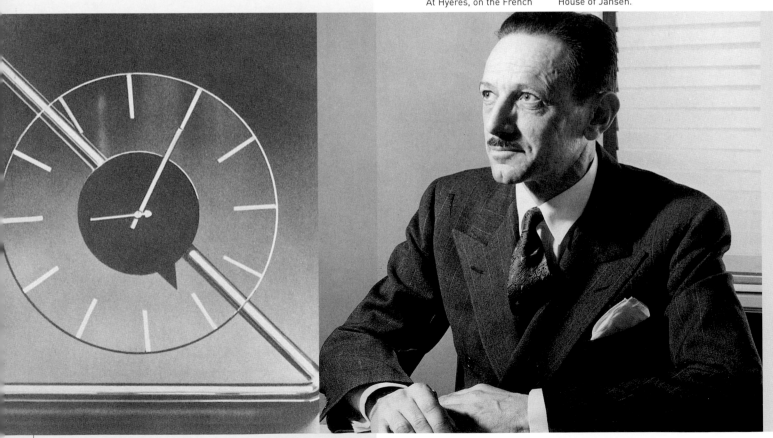

FURNITURE
AND FURNISHINGS

GOVERNMENT EVENTS

MAGAZINES

PROGRESS IN
THE PROFESSION

TECHNICAL AND
SCIENTIFIC ADVANCES

"Dymaxion" car and George Fred Keck's "House of Tomorrow"; the interiors of its "Lumber Industry House" are designed by Wolfgang Hoffmann, son of Josef Hoffmann, and its ten *Design for Living* houses are designed by Gilbert Rohde; on the whole, however, Frank Lloyd Wright thinks the exhibition is passé. The Triennale, formerly in Monza, is held for the first time in Milan; twenty of them will be held there by the end of the century.

Kaare Klint designs his "Safari" chair. Lloyd Manufacturing begins to produce furniture designs by Alfons Bach and Kem Weber. At the Chicago Century of Progress, Herman Miller shows its first modern furniture, designed by Gilbert Rohde.

Franklin Roosevelt becomes president; Adolf Hitler becomes chancellor of Germany. The Twenty-first Amendment to the U.S. Constitution repeals the Eighteenth Amendment (prohibition), stimulating the field of bar and restaurant design.

The Surrealist journal *Minotaure* begins publication in Paris. *Design for Today* begins publication in England, as does *Shelf Appeal*, a showcase of good product design.

The American Institute of Interior Decorators moves its headquarters from Chicago to New York.

The positron (positively charged electron) is discovered.

Chicago unveils a *Century of Progress*; Frank Lloyd Wright unimpressed

1933

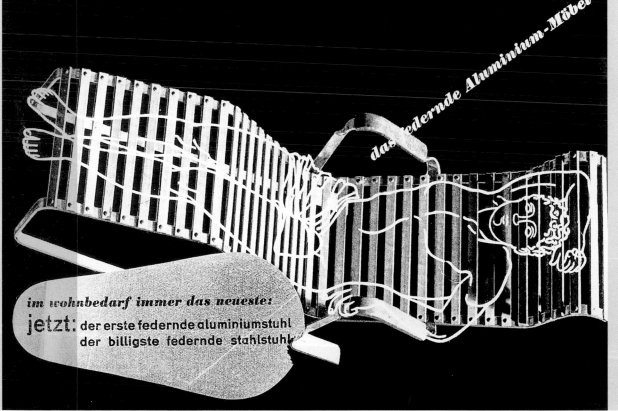

das federnde Aluminium-Möbel

im wohnbedarf immer das neueste:
jetzt: der erste federnde aluminiumstuhl
der billigste federnde stahlstuhl

From left to right:

Gilbert Rohde's clock design for Herman Miller

Gilbert Rohde

An advertisement designed by Bauhaus artist Herbert Bayer for Marcel Breuer's aluminum-framed chaise longue with wood slats

ARCHITECTURE

Frank Lloyd Wright designs the Willey house in Minneapolis. Marcel Breuer designs the Dolderthal apartments, including interiors and furniture, in Zurich. New York's Rockefeller Center, after four years of construction, is completed to the designs of Reinhard & Hofmeister, Harrison & MacMurray, and Hood & Fouilhoux.

BOOKS

Art and Industry by Herbert Read supports the new ideas of Walter Gropius and the Bauhaus. F. R. S. Yorke's *The Modern House* shows models for prefabricated housing by Howe & Lescaze, Richard Neutra, and R. Buckminster Fuller. *Technics and Civilization* by Lewis Mumford, *Art as Experience* by John Dewey, *Twentieth Century Homes* by Raymond McGrath, *Design* by Noel Carrington, *Industrial Art Explained* by John Gloag, and *Modern Furniture and Decoration* by Derek Patmore are published.

CULTURE AT LARGE

Frank Capra's *It Happened One Night* wins all four major Academy Awards. The Dionne quintuplets are born. Cole Porter's *Anything Goes* stars Ethel Merman.

DESIGNERS AND INSTALLATIONS

Austrian designer Josef Frank, recently named artistic director of the Stockholm furniture store Svenskt Tenn, along with Swedish designer Bruno Mathsson and others, will shape and promote "Swedish Modern," its softly curved lines and natural woods opposed to the more rigid geometry and industrial materials of the Bauhaus. The Den Permanente shop is opened in Copenhagen by Kai Bojesen and Georg Jensen. Active members of the Union des Artistes Modernes include Pierre Chareau, Le Corbusier, Pierre Jeanneret, Jean Lurçat, Charlotte Perriand, and Jean Puiforcat. Jean Royère wins a competition for the design of a brasserie in the Hotel Çarlton on Paris's Champs-Élysées. Hungarian architect Pierre Vágó designs an all-metal house in France with aluminum furniture; it will be shown at the 1935 Paris Salon d'Habitation. John Fowler and Sybil Colefax open separate design studios in London. McMillen Inc. redesigns the New York showroom of Steuben Glass. The Rainbow Room opens on the top floor of the RCA Building in New York's Rockefeller Center. Arne Jacobsen designs the Bellevue housing, restaurant, and theater complex in Copenhagen.

EXHIBITIONS

For Chicago's *Century of Progress* exhibition, Walter Dorwin Teague designs the Ford Motor Co. Pavilion. Teague also designs San Diego's *Pacific International Exposition*. The Museum of Modern Art presents *Machine Art*, curated by Philip Johnson; it establishes the museum's design collection. In New York, the Metropolitan Museum of Art's *Contemporary American Industrial Art* exhibition includes a full-scale mock-up of the "streamlined" office of industrial designer Raymond Loewy. Harrod's department store in London shows "Modern Art for the Table," and W. & J. Sloane in New York shows "The House of Years." Josef Hoffmann designs the

Philip Johnson extols machine art

Austrian Pavilion at the Venice Biennale. A retrospective of work by Jacques-Émile Ruhlmann, who died in 1933, is shown at the Pavillon de Marsan in the Louvre. Work of the Omega Workshops (1913–19) is shown at the Bethnal Green Museum, London. The Museum of Modern Art, New York, deplores urban housing conditions in "America Can't Have Housing"; its tenement mock-ups are complete with live cockroaches.

FURNITURE AND FURNISHINGS

Gerrit Rietveld designs his "ZigZag" chair. Russel Wright designs a sixty-piece furniture line for Heywood-Wakefield. Kaare Klint designs a ladderback chair for Fritz Hansen. Bruno Mathsson designs the "Eva" chair for Karl Mathsson; it will later be produced by Dux. The Vitra furniture company is founded in Switzerland by Willi Fehlbaum. Brothers Alberto and Diego Giacometti design bronze lamps, chandeliers, and vases to be sold by Jean-Michel Frank. Gerald Summers designs the one-piece "Bent Plywood Lounge Chair" and the "High-Back Chair," both to be manufactured by his own firm Makers of Simple Furniture. Textile designer Boris Kroll opens his first showroom. Kem Weber designs Bakelite digital clocks for Lawson Time Inc. and his cantilevered "Airline" chair; although he will hand-produce over 250 versions of the chair, he will never find a commercial producer for it.

MAGAZINES

Deutsche Kunst und Dekoration, published in Darmstadt since 1897, folds.

PROGRESS IN THE PROFESSION

In England, the Committee on Art and Industry is succeeded by the Council for Art and Industry; headed by Frank Pick, it is popularly known as the Pick Council.

TECHNICAL AND SCIENTIFIC ADVANCES

William Beebe descends three thousand feet into the ocean in his "bathysphere."

1934

From left to right:

Eliel Saarinen's "Room for a Lady" at the Metropolitan Museum of Art's *Contemporary American Industrial Art* exhibition

Sofa designed by Jean-Michel Frank, as reproduced by Ecart and available through Pucci International

Gerrit Rietveld's "ZigZag" chair

The mirror-ceilinged lounge of the Rainbow Room atop the RCA Building at New York's Rockefeller Center. The interior design is by Mrs. M. B. Schmidt.

Glass objects from the Museum of Modern Art's *Machine Art* exhibition

ARCHITECTURE

Alvar Aalto's library at Viipuri, Finland, is completed, and the three-legged stool he designed for it becomes one of the century's most popular pieces of furniture. Le Corbusier designs a weekend house for himself near Paris, signaling a change to a more natural palette of materials.

BOOKS

Elsie de Wolfe writes her autobiography, *After All*; it will be republished in 1974. Anthony Bertram writes *The House: A Machine for Living In*. H. G. Dowling writes *A Survey of British Industrial Arts*.

CULTURE AT LARGE

George Gershwin composes *Porgy and Bess*. Billie Holiday makes her first recording. Sculptor (and future furniture designer) Isamu Noguchi designs a set for Martha Graham's dance *Frontier*, beginning an association that will last thirty years. The game Monopoly is introduced.

DESIGNERS AND INSTALLATIONS

Ruby Ross Wood hires Billy Baldwin as her assistant. Syrie Maugham is designing the interiors of Wilsford Manor, Wiltshire, for the Hon. Stephen Tennant. Stéphane Boudin of Paris's House of Jansen designs interiors for Sir Henry Channon on Belgrave Square, London. Dorothy Draper designs interiors for the Mark Hopkins Hotel, San Francisco, and the Arrowhead Springs Hotel, Arrowhead Springs, California (near Los Angeles). Franco Albini designs a building and interiors for the Istituto Nazionale delle Assicurazioni in Milan. Wells Coates designs his own apartment in London, and Raymond Loewy and Alexander Girard design their own apartments in New York. Also in New York, Winold Reiss begins designing a series of restaurants for Longchamps, culminating in the 1938 restaurant on the ground floor of the Empire State Building. In Paris, Jean-Michel Frank designs a leather-lined smoking room for perfumer Jean-Pierre Guerlain. The oceanliner *Normandie* is launched with an *appartement de luxe* by Paul Follot; first-class cabins by brothers Tony and Pierre Selmersheim; a first-class doctor's office by Louis Sognot and Charlotte Alix; a dining room by René Prou; other interiors by Dominique, Lucie Renaudot, Pierre Patout, Jean Pascaud, Émile-Jacques Ruhlmann, Jean Dunand, Charles Despiau, Raymond Subes, and Albert-Lucien Guénot; rugs by Ivan Da Silva-Bruhns; lighting by the Paris firm Delisle; silverware by Jean-Émile Puiforcat; bronze doors by Gilbert Poillerat; and chandeliers by Lalique. In 1942 the ship will be destroyed by fire in New York harbor.

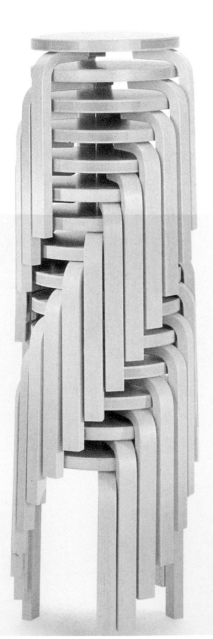

George Nelson interviews European modernists

EXHIBITIONS

At the *Brussels Exposition Internationale et Universelle*, rival pavilions are designed by the Salon des Artistes-Décorateurs and the Union des Artistes Modernes, and there is an elaborate reconstruction of "Old Brussels," complete with cobbled streets. In London, the Royal Academy and the Royal Society of the Arts cosponsor the exhibition *British Art in Industry* at Burlington House, and an exhibition of pottery is seen at the Victoria & Albert.

FURNITURE AND FURNISHINGS

Marcel Breuer designs bent plywood chaise longues for England's Isokon. In Finland, Artek Ltd. is founded for the manufacture of furniture by Alvar Aalto. Edward Fields establishes a company for the production of custom-designed rugs. Russel Wright's "Modern Living" line for Conant Ball is introduced at Macy's; its bleached maple is called "blonde." Jean-Michel Frank's furniture designs for his Argentinian client Jorge Born are shown at the Salon de la Porte de Versailles. Pierre Frey establishes a firm in Paris for the creation of decorative fabrics. Rex Whistler's carpet design for Edward James is woven by the Wilton Royal Carpet Factory.

GOVERNMENT EVENTS

The Federal Arts Project is instituted as part of the U.S. Works Progress Administration.

MAGAZINES

Upholsterer and Interior Decorator changes its name to *Interior Decorator*. From Rome, where he is a fellow at the American Academy, George Nelson begins for *Pencil Points* magazine (later to be *Progressive Architecture*) a series of interviews called "The Architects of Europe Today"; his subjects will include Le Corbusier, Walter Gropius, Ludwig Mies van der Rohe, and Gio Ponti.

PROGRESS IN THE PROFESSION

The Federal Works Progress Administration establishes the Design Laboratory school in New York with Gilbert Rohde as its director, but it will be short-lived. The first degree program in industrial design is offered at the Carnegie Institute of Technology in Pittsburgh.

TECHNICAL AND SCIENTIFIC ADVANCES

Fluorescent lighting is demonstrated at the Illuminating Engineering Society convention in Cincinnati.

1935

From left to right:

Alvar Aalto's three-legged stacking stool for the Viipuri library

Teacart designed of bent wood by Gerald Summers

Chair design by Jean-Michel Frank, as reproduced by Écart and available through Pucci International

Cocktail lounge of the Mark Hopkins Hotel, San Francisco, by Dorothy Draper

Marcel Breuer's chaise longue for Isokon

ARCHITECTURE

After a period of little activity, Frank Lloyd Wright designs the Hanna house, Palo Alto, California, on a hexagonal grid. He also begins the design of the Kaufmann country house Fallingwater, Bear Run, Pennsylvania, which will be finished in 1939, and the S. C. Johnson and Son Administration Building, Racine, Wisconsin, which will be finished in 1946. The firm of Skidmore, Owings, & Merrill is founded. Joseph Urban designs Mar-a-Lago, a house in Palm Beach for Marjorie Merriweather Post; at the end of the century it will be owned by Donald Trump.

BOOKS

Nancy McClelland writes *Furnishing the Colonial and Federal House*. Joseph Applegate writes *The Book of Furniture and Decoration: Period and Modern*. Marta K. Sironen writes *A History of American Furniture*. Russell Hawes Kettell writes *Early American Rooms*. Herbert Read writes *Art and Society*. Nikolaus Pevsner writes *Pioneers of the Modern Movement: From William Morris to Walter Gropius*; it will be revised in 1949 as *Pioneers of Modern Design*. Derek Patmore publishes both *Colour Schemes for the Modern Home* and *I Decorate My Home*.

CULTURE AT LARGE

The Green Hornet debuts on radio. Margaret Mitchell writes *Gone with the Wind*. Samuel Barber composes *Adagio for Strings*.

DESIGNERS AND INSTALLATIONS

Elsie de Wolfe designs a cocktail lounge for New York's Savoy-Plaza Hotel; she is also hired by King Edward VIII to advise on the redecoration of Buckingham Palace, but the job falls through when the king abdicates. Jean-Michel Frank designs a Paris salon for couturier Lucien Lelong. Syrie Maugham designs a London house for Mr. and Mrs. Vincent Paravicini. Lilly Reich designs the Facius apartment in Berlin-Dahlem. Gerrit Rietveld with Truus Schröeder-Schräder designs the Vreeburg Cinema in Utrecht. William Pahlmann becomes head of the antiques and decorating department at Lord & Taylor, where he will pioneer the display of furniture in model room settings. Elsie Cobb Wilson's decorating firm is reorganized as Smyth, Urquhart, & Marckwald with Miriam Smyth in charge. Industrial designer Lurelle Guild "streamlines" a New York showroom for Alcoa. Donald Deskey designs interiors for the Hollywood Turf Club in Inglewood, California. Kem Weber designs the Bixby house and its furniture in Kansas City. Elisabeth Draper establishes her decorating firm; its work will include a New York house for Dwight D. and Mamie Eisenhower, a restoration of the 1832 Old Merchant's House, New York, and, for Ambassador Amory Houghton, interiors of the U.S. embassy in Paris. The Cunard Line puts the *Queen Mary* into service; its chief interior designers are Arthur Davis and Benjamin Wistar Morris; its décor includes paintings by Vanessa Bell, bronze plaques by Maurice Lambert, and printed bathroom textiles by Marion Dorn; the chief contractor for decoration and furnishings is Waring & Gillow of Oxford Street, London.

EXHIBITIONS

In Bristol, the Royal Agricultural Show features an open-plan pavilion by Marcel Breuer and F. R. S. Yorke. The second Milan Triennale features Max Bill's Swiss Pavilion and Franco Albini's "Room for a Man" and "Apartment for Four." The work of textile, carpet, and wallpaper designer Ronald Grierson is shown at London's Redfern Gallery. Also in London, the Royal Institute of British Architects organizes the *Exhibition of Everyday Things*, and Heal's shows modern rooms by Marcel Breuer, Maxwell Fry, Raymond McGrath, Hugh Casson, and others. The Museum of Modern Art, New York, devotes a one-man exhibition to Ludwig Mies van der Rohe, as it will again in 1947, 1960, and 1986.

Dorothy Draper cultivates cabbage roses

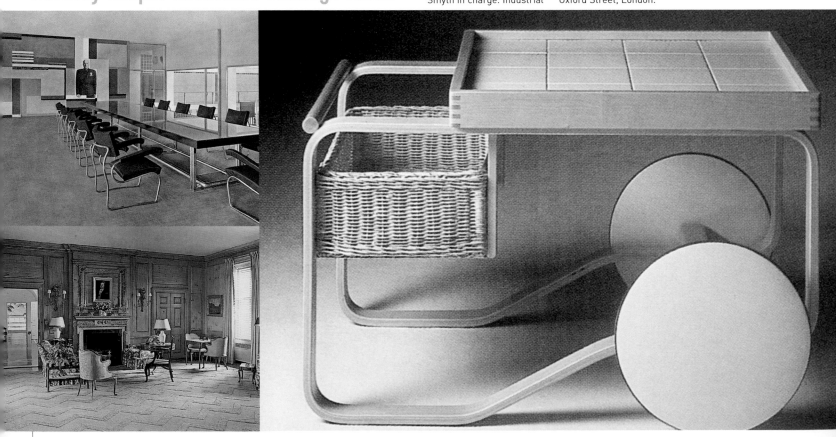

FURNITURE AND FURNISHINGS

Alvar Aalto designs a tea cart, the "400" easy chair, and the "43" lounge chair, all for Artek, and his furniture is exported to the United States for the first time. Salvador Dali designs a loveseat in the shape of Mae West's lips for the residence of Edward James. T. H. Robsjohn-Gibbings designs a lounge chair and ottoman for Widdicomb. Dorothy Draper begins designing fabrics for Schumacher, the most famous of which will be her "Cabbage Rose" design for the Hampshire House hotel in New York. Warren McArthur designs side chairs of tubular aluminum. The "Lariana" chair is designed by Giuseppe Terragni and will later be produced by the Italian manufacturer Zanotta. Dunbar Hay & Co. commissions English painter and designer Eric Ravilious to design a suite of furniture in the "Regency Revival" style. The German ceramics factories of Boch and Villeroy, both founded in the eighteenth century, merge to form Villeroy & Boch. Billy Baldwin's "Slipper Chair," originally designed in Madagascar grass cloth with a white canvas cushion, is reinterpreted in white-piped beige canvas for Ellena du Wolcott Blair's house in Palm Beach, Florida. Boris Kroll founds Kroll Handwovens.

GOVERNMENT EVENTS

King Edward VIII abdicates from the throne of Great Britain and Northern Ireland and is succeeded by George VI. The Spanish Civil War begins.

MAGAZINES

Trend and *Industrial Arts* magazines are founded in England, but *Trend* will last only a few months.

PROGRESS IN THE PROFESSION

The American Institute of Interior Decorators changes its name to the American Institute of Decorators and its acronym from AIID to AID. Peter Behrens is appointed Director of the Department of Architecture at the Prussian Academy in Berlin.

TECHNICAL AND SCIENTIFIC ADVANCES

Owens-Corning introduces fiberglass. Mathematician Alan Turing's paper "On Computable Numbers" establishes the theory of computers.

1936

From left to right.

Giuseppe Terragni's board room for the Casa del Fascio, Como, Italy. The furniture is also Terragni's design.

Residence for Mrs. James Cromwell (Doris Duke), Somerville, New Jersey, by McMillen Inc.

Alvar Aalto's teacart

Founders of a new architecture firm: Louis Skidmore, John O. Merrill, and Nathaniel A. Owings

Alvar Aalto's chaise longue of bent laminated wood

Desk and three-legged chair designed by Frank Lloyd Wright and manufactured by Steelcase for the Johnson Wax interior, Racine, Wisconsin

ARCHITECTURE

Walter Gropius and Marcel Breuer are teaching at Harvard and partners in an architecture practice; it will produce houses for both principals in Lincoln, Massachusetts. Frederick Kiesler designs his "Endless House." Alvar Aalto designs the Savoy Restaurant in Helsinki and some free-form glass vases for its interior. Arne Jacobsen wins a competition for the design of the town hall in Aarhus, Denmark.

BOOKS

Elements of Interior Decoration by Sherrill Whiton, based on his 1916 "Home Study Catalogues in the Decorative Arts," is first published. *Vision and Design* is written by Roger Fry. William Varnum writes *Creative Design in Furniture: Wood, Metal, Glass, and Plastic.* Harold D. Eberlein, Abbot McClure, and Edward S. Holloway write *The Practical Book of Interior Decoration.* Edward Deming Andrews and Faith Andrews write *Shaker Furniture: The Craftsmanship of an American Communal Sect.* Herbert Cescinsky writes *English Furniture from Gothic to Sheraton.*

Raymond McGrath and A. C. Frost write *Glass in Architecture and Decoration.* The editors of *House and Garden* compile *House and Garden's Complete Guide to Interior Decoration*; it will be followed by many later editions. The British government produces a report, *The Working Class Home: Its Furnishings and Equipment.* Nikolaus Pevsner writes *Industrial Art in England.*

CULTURE AT LARGE

Pablo Picasso's *Guernica* protests the cruelties of civil war in Spain. László Moholy-Nagy is appointed the first director of the New Bauhaus in Chicago. *Time* names Wallis Warfield Simpson "Woman of the Year."

DESIGNERS AND INSTALLATIONS

Designer, poet, and sportsman Carlo Mollino designs the Ippica riding club in Turin, Italy; despite protests, it will be razed in 1960. Dorothy Draper designs the Hampshire House hotel, New York. Kem Weber designs the Wedemeyer house, Altadena, California, its interiors, and its built-in furniture. Walter Dorwin Teague designs the Ford showroom in New York. Michael Saphier establishes Michael Saphier Associates; in 1958, it will change its name to Saphier, Lerner, Schindler; in 1962, it will become SLS Environetics. Architect

Wallace Harrison and French designer Jean-Michel Frank collaborate on a New York apartment interior for Mr. and Mrs. Nelson Rockefeller; the living room contains furniture by Frank, andirons and lamps by Diego Giacometti, a mantelpiece by Henri Matisse, and paintings by Pablo Picasso; Rockefeller describes it as "Louis XV—but modern."

Sherrill Whiton outlines *Elements of Interior Decoration*

EXHIBITIONS

FURNITURE
AND FURNISHINGS

GOVERNMENT EVENTS

MAGAZINES

PROGRESS IN
THE PROFESSION

TECHNICAL AND
SCIENTIFIC ADVANCES

The Exposition Internationale des Arts et Techniques is held in Paris; in its Finnish Pavilion, Alvar Aalto's "Savoy Vase" wins first prize for glassware; Robert Mallet-Stevens designs the Pavilion de la Solidarité, the Pavilion de l'Hygiène, the Palais de l'Electricité, the Pavilion de Tabac, and the Café du Brasil; Henry Van de Velde designs the Belgian Pavilion; Josep Lluis Sert designs the Spanish Pavilion; Eric Ravilious decorates the walls of the British Pavilion; Sonia Delaunay contributes two murals; and Jacques Adnet wins the grand prize for the St. Gobain Pavilion. In New York, the Metropolitan Museum of Art shows *Carpets: An International Exhibition of Contemporary Industrial Art,* and in London, the Council of Art and Design, sponsored by the British government, shows *The Working Class Home.*

Frank Lloyd Wright designs the "Barrel" armchair, Gio Ponti designs the "Lotus" armchair for Cassina, and Jacob Jacobsen's "Luxo" adjustable-arm lamp is introduced. Painter Ben Nicholson and sculptor Barbara Hepworth design fabrics for Edinburgh Weavers, an offshoot of England's Morton Sandour Fabrics. British designer Ernest Race establishes Race Fabrics to market his own textile designs hand-woven in India. Samuel Marx, Kem Weber, and Warren McArthur are among the current designers in the "Art Moderne" style. Russel Wright designs "American Modern" tableware for Steubenville Pottery; it will be produced for twenty years.

The U.S. Supreme Court upholds the minimum-wage law for women.

The Decorator's Digest changes its name to *Interior Design and Decoration.* The English *Journal of Decorative Art*, founded in 1881, ceases publication. *Verve* begins publication in Paris and London and will continue until 1960.

In England, a National Register of Industrial Art Designers is established, and the Pick Council publishes the report "Design and Designer in Industry."

Industrial chemist Walter Hume Carothers produces nylon. R. Buckminster Fuller patents the three-wheeled "Dymaxion" car.

1937

From left to right:

A private dining room by Dorothy Draper for the Hampshire House hotel, New York

Dorothy Draper dreaming up the interiors of the Hampshire House.

Nelson Rockefeller apartment, New York, by Jean-Michel Frank

Wood stacking chairs by Marcel Breuer

Serge Chermayeff designs Bentley Wood, a house for himself in Sussex. Ludwig Mies van der Rohe is appointed head of the architecture school at Chicago's Armour Institute, later to be the Illinois Institute of Technology. Walter Gropius is appointed chairman of the architecture school at the Harvard Graduate School of Design. Alvar Aalto's Villa Mairea is being built in Noormarkku, Finland, for his chief patrons, the Gullichsen family.

Bauhaus 1919–1928, edited by Herbert Bayer, Walter Gropius, and Ise Gropius, *Aalto: Architecture and Furniture* by S. Breines and A. L. Kocher, Osbert Lancaster's *Pillar to Post*, Paul Frankl's *Space for Living: Creative Interior Decoration and Design*, Matthew Luckiesh's *Color and Colors*, and Joseph Aronson's *The Encyclopedia of Furniture* are published.

Thornton Wilder's *Our Town* is staged. Alfred Hitchcock films *The Lady Vanishes*. The first issue of *Action Comics* introduces Superman.

Frances Elkins designs interiors for the Zellerbach house in San Francisco. Henry Dreyfuss designs railway car interiors for the *Twentieth Century Limited*, and Raymond Loewy for the *Broadway Limited*. Louis Süe designs interiors for the Paris house of Helena Rubenstein. Jean-Michel Frank designs interiors for the house of Jorge Born in Buenos Aires. Franco Albini begins designing interiors and furniture for his own apartment in Milan. John Fowler joins Sybil Colefax to form the London decorating firm Colefax & Fowler. In the Netherlands, Piet Zwart designs a kitchen for the Bruynzeel Company. Elsie de Wolfe helps the Duchess of Windsor redecorate the Château de la Croë at Cap d'Antibes, France.

Bauhaus 1919–1928, curated by Bauhaus faculty member Herbert Bayer, opens at the Museum of Modern Art, New York, as does a show of design by Alvar Aalto. A Surrealist exhibition is held in Paris. Scalamandré's floral stripe in bouclé cotton wins the gold medal at Paris's *Exposition des Arts et Metiers*. For the *Swiss National Exhibition* in Zurich, Hans Coray of Switzerland designs the "Landi" chair of aluminum alloy; it will be the most popular outdoor chair of the century, particularly after Zanotta begins to manufacture it in the 1980s. The design work of Marcel Breuer is shown at Harvard's Graduate School of Design, where he has been teaching for a year.

Hans Knoll founds furniture company

FURNITURE AND FURNISHINGS

The Hardoy or "Butterfly" chair, with a canvas or leather sling on a frame of steel rods, is designed by Jorge Hardoy, Antonio Bonet, and Juan Kurchan. Jean-Michel Frank designs furniture for the Paris house of Helena Rubenstein, and, for Frank's Paris boutique, Emilio Terry designs furniture of white stucco in Baroque scrollwork forms. Lilly Reich designs furniture for the Wolf house in Guben, Germany. Marion Dorn's curtain fabrics are in the first-class lounge of the liner *Orcades*. Hendrik Van Keppel and Taylor Green establish a design office in Los Angeles; its best-known products will be metal-framed outdoor furniture strung with cords. Billy Baldwin produces his

"Slipper Chair" in white sailcloth stenciled with yellow orchids for John King Reckford's house, Montego Bay, Jamaica. Hans Knoll establishes a furniture company in New York called HG Knoll. Franco Albini designs a desk that will be marketed by Gavina in Italy and by Knoll in the United States. Boris Kroll establishes Cromwell Designs for his fabrics; he will change the company's name to Boris Kroll in 1946. Hans Coray designs the "Spartana" chair. Erwine and Estelle Laverne establish Laverne Originals, using as their studio the Oyster Bay, New York, estate formerly owned by Louis Comfort Tiffany.

GOVERNMENT EVENTS

Adolf Hitler appoints himself Germany's war minister.

MAGAZINES

John Entenza buys a magazine called *California Arts and Architecture*; he will drop the "California" and make the magazine a showcase for modern design.

PROGRESS IN THE PROFESSION

The American Designers Institute is founded. Most of its members are designers of home furnishings, but it will later lead to the formation of the Industrial Designers Institute.

TECHNICAL AND SCIENTIFIC ADVANCES

Nylon and Teflon are both developed by DuPont. The first Xerox photocopy is made.

1938

From left to right:

Franco Albini's desk design

Hans Knoll

Frank Lloyd Wright's Taliesin West, near Scottsboro, Arizona

Alvar Aalto's Villa Mairea

Walter Gropius and Marcel Breuer design the Frank house in Pittsburgh and Breuer's own house in Lincoln, Massachusetts. The Museum of Modern Art, New York, moves into a new building by Philip L. Goodwin and Edward Durell Stone.

Decorating Is Fun! is written by Dorothy Draper. *Duncan Phyfe and the English Regency* is written by Nancy McClelland. *Homes, Sweet Homes* is written by Osbert Lancaster. Emily Genauer writes *Modern Interiors Today and Tomorrow: A Critical Analysis of Trends in Contemporary Décor as Seen at the Paris Exposition of Arts and Techniques and Reflected at the New York World's Fair.* Sir Patrick Abercrombie edits *The Book of the Modern House.*

Judy Garland stars in *The Wizard of Oz.* John Steinbeck writes *The Grapes of Wrath.* Aaron Copland composes the ballet *Billy the Kid.*

Syrie Maugham designs an apartment for herself in London. Lilly Reich designs interiors for the Schäppi apartment in Berlin and furniture for the Crous house in Berlin-Südende. Ogden Codman, Jr., begins work on La Leopolda, a château for himself at Villefranche-sur-Mer, France. At Versailles, Stéphane Boudin of the House of Jansen decorates Elsie de Wolfe's Villa Trianon for a circus party.

"Streamline" design in New York and San Francisco

EXHIBITIONS

The New York World's Fair opens, popular features being the Ford Pavilion's lounge designed by Walter Dorwin Teague, and the House of Jewels, designed by Donald Deskey, a beautiful one being Alvar Aalto's Finnish Pavilion, other notable ones being the Swedish Pavilion by Sven Markelius and the French Pavilion by Pierre Patout and Robert Expert, and instructive ones being Henry Dreyfuss's "Democracity" (seen from moving ramps within a structure called the Perisphere), and Norman Bel Geddes's "Futurama."

The Golden Gate International Exhibition in San Francisco opens on the newly constructed Treasure Island, and, like the New York fair, it exults in "streamline" design. Abroad, there is a Swiss National Exposition in Zurich and the Salon de la Société des Artistes-Décorateurs in Paris; among the Paris exhibitors is Jean Royère. The Museum of Modern Art, New York, presents *Houses and Housing: Industrial Design*.

FURNITURE AND FURNISHINGS

Modern art invades modern furniture design as Finn Juhl surprises the Danish guild of cabinetmakers with a sofa whose outlines are derived from the paintings of Jean Arp. Elsie de Wolfe designs (or, at least, popularizes, for her authorship of the design will later be disputed) a side chair made of Lucite, a product recently developed by DuPont. Russel Wright turns to ceramics, producing the "American Modern" line for Steubenville Pottery. Walter Dorwin Teague designs a steel-based grand piano for Steinway. Sculptor Isamu Noguchi designs a table with a free-form glass top for the house of Museum of Modern Art president A. Congers Goodyear; it will later be produced by Herman Miller.

GOVERNMENT EVENTS

Hitler invades Poland.

MAGAZINES

The French periodical *Art et décoration*, founded in 1898, ceases publication.

TECHNICAL AND SCIENTIFIC ADVANCES

Polyethylene is invented.

1939

From left to right:

Foyer of Syrie Maugham's own London flat has striped paper, blackamoor torch-bearers.

Living room, Marcel Breuer's own house in Lincoln, Massachusetts

Alvar Aalto's Finnish Pavilion for the New York World's Fair

Russel Wright's "American Modern" pottery for Steubenville

Gunnar Asplund designs the Woodland Crematorium in Stockholm, including its interiors and furniture. Ludwig Mies van der Rohe begins his work on the campus of the Illinois Institute of Technology. George Nelson designs the Sherman Fairchild house in New York; *The New Yorker's* "Talk of the Town" reports that "it has ramps instead of staircases, electrically operated Venetian blinds on the outside of the window panes," and "a living-room floor of teakwood mounted on rubber springs to provide resiliency." Peter Behrens dies at seventy-two.

Willis H. Carrier and others write *Modern Air Conditioning, Heating, and Ventilating*. Also published are *Design This Day: The Technique of Order in the Machine Age* by Walter Dorwin Teague, *The Modern House in America* by James and Katherine Morrow Ford, and *Masterpieces of English Furniture and Clocks* by Robert Wemyss Symonds.

Raymond Loewy designs the Lucky Strike cigarette package. Ernest Hemingway writes *For Whom the Bell Tolls*. Orson Welles films *Citizen Kane*. Ethel Merman is *Panama Hattie*. McDonald's sells its first hamburger. Painted prehistoric caves are discovered at Lascaux, France.

Elsie de Wolfe moves from France to Beverly Hills, California; for her house, which she calls After All, she commissions some furniture designs from a young decorator, Tony Duquette, whose previous work has been display designs for Bullock's department store and for the salon of fashion designer Adrian. Dorothy Draper designs the Mayflower Hotel in Washington, D.C., and the Camellia House restaurant in Chicago's Drake Hotel, and begins her own radio show, *Lines about Living.* Kem Weber completes interiors for the Walt Disney Studios in Burbank, California. Carlo Mollino designs the Casa Devalle in Turin, Italy. Lilly Reich renovates the Büren house in Berlin-Dahlen. Charlotte Perriand is invited by the Japanese Ministry of Trade to advise on arts and crafts. *Colliers* magazine sponsors a

Dorothy Draper on the air

model house in Rockefeller Center designed by Edward Durell Stone with interiors by Jens Risom. McMillen Inc. opens a design studio in Houston, which will close in 1943, and a townhouse for its own use in New York.

George Nelson designs the *40 under 40* exhibition for the Architectural League of New York. The *Organic Design in Home Furnishings* competition is announced by the Museum of Modern Art, New York; the competition's director, Eliot Noyes, declares that "A new way of living is developing . . . and this requires a fresh approach to the design problems and a new expression."

Bruno Mathsson designs a chaise longue of canvas webbing on a molded-birch frame. Franco Albini introduces the "Tensistructure" bookcase suspended on cables. Achille Castiglioni designs the "Leonardo" table base for Zanotta. William Lescaze designs furniture for John Stuart Inc. Richard Neutra designs the "Camel" table for his Sidney Kahn house in San Francisco. Dorothy Draper designs "Stylized Scroll" fabric for Waverly.

Winston Churchill becomes British prime minister.

Interior Decorator, founded in 1888 as *The Upholsterer*, changes its name to *Interiors*.

R. Buckminster Fuller designs a two-piece prefabricated metal bathroom.

From left to right:

Stephen Lynch Jr., residence, Miami Beach, by William Pahlmann

Dorothy Draper's Camellia House restaurant in the Drake Hotel, Chicago

The Leonardo trestle table designed by Achille Castiglioni

Swimming pool on the SS *America* by Smyth, Urquhart, & Marckwald

Erik Bryggman designs a cemetery chapel in Turku, Finland. Walter Gropius and Marcel Breuer design the Chamberlain cottage, Weyland, Massachusetts. Grand Coulee Dam is the first structure to exceed the volume of the Great Pyramid of Cheops.

After working in Tokyo, Charlotte Perriand (with Junzo Sakakura) edits *Contact with Japanese Art: Selection, Tradition, Creation.* Also published are *Space, Time, and Architecture* by Sigfried Giedion, *Organic Design in Home Furnishings* by Eliot Noyes, *The Book of Furniture and Decoration* by Joseph Aronson, *Outline History of Furniture* by Ole Wanscher, and *Hispanic Furniture* by Grace Hardendorff Burr.

Orson Welles's *Citizen Kane* is on the screen. Virginia Woolf's *Between the Acts* is published shortly after her suicide. James Joyce dies. The National Gallery of Art opens in Washington. The "Chemex" coffeemaker is patented by German designer Peter Schlumbohm.

French designer Jean-Michel Frank commits suicide at age forty-six. Designer and antique dealer Madeleine Castaing opens a shop on the rue du Cherche Midi, Paris. T. H. Robsjohn-Gibbings designs interiors for Nieman-Marcus, Dallas. Dorothy Draper designs the Coty beauty salon in New York, and an article in *Harper's Bazaar* describes her as "brisk, iconoclastic, inventive, unapologetic, and successful." Charles and Ray Eames set up a design studio in their Los Angeles apartment.

For the Museum of Modern Art, New York, John McAndrew and Elizabeth Mock curate the exhibition *What Is Modern Architecture?* and write a book with the same title. For the Architectural League of New York, George Nelson designs the *Versus* exhibition.

The Museum of Modern Art, New York, sponsors the competition and exhibition *Organic Design in Home Furnishings.* The winning team in two of the nine categories is Eero Saarinen and Charles Eames; other winners include Harry Weese and Benjamin Baldwin, Oscar Stonorov and Willo von Moltke, Carl Koch, Hugh Stubbins, Antonin Raymond, Marianne Strengell, and Bernard Rudofsky. Jens Risom designs the first chair to be produced (not just marketed) by Hans Knoll. Captain Roger E. Brunschwig joins the French Free Forces in London, leaving the directorship of Brunschwig & Fils to his American wife, Zelina; the fabric company will eventually be managed by Zelina's nephew and niece, Thomas Peardon and Murray Douglas.

World War II begins.

Dorothy Draper directs *Good Housekeeping*'s Studio of Architectural Building and Furnishing. *Du* is founded in Zurich.

The American Institute of Decorators, with *Interior Design* magazine and the Public Buildings Administration, sponsors a "Competition for the Design of Interiors in Defense Housing Projects."

British inventor Frank Whittle develops a jet engine for aircraft.

Sigfried Giedion's text legitimizes modernism

1941

From left to right:

Jens Risom's furniture for Knoll with seats of woven webbing

Maison Coty, a New York beauty salon by Dorothy Draper

The *Organic Design in Home Furnishings* selections exhibited

Eileen Gray's rug design "La Bastide Blanche," as reproduced by Écart and available through Pucci International

Judging the Museum of Modern Art's *Organic Design in Home Furnishings* competition: seated, left to right: Edward Durell Stone, Catherine K. Bauer, Alfred H. Barr, Jr., Frank Parrish; standing: Marcel Breuer, Eliot Noyes, Edgar Kaufmann, jr.

ARCHITECTURE

Arne Jacobsen and Eric Møller complete the design of the town hall in Aarhus, Denmark. Oscar Niemeyer (with Lucio da Costa and Affonso Reidy) designs the Church of St. Francis of Assisi at Pampulha, Brazil. Richard Neutra completes the design of the Nesbit house in Brentwood, California. Oscar Niemeyer and Lucio da Costa design the Ministry of Education and Health in Rio de Janeiro. The Pentagon, at 6.5 million square feet, is the largest office building in the world.

BOOKS

James and Katherine Morrow Ford write *Design of Modern Interiors*. Charlotte Perriand's 1941 book is republished in the United States as *Contact with Japan*. Herbert Read writes *Education through Art*.

CULTURE AT LARGE

Ingrid Bergman and Humphrey Bogart star in *Casablanca*. Bing Crosby introduces Irving Berlin's "White Christmas." Albert Camus writes *The Stranger*. Richard Rodgers and Oscar Hammerstein's *Oklahoma!* is staged. Novelist Ayn Rand's *The Fountainhead* and T. S. Eliot's *Four Quartets* are published. Piet Mondrian paints *Broadway Boogie-Woogie*.

DESIGNERS AND INSTALLATIONS

Hecor Guimard dies at seventy-five and Gustav Stickley dies at eighty-four. Piero Fornasetti, a protégé of Gio Ponti, designs frescoes for the Palazzo Bo, Padua. Kem Weber designs interiors and furniture for the Bismarck Hotel, Chicago. William Odom ("Mr Taste"), president of the Parsons School of Design, dies in his fifties and is succeeded by Van Day Truex. Frederick Kiesler designs the Art of This Century gallery in New York. Lilly Reich designs interiors and furniture for the Jürgen Reich apartment in Berlin; the next year, her studio will be destroyed by bombs. Dorothy Draper designs

apartments at New York's Savoy Plaza Hotel. At the Neiman-Marcus store in Dallas, Eleanor Lemaire designs a private office for Stanley Marcus. Tony Duquette designs sets for Vincente Minnelli's film *Ziegfeld Follies of 1944*. Hans Wegner leaves the architecture and design firm of Arne Jacobsen and opens his own office.

The Metropolitan Museum of Art, New York, shows an *Exhibition of Modern British Crafts*. Focusing on the war effort, the Museum of Modern Art, New York, stages the exhibitions *Wartime Housing* and *Useful Objects in Wartime under $10*. Marcel Duchamp's "Mile of String" exhibition design entangles the art in the *First Papers of Surrealism* exhibition, New York. A Greek Revival exhibition at the Metropolitan Museum of Art, New York, includes furniture by Duncan Phyfe and Honoré Lannuier.

Frederick Kiesler designs furniture in free-form shapes with wood sides and leatherette seating surfaces. Arne Jacobsen designs wallcoverings and fabrics for the C. Oleson Co. Richard Neutra designs the "Boomerang" chair for his Nesbit house in Brentwood, California. Gilbert Rohde designs the Executive Office Group for Herman Miller. In wartime England, the government-sponsored "Utility Furniture" becomes available, its designers including Edwin Church and Herbert Cutler. More elaborate furniture will not be available until market controls are lifted in 1948. Florence Knoll joins her husband's furniture company and forms the Knoll Planning Unit; it will be active until 1971.

Americans land at the Japanese-occupied island of Guadalcanal. The Japanese capture Singapore. Mahatma Gandhi demands independence for India and is arrested. Germany's Sixth Army surrenders at Stalingrad.

John Entenza has the California-based *Arts and Architecture* redesigned by Alvin Lustig and begins publishing a series of "Case Study Houses" that will become famous; a frequent contributor of cover designs will be Ray Eames. Because of the war, *Interior Design and Decoration* suspends publication; it will resume in 1949.

Enrico Fermi splits the atom. Magnetic recording tape is invented. Radiant floor heating and the principles of solar energy are developed by George Fred Keck. Earl Tupper develops a technique for the injection molding of polyethylene; Tupperware parties will follow. The Mark I computer (or Automatic Sequence Controlled Calculator) is developed by Howard Aiken and will be installed at Harvard University the following year. It contains five hundred miles of wiring.

Wartime shortages, cutbacks, economies

1942–43

From left to right:

Russel Wright in his home office, New York

Herman Miller advertisement for Gilbert Rohde's Executive Office Group

Florence Schust Knoll

Living room vignette designed by George Stacey

Amancio Williams builds a house atop a bridge at Mar del Plata, Argentina.

T. H. Robsjohn-Gibbings's *Good-bye, Mr. Chippendale,* Gyorgy Kepes's *Language of Vision,* Ole Wanscher's *English Furniture, c. 1680–1800,* and Gustav Ecke's *Chinese Domestic Furniture* are published.

Martha Graham dances to Aaron Copland's *Appalachian Spring.* George Orwell writes the fable *Animal Farm,* and Jean-Paul Sartre writes the existentialist drama *No Exit.* Francis Bacon paints *Three Studies for Figures at the Base of a Crucifixion.* The American Abstract Artists, attacking the Museum of Modern Art's focus on European painting, circulates a flyer asking, "How Modern Is the Museum of Modern Art?"

Gilbert Rohde dies at sixty. In New York, Franklin Hughes redesigns the Monte Carlo supper club, originally designed by Dorothy Draper; meanwhile, Draper designs the Quintandinha resort at Petrópolis, near Rio de Janeiro, and one of her fabrics, "Braziliance," will be manufactured by Schumacher. In Chicago, Raymond Anthony Court redesigns the Stevens Hotel after its wartime use by the army, and Samuel A. Marx transforms the dining room of the Ambassador East Hotel into the Pump Room. In Paris, designer Jean Royère opens a studio and shop; he will later establish branches in Cairo, Beirut, Teheran, and São Paulo. George Nelson, working for *Fortune* magazine in New York, designs his own office there, the custom furniture including his first slat bench.

The Museum of Modern Art, New York, shows *Design for Use* with an exhibition design by Serge Chermayeff.

Charles and Ray Eames, designing in partnership in Los Angeles, produce a child's chair for the Evans Products Co. Hans Wegner designs his "Chinese" chair. George Nelson and Henry Wright design the "Storagewall," which is featured in *Life* magazine. Hans Knoll invites Charles Eames, Eero Saarinen, Ralph Rapson, and Serge Chermayeff to design furniture for his "Equipment for Living" line. Knoll also produces a three-legged table lamp by sculptor Isamu Noguchi. The "Barwa" chair is designed by Barolucci and Waldheim.

London suffers German air raids. On D-Day, Allied forces land at Normandy beaches. The U.S. Home Loan Guarantee program helps provide housing for returning war veterans.

The July issue of *Arts and Architecture* is devoted to prefabrication, an idea much in the air; the issue's editors are Charles and Ray Eames, Eero Saarinen, R. Buckminster Fuller, and Herbert Matter. *Pencil Points*, founded in New York in 1920, changes its name to *Progressive Architecture*.

In England, the Council of Industrial Design (CoID) is established; it will be renamed the Design Council in 1972. Dorothy Draper's $30,500 fee for designing the Quintandinha resort sets a record for commercial design.

The first nonstop flight is made from England to Canada.

T. H. Robsjohn-Gibbings says *Good-bye, Mr. Chippendale*

1944

From left to right:

Bruno Mathsson's "Pernilla 1" lounge chair of molded beech plywood

Hans Wegner's "Chinese" chair of ash with a woven cord seat

The Pump Room of the Ambassador East Hotel, Chicago, designed by Samuel A. Marx

Marcel Breuer, having left his partnership with Walter Gropius, designs the Geller house on Long Island, its interiors, and its furniture. Edwin Lutyens dies.

George Nelson and Henry Wright collaborate on a best-seller, *Tomorrow's House: How to Plan Your Post-War Home Now.* The Museum of Modern Art publishes Elizabeth B. Mock's *Tomorrow's Small House.* Derek Patmore writes *Colour Schemes and Modern Furnishing.* Osbert Lancaster's 1939 *Homes, Sweet Homes* is published in the United States.

Benjamin Britten composes *Peter Grimes*, Evelyn Waugh writes *Brideshead Revisited*, and Tennessee Williams's *The Glass Menagerie* is staged.

George Nelson and Henry Wright describe *Tomorrow's House*

DESIGNERS AND INSTALLATIONS	EXHIBITIONS	FURNITURE AND FURNISHINGS	GOVERNMENT EVENTS	MAGAZINES	TECHNICAL AND SCIENTIFIC ADVANCES

Alvin Lustig designs the New York headquarters for *Look* magazine. J. Monroe Hewlett's astronomical mural on the ceiling of Grand Central Terminal is repainted. Kem Weber designs a house and studio for himself, including interiors and furniture, in Santa Barbara, California. Dorothy Draper designs the Versailles Dinner Club, New York. In *Yolanda and the Thief*, Fred Astaire dances in sets designed by Tony Duquette. Eva Zeisel designs her "Museum White" dinnerware for the Museum of Modern Art, New York.

At New York's Museum of Modern Art, Bernard Rudofsky, the museum's first and only director of its Department of Apparel Research, curates an exhibition examining the question *Are Clothes Modern?* Rudofsky's book of the same name will be published in 1947.

Isamu Noguchi begins designing his Akari paper lanterns; he will eventually design more than 150 different shapes, and more than 100 will still be in production (by Ozeki & Co.) at the end of the century. Finn Juhl designs his "Teak" chair. Ernest Race, with J. W. Noel Jordan, establishes Race Furniture in London; one of its first products is the "BA" chair of sand-cast aluminum salvaged from fighter planes; more than 250,000 will be sold. Paul McCobb establishes his own design firm. Bloomingdale's department store in New York opens a modern furniture department; it shows pieces by Jens Risom, Abel Sorensen, and Ralph Rapson, all manufactured by Knoll. Charles and Ray Eames are designing their "LCW" (lounge chair wood), which *Time* magazine in 1999 will call "the chair of the century."

World War II ends. The Arab League is formed.

Gio Ponti founds the Italian journal *Lo Stile*. Ponti also establishes the Associazione per l'Architettura Organica and begins editing its magazine, *Metron*.

ENIAC (the Electronic Numerical Integrator and Computer) is designed at the University of Pennsylvania; filling a large room, it weighs thirty tons and contains eighteen thousand vacuum tubes. The atomic bomb is developed. There are five thousand television sets in American homes.

1945

From left to right:

Two of Noguchi's "Akari" lights

Noguchi's glass-topped coffee table, designed in 1939 and now in production by Herman Miller

Finn Juhl's "Teak" chair

The Eameses' molded-plywood "LCW" chair, to be produced by Herman Miller in 1946

A version of R. Buckminster Fuller's "Dymaxion" industrialized house design of 1927 is built in Witchita, Kansas. Ludwig Mies van der Rohe's work on the I.I.T. campus continues with the completion of the Alumni Memorial Hall. Richard Neutra designs a house for Edgar Kaufmann in Palm Springs, California. Frank Lloyd Wright's S. C. Johnson & Co. Administration Building is finished in Racine, Wisconsin.

Elizabeth B. Mock's *If You Want to Build a House* and Ole Wanscher's *History of the Art of Furniture* are published.

Dr. Benjamin Spock's *Common Sense Book of Baby and Child Care* is published. Eugene O'Neill's *The Iceman Cometh* is staged and Carson McCullers's *The Member of the Wedding* is published.

SOM designs the Terrace Plaza Hotel, Cincinnati; it has interior design and custom furniture by SOM's Benjamin Baldwin and Ward Bennett and murals by Saul Steinberg and Joan Miró. Ronald Tree buys the London decorating firm of Colefax & Fowler as a farewell gift to his wife, Nancy (the future Nancy Lancaster), after their divorce. John Fowler and Mrs. Lancaster will operate the firm together, but their differing tastes will cause them to be called "the unhappiest unmarried couple in England." In Mount Kisco, New York, Syrie Maugham designs interiors of the Castle for Mrs. DeWitt Wallace. For the Greyhound Bus Co., Raymond Loewy designs the Scenicruiser and its interior. William Pahlmann opens his own design firm in New York and begins writing a newspaper column, "A Matter of Taste."

Eames furniture admired in New York

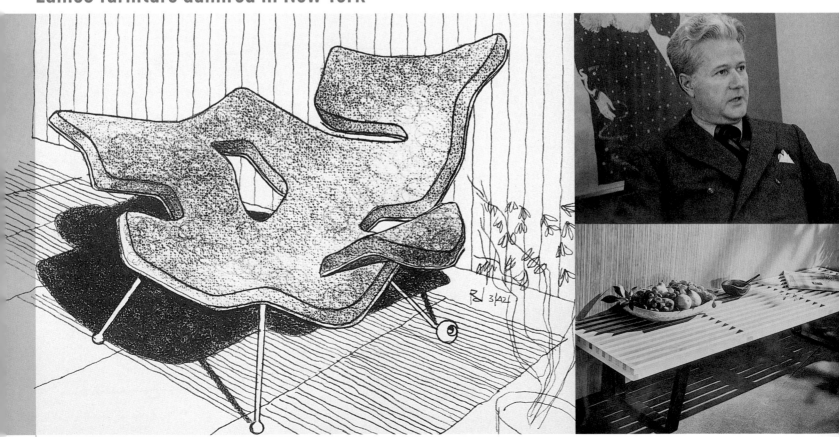

EXHIBITIONS

New Furniture Designed by Charles Eames is seen in February at the Architectural League of New York and the following month at the Museum of Modern Art; George Nelson, just appointed design director of Herman Miller, takes his employer to see the show and insists that Miller hire Eames as well; they do. *Ideas for Better Living* is seen at the Walker Art Center, Minneapolis, and *Useful Objects for the Home* at the Akron Art Institute. In New York, the Metropolitan Museum of Art shows *Modern Swedish and Danish Decorative Arts.* The Museum of Modern Art, New York, shows *Modern China by Eva Zeisel.* In London, the Council of Industrial Design organizes the exhibition *Britain Can Make It* and Maxwell Fry and Jane Drew exhibit a modern kitchen at the Victoria & Albert.

FURNITURE AND FURNISHINGS

George Nelson's first collection for the Herman Miller company includes the slat bench, which will still be in production at the century's end. Also for Miller, Isamu Noguchi designs the "IN 70" sofa and the "IN 71" ottoman, and Charles and Ray Eames prepare for the production of their "LCW" and design a folding wood screen with canvas hinges. Eero Saarinen designs the "Grasshopper" upholstered lounge chair for Knoll. Eva Zeisel designs the "Town and Country" line of ceramic tableware. Jens Risom establishes Jens Risom Design in New York, which will be active until 1973, when he will become CEO of Design Control in New Canaan, Connecticut; despite fashions for plastic and metal furniture, Risom will continue to work in wood. The Hitchcock Chair Co. is formed to produce reproductions of the nineteenth-century stenciled wood chairs by Lambert Hitchcock. Newlyweds Nanna and Jørgen Ditzel establish a studio in Copenhagen for the production of furniture, jewelry, tableware, and fabrics. Jean Prouvé opens his own furniture factory in a suburb of Nancy and will manage it until 1952. In England, artist Graham Sutherland designs fabrics for Helios Ltd.; they will later be reproduced by Warner & Sons Ltd.

GOVERNMENT EVENTS

The United Nations General Assembly holds its first meeting in London.

MAGAZINES

The Walker Art Center, Minneapolis, begins publishing the *Everyday Art Quarterly*; in 1954 it will change its name to *Design Quarterly.*

TECHNICAL AND SCIENTIFIC ADVANCES

CADD (computer-aided drafting and design) gains a presence in the drafting rooms of architects and interior designers.

1946

From left to right:

Ralph Rapson's "Chair of Tomorrow," a design presented to Knoll but never produced

Jens Risom

George Nelson's slat bench for Herman Miller

Armchair by Alvar Aalto

Restaurant of the Terrace Plaza Hotel, Cincinnati, by Benjamin Baldwin and Ward Bennett of SOM. The wraparound mural is by Joan Miró.

ARCHITECTURE

Marcel Breuer designs the Robinson house, Williamstown, Massachusetts, and a house for himself in New Canaan, Connecticut. Alvar Aalto designs the Baker House dormitory for M.I.T. in Cambridge, Massachusetts. Frank Lloyd Wright designs the V. C. Morris gift shop in San Francisco, a forerunner of the Guggenheim Museum. Luis Barragán designs his own house in the Tacubaya section of Mexico City.

BOOKS

T. H. Robsjohn-Gibbings writes *Mona Lisa's Moustache*. László Moholy-Nagy writes *Vision in Motion*. Meyric Rogers writes *American Interior Design*. Paul László writes *Album of Modern Design*. Gordon Logie explains modern production techniques in his *Furniture from Machines*, and Gordon Russell tells *The Story of Furniture*.

CULTURE AT LARGE

Tennessee Williams writes *A Streetcar Named Desire*. Malcolm Lowry writes *Under the Volcano*. Jackson Pollock produces his first major poured paintings.

DESIGNERS AND INSTALLATIONS

Dorothy Draper designs interiors for the Greenbrier Hotel in White Sulphur Springs, West Virginia. Madeleine Castaing moves her Paris shop and studio to the corner of the rue Bonaparte and the rue Jacob, paints the exterior black, and fills it with museum-quality antiques and flea-market curiosities. In East Hampton, New York, French architect Pierre Chareau designs the studio of painter Robert Motherwell in the shell of a war-era Quonset hut. Ward Bennett (born Howard Bennett Amsterdam) establishes himself as an interior designer with a New York penthouse design for Harry Jason. Jens Risom designs a New York showroom for Knoll. Ruth Adler Schnee establishes her workshop for hand-screened fabric. Charles Eames designs a Herman Miller showroom in Los Angeles. French president Vincent Auriol commissions Suzanne Guiguichon and Jacques Adnet to design rooms in the Château Rambouillet and the Palais d'Élysée. Wells Coates designs airplane interiors for BOAC. In Brazil, Lina Bardi Bo begins designing interiors for the Museu de Arte de São Paulo. Vladimir Kagan designs a delegates' cocktail lounge for the United Nations headquarters at Lake Success, New York.

Office furniture makers unite

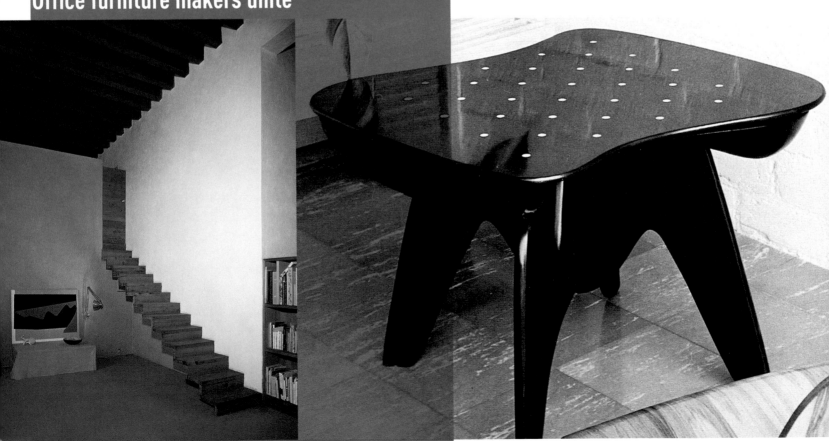

EXHIBITIONS

FURNITURE
AND FURNISHINGS

GOVERNMENT EVENTS

PROGRESS IN
THE PROFESSION

TECHNICAL AND
SCIENTIFIC ADVANCES

At the Museum of Modern Art, New York, Edgar Kaufmann, jr., presents *Modern Rooms of the Last Fifty Years*, and Philip Johnson curates *The Architecture of Mies van der Rohe*. In Edinburgh, the Council of Industrial Design presents *Enterprise Scotland*. American museums are eager to show the public the new possibilities in postwar residential design and furniture. The Albright Art Gallery in Buffalo shows *Good Design Is Your Business*; the Newark Museum shows *Decorative Arts Today*; the Munson-Williams-Proctor Institute, Utica, New York, shows *The Modern House Comes Alive*; and the Rhode Island School of Design shows *Furniture of Today*.

Dennis Young uses a "seating box" of modeling clay to record the body shapes and postures of sixty-seven models as a basis for the design of his "Shell Chair" for Design London; it is an early step toward what will be called ergonomic design. Hans Wegner's "Peacock" chair is designed for Johannes Hansen and shown at the Copenhagen Cabinetmakers' Guild. Ilmari Tapiovaara designs the "Domus" chair for a Helsinki dormitory. Josef Frank designs a mahogany chair for Stockholm's Svenskt Tenn. Edward Wormley designs the "Listen-to-Me" chaise for Dunbar. The fabric designs of Marianne Strengell are introduced by Knoll. Isamu Noguchi designs a chess table with movable pockets for the chess pieces for Herman Miller. Also for Miller, Charles and Ray Eames design a fiberglass shell chair on a base of thin metal rods. For the Howard Miller Clock Co., George Nelson designs the "4755" wall clock, popularly known as the "Ball Clock." George Hanson designs a wall-mounted swing-arm lamp that will be manufactured for decades by Hinson & Co.

India is proclaimed independent from Great Britain and is partitioned into India and Pakistan. The United Nations mandates that Palestine be partitioned into Arab and Jewish states.

The National Office Furniture Association is established.

There are now one million television sets in American homes.

1947

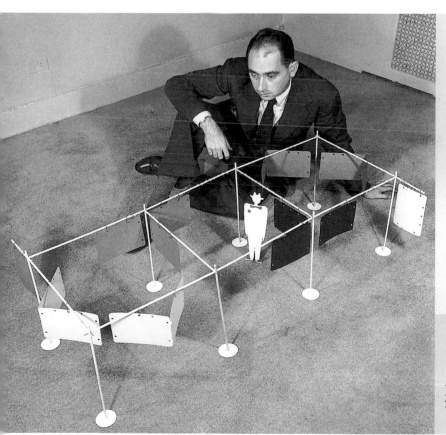

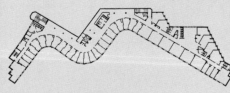

From left to right:

Interior of Luis Barragán's own house, Mexico City

Isamu Noguchi's chess table for Herman Miller

George Nelson with a model of his "StrucTube" display system

Hans Wegner's "Peacock" chair

Plan of the Baker House dormitory for M.I.T., Cambridge, Massachusetts, by Alvar Aalto

Pietro Belluschi designs the Equitable building in Portland, Oregon. Richard Neutra designs the Tremaine house in Montecito, California, and designs bentwood chairs for its interior. The Museum of Modern Art holds a symposium asking, "What Is Happening to Modern Architecture?"; answering the question are Peter Blake, Marcel Breuer, Walter Gropius, George Nelson, Henry-Russell Hitchcock, and Alfred Barr. Vienna-born Harry Seidler, having studied at Harvard and worked for Breuer, arrives in Australia and designs a house for his mother.

Siegfried Giedion explores the interaction of industry and design in *Mechanization Takes Command*. Catherine and Harold Sleeper's *The House for You*, and Rudolph Rosenthal and Helena L. Ratzka's *The Story of Modern Applied Art* are published. George Nelson compiles a catalog for the Herman Miller Co. showing furniture designs by himself and by Charles Eames, Isamu Noguchi, and Paul László; with unprecedented candor, furniture dimensions are given; with unprecedented cheek, the catalogs are sold, not given away. A second catalog will be produced in 1952.

Norman Mailer writes *The Naked and the Dead*, and Truman Capote writes *Other Voices, Other Rooms*. George Balanchine becomes artistic director of the New York City Ballet.

Gio Ponti designs the swimming pool and the interiors of the Hotel Royal, San Remo, Italy. Also in Italy, Joe Colombo, Bruno Munari, and Gillo Dorfles found the Movimento Arte Concreta. Donald Deskey designs stateroom interiors and public rooms for the SS *Argentina*. A Chicago showroom for Herman Miller, designed by George Nelson, features the first rudimentary version of track lighting, developed by an employee of the Nelson office, designer Jack Dunbar. Edgar Kaufmann, jr.'s *Interiors* article about Danish designer Finn Juhl is "the first report of Juhl's work to be published out-

Nelson improvises track lighting

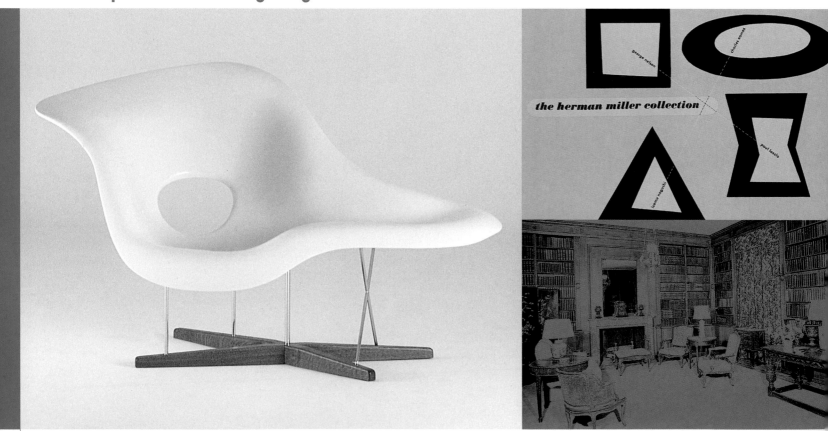

side of Denmark." The annual Scandinavian Furniture Fair is instituted in Copenhagen. Gerald Luss and others establish the design firm Designs for Business. Benjamin Baldwin establishes his own design practice in New York; he will move to Chicago in 1955.

American entrepreneur Jim Thompson establishes Thai Silk, revolutionizing traditional weaving techniques, color palettes, and merchandising methods; Thompson will mysteriously vanish in 1967. Harvey Probber opens a New York showroom for his own modular seating designs. Modern Products is founded, and will later change its name to Haworth Inc. For Herman Miller, Charles and Ray Eames design molded-plywood chairs, molded fiberglass-reinforced plastic chairs, and the "Aluminum Group." Eero Saarinen's "Womb" chair is introduced by Knoll. Kartell introduces nesting plastic tables by Giotto Stoppino. Baker introduces a Far East collection based on classical Chinese furniture. New York's Museum of Modern Art holds an *International Competition for Low-Cost Furniture.*

The State of Israel is created. War breaks out between the new state and its Arab neighbors.

The American Institute of Decorators gives its first award for woven fabrics to Maria Kipp.

NÉON, a journal of Surrealist art and literature, is founded in Paris.

Antibiotics are produced. The two-hundred-inch reflecting telescope on Mount Palomar is built.

1948

From left to right:

"La Chaise" by Charles and Ray Eames

George Nelson's catalog for Herman Miller; the cover design is by Irving Harper of the Nelson office.

Elisabeth Draper's library design for Dwight D. Eisenhower, Morningside Drive, New York

Rose Seidler house, Wahroonga, New South Wales, Australia, designed by Harry Seidler, who also painted the mural. It will later be owned by the Historic Houses Trust of New South Wales.

Eero Saarinen's "Womb" chair for Knoll

Frank Lloyd Wright accepts the gold medal of the American Institute of Architects, saying, "Well, it's about time." Charles and Ray Eames build their studio-house in Pacific Palisades, California. Philip Johnson builds his Glass House in New Canaan, Connecticut.

Peter Blake writes *Marcel Breuer: Architect and Designer*.

Arthur Miller writes *Death of a Salesman*, George Orwell writes *1984*, and Richard Rodgers and Oscar Hammerstein write *South Pacific*. Lee Strasberg becomes artistic director of the Actors' Studio.

A renovation of the White House is begun by Charles T. Haight, director of interior decoration for B. Altman & Co.; it will be finished in 1952. Carlo Mollino designs interiors for the Casa Orengo, Turin, Italy. Alvar Aalto designs the Woodberry Poetry Room at Harvard University, Cambridge, Massachusetts. James Amster designs the New York showroom of d'Orsay Perfumes. The firm of Warner-Leeds designs the Paris Theatre and the Bonniers store, both in New York. The September issue of *Interiors* investigates the "current pet problem" of how to arrange furniture around a television set. William Pahlmann designs a series of spaces for Bonwit Teller, Chicago. In New York, designer Tom Lee founds Tom Lee Ltd.

Modernism shown by Girard in Detroit, by Breuer in MoMA garden

EXHIBITIONS

An Exhibition for Modern Living is curated by Alexander Girard at the Detroit Institute of the Arts. Celebrating its twentieth anniversary, the Museum of Modern Art in New York shows *Timeless Aspects of Modern Art* and *Modern Art in Your Life*. Marcel Breuer builds an exhibition house in the museum garden. MoMA also presents its first exhibition devoted to a single textile artist, Anni Albers. *Design in Use: USA* tours Europe, showing the textile designs of Ruth Adler Schnee.

FURNITURE AND FURNISHINGS

Carlo Mollino designs furniture as well, curving wood into the "Arabesque" line. Hans Wegner's "De runde stol" ("The Round Chair)," an armchair of teak and split cane, is manufactured by Johannes Hansen in Copenhagen; in the United States it will be called simply "The Chair," and *House Beautiful* will declare it "the most beautiful object of the year." For Herman Miller, George Nelson designs the Executive Office Group and Isamu Noguchi designs a dining table, a coffeetable, and biomorphic sofas and ottomans. Ray Komai designs a molded plywood shell chair for J. G. Furniture. Winchendon presents the "Planner Group" low-cost furniture collection by Paul McCobb,

and Widdicomb introduces an upholstered sectional sofa by T. H. Robsjohn-Gibbings. Pier Giacomo Castiglioni and his brothers Livio and Achille design the "Turbino" desk lamp for Arredoluce. Hungarian-born textile designer Eszter Haraszty is director of Knoll Textiles, a position she will hold until she resigns in 1955; she will create unusual color combinations (such as pinks with oranges), and her own fabrics will include "Transportation Cloth," "Knoll Stripes," and "Fibra."

GOVERNMENT EVENTS

The Chinese People's Republic is founded by Mao Tse-Tung. Germany is split into eastern and western zones. The Irish Free State is formed. The North Atlantic Treaty Organization is established.

MAGAZINES

England's Council of Industrial Design begins publishing *Design*. Raymond Loewy appears on the cover of *Time*.

TECHNICAL AND SCIENTIFIC ADVANCES

Union Carbide introduces modacrylic fibers. Sir Geoffrey de Havilland designs the "Comet" airplane. The USSR tests an atomic bomb. *Popular Mechanics* magazine predicts that "computers in the future may weigh no more than 1.5 tons."

1949

From left to right:

The Grand Salon, Bonwit Teller, Chicago, by William Pahlmann

"The Chair" by Hans Wegner

George Nelson's tray table for Herman Miller

Isamu Noguchi's curvaceous furniture for Herman Miller

Finn Juhl's "Double Chieftain" chair

THE '50s

The decade begins with a series of four annual *Good Design* exhibitions curated by Edgar Kaufmann, jr. Seen at both New York's Museum of Modern Art and Chicago's Merchandise Mart, they are announced as "A Joint Program to Stimulate the Best Modern Design of Home Furnishing," and Kaufmann explains that by placing such a show "at the core of American commerce, a new and crucial audience has been gained for progressive modern design." The shows display a selection of well-designed but inexpensive furniture, fabric, and household goods and are themselves examples of modern exhibition design, the designers chosen by Kaufmann being Charles and Ray Eames for the 1950 show, Finn Juhl for 1951, Paul Rudolph for 1952, and Alexander Girard for 1953. But the consumption of goods, however well designed, begins to be questioned. Mid-decade, architect, designer, curator, and iconoclast Bernard Rudofsky examines the conventions of the modern house in his book *Beyond the Picture Window*. Citing the sparely furnished Japanese house as an ideal, he says that "An innately vacant room never breathes the sort of tiredness peculiar to our well-furnished ones." The '50s close with another remarkable exhibition that takes modern design beyond the so-called Iron Curtain. *The American National Exhibition* in Moscow features exhibition and pavilion designs by George Nelson, an architecture exhibit curated by Peter Blake, a fabric exhibit designed by Tom Lee, Edward Steichen's *Family of Man* photographic exhibit, a gold-anodized geodesic dome by R. Buckminster Fuller, and, inside the dome, a seven-screen audiovisual presentation of American life by Charles and Ray Eames.

Frank Lloyd Wright's
Guggenheim Museum, New
York, finished in 1959

ARCHITECTURE

Walter Gropius and the Architects Collaborative design the Harvard Graduate Center in Cambridge, Massachusetts. Ludwig Mies van der Rohe's Farnsworth house is finished in Plano, Illinois. Bruce Goff's Bavinger house is begun in Norman, Oklahoma; it will be finished in 1955. Frank Lloyd Wright's 1904 Larkin Building is sold for $5,000 to be demolished for a garage.

BOOKS

Edgar Kaufmann, jr., writes *What Is Modern Design?* and *Prize Designs for Modern Furniture*, both published by the Museum of Modern Art. Le Corbusier publishes the first of two books on his proportioning system, *The Modulor*. Edwin O. Christensen compiles *The Index of American Design* for the National Gallery of Art.

CULTURE AT LARGE

On Broadway are William Inge's play *Come Back, Little Sheba* and Frank Loesser's musical *Guys and Dolls*. On the movie screen are Joseph Mankiewicz's *All about Eve* and Billy Wilder's *Sunset Boulevard*.

DESIGNERS AND INSTALLATIONS

William Pahlmann designs the Bronzini shop, New York. T. H. Robsjohn-Gibbings designs a New York apartment for Victor Ganz. In San Remo, Italy, Gio Ponti and Piero Fornasetti design the interiors of a casino, and in Genoa Franco Albini renovates the interiors of the Palazzo Bianco. Warner-Leeds designs interiors for the Caribe Hilton in San Juan, Puerto Rico. Elsie de Wolfe dies at eighty-five; her protégé Tony Duquette will later become president of the Elsie de Wolfe Foundation. Ruby Ross Wood dies at seventy-one; Billy Baldwin, who has worked for Wood for fifteen years, forms his own firm, Baldwin Inc.; it will later operate under the names Baldwin & Martin and Baldwin & Smith; Baldwin's clients will include Greta Garbo, Barbara Hutton, Paul Mellon, and Hattie Carnegie. Sybil Colefax dies at seventy-five.

London's Institute of Contemporary Arts celebrates Pablo Picasso's seventieth birthday. The Museum of Modern Art, New York, prepares a traveling exhibition for Europe, *Design for Modern Use: Made in the USA*; it is designed by Alexander Girard. Carlo Mollino designs a room setting for the *Italy at Work* exhibition at the Brooklyn Museum. The first *Good Design* show is at New York's Museum of Modern Art and Chicago's Merchandise Mart.

Herman Miller begins marketing the "Eames Storage Unit" and Isamu Noguchi's round table on a base of chrome rods. Harry Bertoia designs his wire mesh chairs for Knoll. Textile artist D. D. (Doris) Tillett designs and produces "Queen Anne's Lace," a fabric that will be sold for more than thirty years. The Castiglioni brothers design the "Taraxacum" hanging lamp for Flos, and Achille Castiglioni the "Bramante" table base for Zanotta. Franco Albini designs wicker armchairs named "Gala" and "Margherita." Jean Prouvé designs the "Antony" chair of molded plywood with steel legs. Joseph-André Motte designs the "Tripode" chair of steel, wood, and rattan for Rousier. Carlo Mollino designs the "Arabesque" table for F. Apelli and L. Varesio. Tommi Parzinger designs a lacquered cabinet in the "Chinese Modern" style. Ralph Rapson and his wife, Mary, open the Rapson-Inc. shop at 282 Dartmouth Street, Boston; one of the first modern design shops in the United States, it sells Arzberg porcelain, Noguchi lamps, George Nelson clocks, jewelry by Harry Bertoia, and furniture by Bruno Mathsson, Arne Jacobsen, Eero Saarinen, Charles and Ray Eames, and Rapson himself; they will sell the shop in 1954. Throughout the decade, T. H. Robsjohn Gibbings will design furniture for Widdicomb, and Edward Wormley will design furniture for Dunbar.

The Korean War begins.

Interior Design and Decoration, which had resumed publication the previous year, changes its name to *Interior Design*.

DuPont introduces acrylic fibers. There are 1.5 million television sets in the United States; a year later there will be 15 million.

Edgar Kaufmann, jr., curates *Good Design*

1950

From left to right:

The Eameses' "DAR" chair for Herman Miller with a shell of glass-reinforced polyester

Chairs by Harry Bertoia for Knoll

"Eames Storage Units" for Herman Miller

The *Good Design* installation at the Museum of Modern Art, curated by Edgar Kaufmann, jr., and designed by Charles and Ray Eames.

Ganz apartment, New York, designed by T. H. Robsjohn-Gibbings

ARCHITECTURE

Ludwig Mies van der Rohe's apartment blocks at 860 and 880 Lake Shore Drive are finished in Chicago. Alvar Aalto's Baker House dormitory is finished for M.I.T. in Cambridge, Massachusetts. Le Corbusier is designing the government buildings at Chandigarh, India.

BOOKS

Sherrill Whiton's *Elements of Interior Decoration* is republished as *Elements of Interior Design and Decoration*. F. R. S. Yorke and Penelope Whiting write *The New Small House*. Russel and Mary Wright offer *A Guide for Easier Living*. Raymond Loewy advises *Never Leave Well Enough Alone*. Norman Cherner explains *Making Your Own Modern Furniture*, and Mario Dal Fabbro tells *How to Build Modern Furniture*. Ernö Goldfinger writes *British Furniture of Today*, and Frank Lewis writes *British Textiles*.

CULTURE AT LARGE

J. D. Salinger's *Catcher in the Rye* is published. Benjamin Britten composes *Billy Budd*. John Huston's *The African Queen* is released.

DESIGNERS AND INSTALLATIONS

Winterthur is established as a public museum of period rooms, furniture, and decorative arts by Henry Francis du Pont. Piero Fornasetti designs interiors for the Dulciora bakery in Milan. Tony Duquette designs a fashion salon for Adrian in Beverly Hills. The first International Design Conference is held at Aspen, Colorado; the conferences will continue annually through the end of the century. Finn Juhl designs a line of furniture for Baker, designs the Trusteeship Council Chamber of the United Nations, and is invited by Edgar Kaufmann, jr., to design his *Good Design* exhibition. Also at the United Nations, Sven Markelius designs a hall for the Economic and Social Council.

EXHIBITIONS

The Milan Triennale is dominated by "Danish Modern" and other designs from Scandinavia, as will be a succession of future Triennales. Also at the Triennale, however, the architecture firm BBPR creates the exhibition *The Form of the Useful*. The Festival of Britain opens in London; shown are furniture designs by a new generation of English designers, including Dennis Young and Ernest Race, and an entertainment complex is designed by Ernö Goldfinger; Wells Coates designs the Telekinema; Robin Day designs the Homes and Gardens Pavilion, upholstering the furniture in fabric designed by his wife, Lucienne Day; the fabrics of Swiss weaver Marianne Straub are also shown. Edgar Kaufmann, jr.'s second *Good Design* exhibition is seen at New York's Museum of Modern Art and Chicago's

Merchandise Mart. Zurich's Kunstgewerbeschule presents an exhibition of Finnish design. Tony Duquette is the first American to have a one-man show at the Musée des Arts Décoratifs, Paris.

FIT offers interior design curriculum

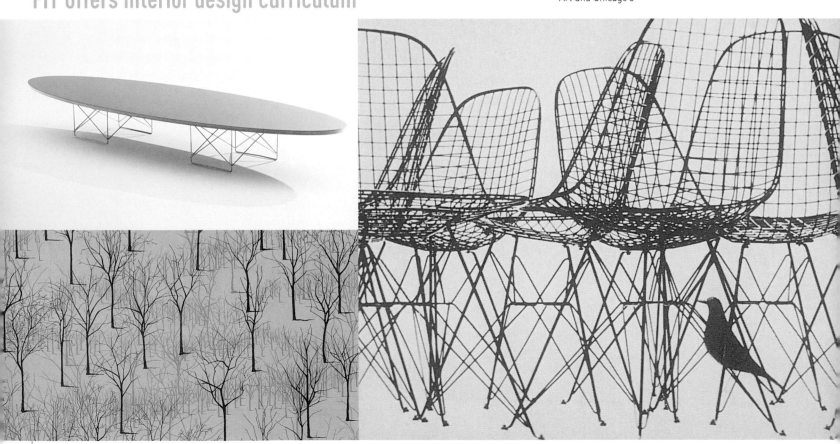

FURNITURE AND FURNISHINGS

Alexander Girard is named color consultant for the General Motors Research Center and begins to design textiles for Herman Miller. Marcel Breuer adapts his earlier desk design with cantilevered file drawers for his own second house in New Canaan, Connecticut; it will be manufactured by Gavina in Milan. Marco Zanuso designs the "Lady" chair for Arflex. In Helsinki, Armi Ratia founds the Marimekko fabric company. Charles and Ray Eames design the elliptical "surf-board" table for Herman Miller. Paul McCobb designs his "Predictor Group." Artemide is founded in Milan.

GOVERNMENT EVENTS

A U.S.–Japan peace treaty is signed in San Francisco.

HONORS AND AWARDS

The Lunning Prize for design is established by Frederick Lunning of Georg Jensen; its first recipients are Hans Wegner and Tapio Wirkkala; the prize will be given annually through 1970.

MAGAZINES

In Buenos Aires, Tomas Maldonado edits *Nueva Vision*. For *Look* magazine, T. H. Robsjohn-Gibbings designs the "Bathroom of 1960."

PROGRESS IN THE PROFESSION

The Fashion Institute of Technology, New York, introduces a curriculum for interior design. In Grand Rapids, Michigan, the American Institute of Decorators celebrates its twentieth anniversary.

TECHNICAL AND SCIENTIFIC ADVANCES

Electric power is produced from atomic energy. The IAS computer is completed at Princeton's Institute for Advanced Study.

1951

From left to right:

Eames elliptical table for Herman Miller

William Pahlmann's "Still Trees" printed silk for F. Schumacher

Wire chairs by Charles and Ray Eames, as photographed by Charles, with a carved wooden dove

Ward Bennett's New York apartment for himself

Finn Juhl's exhibition design for MoMA's *Good Design* show

Apartment at 840 Park Avenue, New York, by Elisabeth Draper

ARCHITECTURE

Le Corbusier's Unité d'Habitation apartment block in Marseilles is completed. Lever House, New York, is designed by Gordon Bunshaft of Skidmore, Owings, & Merrill, with interiors by Raymond Loewy. Alexander Girard designs the Rieveschel house in Grosse Pointe, Michigan, and, with Eero Saarinen, the Irwin Miller house in Columbus, Indiana. Marcel Breuer designs the Caesar cottage in Lakeville, Connecticut, and the De Bijenkorf department store in Rotterdam.

BOOKS

Design books of the year include: William J. Hennessey's *Modern Furnishings for the Home*, which will be republished in 1997; Max Bill's *Form: A Balance-Sheet of Mid-Twentieth-Century Trends in Design*; George Nelson's *Living Spaces*; Joseph Downs's *American Furniture (Queen Anne and Chippendale Periods)* in the Henry F. du Pont Winterthur Museum; Thomas Howarth's *Charles Rennie Mackintosh and the Modern Movement*; and, in a more philosophical vein, Susanne Langer's *Feeling and Form: A Theory of Art*.

CULTURE AT LARGE

Samuel Beckett writes *Waiting for Godot*. Ralph Ellison writes *Invisible Man*. Gene Kelly dances in *Singin' in the Rain*.

DESIGNERS AND INSTALLATIONS

Gio Ponti designs the Turin, Italy, headquarters for the Burroughs Adding Machine Co., and, with Piero Fornasetti, interiors for the ship *Andrea Doria*. Franco Albini and Franca Helg begin the conversion of Genoa's Palazzo Rosso into a museum. Billy Baldwin designs the America's Cup sailing trophy and a fluted wood stand to support it. I. M. Pei designs the New York offices of Webb & Knapp. Dorothy Draper designs the interior of the Packard automobile.

Alexander Girard begins a textile program for Herman Miller. Walter Hoving, the new president of Tiffany & Co., hires Van Day Truex, who has been president of the Parsons School of Design for the last decade, as the company's design director, instructing him that Tiffany should sell nothing that Truex himself would not want to own. Marcel Breuer designs a New York showroom for Scarves by Vera.

EXHIBITIONS

In London, the Victoria & Albert shows *Exhibition of Victorian and Edwardian Decorative Arts*. The Museum of Modern Art, New York, and the Merchandise Mart, Chicago, show Edgar Kaufmann, jr.'s third *Good Design* selections; the exhibition design is by Paul Rudolph. The Kunstgewerbeschule, Zurich, shows *Um 1900: Art Nouveau und Jugendstil*. The products and graphics of the Olivetti Corporation are shown at the Museum of Modern Art, New York.

Jack Lenor Larsen, after training at Cranbrook, opens his textile design studio in New York; one of his first commissions is for fabric for New York's Lever House. Boris Kroll introduces his "Caribbean" fabric collection. Arne Jacobsen's three-legged "Myren" ("Ant") stacking chair is introduced by Fritz Hansen; more than a million will be sold, and it will appear on a Danish postage stamp. Jacques Guillon designs a dining chair of nylon cord strung on a frame of laminated wood. Katavolos, Kelley, and Littell design the three-legged "T Chair" for Laverne. Harry Bertoia's wire-shell "Diamond" chairs and slat benches are introduced by Knoll. Elinor Forbes, design director of

the Gump's store in San Francisco, designs a "bamboo" chair for McGuire. Franco Albini designs his cross-legged "Fiorenza" armchair for Arflex. Finnish designer Ilmari Tapiovaara designs the "Lukki I" stacking chair for Lukkiseppo; it is used in Olivetti's Helsinki showroom; Tapiovaara is also given a one-person exhibition in Chicago. Alvar Aalto designs pendant lighting for Artek, Greta von Nessen (widow of Walter von Nessen) designs the versatile "Anywhere" lamp, and George Nelson designs his "Bubble Lamps" for Howard Miller. Hans Coray designs the aluminum-on-steel "Landa" chair for Zanotta.

Elizabeth II is crowned queen of England.

Eleanor McMillen Brown is made a chevalier of the Legion of Honor.

Idea (International Design Annual) is established in Japan. The first issue of *Perspecta*, the Yale architecture journal, notes "three new and important directions in modern architecture—the work of Paul Rudolph, of Philip Johnson, and of Buckminster Fuller." *Progressive Architecture* begins its annual design awards program.

The contraceptive pill is made available.

Rudolph, Johnson, "Bucky" Fuller called leaders in new directions 1952

From left to right:

Raymond Loewy's second-floor cafeteria design for Lever House

Bertoia's "Diamond" chair for Knoll

Alexander Girard's "Double Triangles" fabric pattern for Herman Miller

Marcel Breuer's Caesar cottage, Lakeville, Connecticut

George Nelson phonograph cabinet and sofas for Herman Miller

ARCHITECTURE

Marcel Breuer and his partner Hamilton Smith begin work on a complex of buildings for St. John's Abbey, Collegeville, Minnesota; the work will continue through 1968. Felix Candela designs the Church of the Virgin Milagrosa in Mexico City. Alvar Aalto designs the town hall in Säynätsalo, Finland.

BOOKS

George Nelson writes *Chairs* and *Display*. Robert Woods Kennedy writes *The House and the Art of Its Design*. Edgar Kaufmann, jr.'s 1950 *What Is Modern Design?* is followed by the more specific *What is Modern Interior Design?* Kaufmann's answers are suggested by his chapter headings: Comfort, Quality, Lightness, Harmony, The Machine, and Nature. Sir Ambrose Heal writes *London Furniture Makers, from the Restoration to the Victorian Era, 1660–1840*. David Joel explores *The Adventure of British Furniture, 1851–1951*, including designs by his wife, Betty Joel; his book will be revised in 1969 as *Furniture Design Set Free: The British Furniture Revolution from 1851 to the Present Day*.

CULTURE AT LARGE

Raymond Loewy designs the Studebaker. Marilyn Monroe stars in *Gentlemen Prefer Blondes*.

DESIGNERS AND INSTALLATIONS

Frances Elkins dies. The French designer Lelen designs a Paris apartment for the Comtesse de Lonlay. Also in Paris, Jean Royère redesigns Fouquet's restaurant on the Champs-Élysées. Kem Weber designs the Gray house and its interiors in Montecito, California. A year out of art school, David Hicks creates some boldly colored rooms in his mother's house at South Eaton Place, London; *House and Garden* will publish the rooms, launching Hicks's career. Oliver Messel designs suites at London's Dorchester Hotel. Tom Lee Ltd. designs New York showrooms and offices for the jewelers D. Lisner & Co. Benjamin Baldwin and William Machado design an office/studio for themselves in Montgomery, Alabama. Philip Johnson designs the penthouse dining room and lounge for the Museum of Modern Art, New York.

Architect Benjamin Thompson opens the first Design Research shop in Cambridge, Massachusetts. Van Day Truex upholsters his New York apartment with mattress ticking, dubbing the effect "peasant chic."

EXHIBITIONS

Alexander Girard designs the last of Edgar Kaufmann, jr.'s *Good Design* exhibitions for the Museum of Modern Art, New York, and the Merchandise Mart, Chicago.

Edgar Kaufmann jr.'s book asks

FURNITURE AND FURNISHINGS

Gio Ponti designs the "Distex" armchair for Cassina. Hans Wegner designs the "Valet" chair for PP Møbler. French designer Jacques Adnet designs a bar wrapped in Hermès leather. Pierre Paulin designs the plastic "Chair 157" for Artifort. Serge Mouille designs a three-legged floor lamp of steel rods. Antti Nurmesniemi designs a sauna stool for the Palace Hotel, Helsinki. Laura Ashley Ltd., a retailer of clothing and home furnishings, opens for business, specializing in romantic small-scale prints; thirty years later, it will have almost two hundred outlets all over the world.

GOVERNMENT EVENTS

The U.S. Congress creates a new cabinet post, the Secretary of Health, Education, and Welfare.

HONORS AND AWARDS

The AID's "Rooms of the Year" include work by Adele Faulkner, Mildred Irby, and John C. Frear. The Home Fashions League Trailblazer Award goes to Paul McCobb.

MAGAZINES

The Los Angeles chapter of the AID begins publishing a newsletter; in 1955 it will take the name *Designers West*, and in 1965 it will become an independent magazine. In France, *Esthétique Industrielle* begins publication. *Stile Industria* is founded and will be published until 1962.

PROGRESS IN THE PROFESSION

The Incorporated Institute of British Decorators adds "and Interior Designers" to its name.

TECHNICAL AND SCIENTIFIC ADVANCES

James Watson and Francis Crick propose the "double helix" model for the molecular structure of DNA. DuPont introduces polyester.

1953

What Is Modern Interior Design?

From left to right:

Living room at 1 Sutton Place South, New York, by Smyth, Urquhart, & Marckwald

Steel floor lamp by Serge Mouille

"Ant" chair designed by Arne Jacobsen for Fritz Hansen, later available through ICF, becoming a best-seller

The Blue Room of the White House, Washington, D.C., is hung with a fabric chosen for the room by Stanford White in 1902 and made by F. Schumacher.

"Circles" fabric by Alexander Girard for Herman Miller

Hans Wegner's "Valet" chair

ARCHITECTURE

Architectural Record begins publication of its "Record Houses." Louis Kahn designs the Yale University Art Gallery in New Haven, Connecticut. Skidmore, Owings, & Merrill design the Manufacturers Hanover Bank in New York. Alison and Peter Smithson design a modern school in Hunstanton, Norfolk, England. Edward Durell Stone designs the U.S. embassy in New Delhi. Morris Lapidus designs the Fontainebleu Hotel in Miami Beach. Eliot Noyes designs his own house in New Canaan, Connecticut, and the prototype "Wonder House" for General Electric. In Hobe Sound, Florida, Noyes erects "bubble" structures of concrete sprayed on inflated balloons. In Havana, Max Borges builds the Tropicana nightclub of concrete shells.

BOOKS

T. H. Robsjohn-Gibbings publishes *Homes of the Brave*; like his earlier *Goodbye, Mr. Chippendale*, it is illustrated with drawings by *New Yorker* cartoonist Mary Petty. George Nelson writes *Storage*. Frank Lloyd Wright writes *The Natural House*. Russell Lynes writes *The Tastemakers*. Cecil Beaton writes *The Glass of Fashion*. Ray Faulkner writes *Inside Today's Home*. Albert H. Munsell writes *A Color Notation*. Rudolph Arnheim writes *Art and Visual Perception: A Psychology of the Creative Eye*. Nanna and Jorgen Ditzel write the bilingual *Danske stole—Danish Chairs*. Mario del Fabbro writes *Furniture for Modern Interiors*. Francis de N. Schroeder, editor in chief of *Interiors*, writes *Anatomy for Interior Designers*.

CULTURE AT LARGE

Dylan Thomas publishes *Under Milk Wood*. Bill Haley and the Comets record "Rock around the Clock." Francis Bacon reinterprets Velasquez's portrait of Leo X in his *Head Surrounded by Sides of Beef*.

DESIGNERS AND INSTALLATIONS

For New York's Metropolitan Museum of Art, Dorothy Draper designs a pool-centered cafeteria with figures sculptured by Carl Milles. Davis Allen, at Skidmore, Owings, & Merrill since 1950, designs penthouse offices for Manufacturers Hanover Trust, New York. The Italian architecture firm BBPR designs New York offices and a showroom for Olivetti. Gerald Luss of Designs for Business designs a New York office for Tower Fabrics; it employs cinderblock partitions, and its furnishings from Dux are imported from Sweden by George Tanier. Antiques dealer and designer Yale R. Burge designs his own duplex apartment in New York. In Nancy, France, Jean Prouvé designs a house for himself plus all its interiors and furniture. Designer James Amster, employing muralist Vertés, designs the three-hundred-foot-long Peacock Alley restaurant in New York's Waldorf-Astoria. Victor Gruen designs interiors for Dayton's department store in Rochester, Minnesota. Elisabeth Draper designs interiors for SOM's Nassau Hospital on Long Island. Alexander Girard transforms two adobe shells into his own house in Santa Fe, New Mexico. Everett Brown designs suites for two Chicago hotels, the Sherman and the Ambassador East.

EXHIBITIONS

The Merchandise Mart, Chicago, presents *Five Years of Good Design*, a retrospective of Edgar Kaufmann, jr.'s *Good Design* shows, with a hundred objects from the two thousand the shows have exhibited. At the tenth Milan *Triennale*, Gio Ponti designs a "One Room Apartment," and textiles by Lucienne Day are awarded a grand prize. A Japanese house, its parts imported from Nagoya, is built in the sculpture garden of New York's Museum of Modern Art. *House Beautiful* prepares an exhibition and a special issue, *Design in Scandinavia*.

FURNITURE AND FURNISHINGS

Hans Knoll is killed in an auto accident at forty-one, and his wife, Florence Knoll, becomes the director of their furniture company. For Herman Miller, George Nelson designs the "Steelframe Group" of storage units and Charles and Ray Eames design the "Sofa Compact." Elinor Forbes designs a line of rawhide-wrapped rattan furniture for the McGuire Company. Boris Kroll introduces the "Orient" fabric collection, and Schumacher introduces its "Spanish Collection." Van Day Truex designs the "Dionysus" decanter for Baccarat. Marco Zanuso designs the "Sleep-o-matic" sofa for Arflex. Franco Albini designs the "Luisa" armchair. Harvery Probber is producing his "Sert" modular seating group.

GOVERNMENT EVENTS

The U.S. Supreme Court rules school segregation unconstitutional.

HONORS AND AWARDS

The Italian design prize called the Premio Compasso d'Oro is established by Aldo Borletti of the La Rinascente department store chain.

MAGAZINES

Industrial Design, previously a department of *Interiors* magazine, begins independent publication. The Swiss quarterly *Intérieur* is published by the Association of Swiss Interior Designers and the Association of Swiss Industrial Designers.

PROGRESS IN THE PROFESSION

The U.S. Supreme Court, in *Stein vs. Mazer*, rules that a mass-produced lamp base is protected by copyright from imitation.

TECHNICAL AND SCIENTIFIC ADVANCES

The Celanese Corporation introduces triacetate fibers. RCA introduces the color television set. The U.S. submarine *Nautilus* is converted to nuclear power. R. Buckminster Fuller patents the geodesic dome.

Japanese house grows in MoMA garden

1954

From left to right:

Olivetti showroom, New York, by BBPR

The Eames "Sofa Compact" for Herman Miller

George Nelson's "Thin Edge 54" daybed for Herman Miller

George Nelson's clock design, one of a continuing series for the Howard Miller Clock Co.

Drawing by Mary Petty for T. H. Robsjohn-Gibbings's *Homes of the Brave*

Morris Lapidus's Fontainebleau Hotel, Miami Beach

125

Le Corbusier's Notre-Dame-du-Haut chapel is finished at Ronchamp, France. Eduardo Catalano designs a house for himself in Raleigh, North Carolina, with a hyperbolic paraboloid roof. Arne Jacobsen designs a building and its interiors for Jesperson & Son in Copenhagen and a town hall and its interiors and furniture for Rødovre, Denmark. Alvar Aalto designs the Pension Bank in Helsinki, its interiors, and its furniture.

William Pahlmann, at the height of his career, writes *The Pahlmann Book of Interior Decorating*. Bernard Rudofsky writes *Beyond the Picture Window*. Robert Wemyss Symonds describes *Furniture Making in Seventeenth and Eighteenth Century England*. Aldo Tanchis writes *Design as Art*. Industrial designer Henry Dreyfuss writes *Designing for People*. Katherine Morrow Ford and Thomas Creighton write *Designs for Living*.

Vladimir Nabokov conceives *Lolita*, and Kay Thompson *Eloise*.

Billy Baldwin designs apartment 33A in the Waldorf-Astoria Towers for Cole Porter and his wife; for its library, he designs brass bookcases with ebony shelves, standing against walls of tortoise-shell-finished leather. Syrie Maugham dies at age seventy-six. Designs for Business, of which Gerald Luss has been director of design since 1948, designs a New York headquarters for Olin Mathieson. The same firm also designs interiors for the Long Island Jewish Hospital, and Maria Bergson designs interiors for the North Shore Hospital in Manhasset, New York. Michael Saphier designs the New York offices of Sabena Belgian Airlines. Alvin Lustig designs the Wilheim apartment in New York. Model apartments for New York's Brevoort building are designed by Yale R. Burge, Dora Brahms, Ellen Lehman McCluskey, and Bertha Schaefer. Gio Ponti designs interiors of the Villa Planchart in Caracas, Venezuela. William Pahlmann redesigns Miami's Columbus Hotel, using woven blinds by Dorothy Liebes and pine paneling. Vladimir Kagan, using his own furniture designs, designs an apartment for himself in New York, and Henri Jova designs an apartment for himself in Atlanta.

The Museum of Modern Art, New York, shows *Textiles and Ornamental Arts of India* within an exhibition design by Alexander Girard. The Takashimaya department store in Tokyo shows the furniture designs of Charlotte Perriand, including her "Synthèse des Arts, Tokyo" chair.

Ronchamp heralds more tactile modernism

FURNITURE AND FURNISHINGS

DuPont commissions custom fabric designs from Dorothy Liebes, and Boris Kroll presents his "Mediterranean" textile collection. George Nelson designs the "Coconut" chair for Herman Miller. Sori Yanagi designs his plywood "Butterfly" stool; it will be manufactured by Akane Shokai. Arne Jacobsen begins designing lighting fixtures for Louis Poulsen. For Fritz Hansen, Jacobsen designs the "3107" chair, and Poul Kjærholm designs the "PK 61" coffeetable and "PK 1" side chair. Frank Lloyd Wright designs are used for Schumacher's "Taliesin" fabric collection, a furniture collection for Heritage-Henredon, and rugs for Karastan. Russel Wright designs a line of school furniture for Samsonite. Florence Knoll designs her "Parallel Bar" series of metal-frame tables and seating. In France,

Charlotte Perriand and Jean Prouvé begin a collaboration in furniture design that will last almost twenty years.

GOVERNMENT EVENTS

In Montgomery, Alabama, seamstress Rosa Parks refuses to give her bus seat to a white man and is arrested; in 1999, she will be honored by Congress.

HONORS AND AWARDS

The Hardwood Institute's annual award for furniture design goes to Paul McCobb, as it will again in 1958.

MAGAZINES

The German magazines *Möbel + Décoration* and *Die Innenarchitektur* are combined to form *Möbel Interior Design*. The Danish magazine *Mobilia* is founded.

PROGRESS IN THE PROFESSION

The American Institute of Decorators publishes a *Manual of Professional Practice*.

1955

From left to right:

Le Corbusier's chapel at Ronchamp, France

Arne Jacobsen's stair for the Jespersen building, Copenhagen

Diagram from Henry Dreyfuss's *Designing for People*

Alexander Girard's exhibition design for MoMA's *Textiles and Ornamental Arts of India*

Aalto's cantilevered chair for the National Pension Bank, Helsinki

ARCHITECTURE

Jørn Utzon of Denmark wins an international competition for the design of an opera house in Sydney, Australia; it will not be completed until 1973. Ludwig Mies van der Rohe designs Crown Hall for the Illinois Institute of Technology, Chicago. Le Corbusier designs the Maisons Jaoul at Neuilly-sur-Seine, France, and his High Court in Chandigarh, India, is completed. Eero Saarinen designs the General Motors Technical Center in Warren, Michigan, with Alexander Girard as color consultant and with textile designs by Marianne Strengell. Ulrich Franzen designs a house for himself in Rye, New York.

BOOKS

Donald A. Wallance writes *Shaping America's Products*. Stephan Tschudi Madsen writes *Sources of Art Nouveau*.

CULTURE AT LARGE

Elvis Presley records his hit single "Heartbreak Hotel" and appears on Ed Sullivan's television show. The musical *My Fair Lady* is based on George Bernard Shaw's 1914 *Pygmalion*; it is enhanced by the sets of Oliver Smith, the lighting of Abe Feder, and the costumes of Cecil Beaton, who will design both sets and costumes for the 1965 film version.

DESIGNERS AND INSTALLATIONS

After study at the Rudolf Schaeffer School and a four-year partnership with Frances Milhailoff, Michael Taylor opens a practice of his own in San Francisco; his clients will include Maryon Lewis, Nan Kempner, Steve Martin, and Norton Simon and Jennifer Jones. David Hicks and Tom Parr establish the design firm Hicks & Parr; after 1960, Hicks will practice on his own, designing carpets and textiles as well as interiors. Oliver Messel designs the Pavilion Room at London's Dorchester Hotel. Billy Baldwin's stage set for William Douglas-Home's *The Reluctant Debutante* is an Adam-style drawing room in lilac and white. Benjamin Baldwin and William Machado design an apartment for themselves in Chicago. Eszter Haraszty designs Knoll's Paris headquarters, including an apartment for transient executives. The Design Centre is opened in London by the British Council of Industrial Design. Josef Hoffmann dies in Vienna at age eighty-six. In New York, Fredrick Kiesler and Armand Bartos design the World House Gallery.

Michael Taylor, David Hicks open offices

EXHIBITIONS

The City Art Galleries, Manchester, England, present *Modern Italian Design*, and the Whitechapel Gallery, London, presents *This Is Tomorrow* with exhibition design by Ernö Goldfinger. Also in London, architects Alison and Peter Smithson design the "House of the Future" for the *Ideal Home* exhibition, including their own furniture designs of steel and clear plastic. Ionel Schein's all-plastic model house is shown at the Salon des Ménagers in Paris. In New York, the Museum of Modern Art shows *Textiles USA*.

FURNITURE AND FURNISHINGS

For Herman Miller, Charles and Ray Eames design their molded plywood and leather lounge chair and ottoman, and George Nelson designs his "Marshmallow" sofa. Poul Kjærholm designs the "PK 22" chair for Fritz Hansen. Alvar Aalto designs the "A 805" floor lamp for Artek. The Italian architecture firm BBPR designs the "Spazio" system of metal office furniture for Olivetti. Boris Kroll presents his "Etruscan" fabric collection. Edward Wormley's "Anchor Collection" for Dunbar is vaguely Art Nouveau in inspiration and has Tiffany tiles set into table tops.

GOVERNMENT EVENTS

The liner *Andrea Doria* is hit by the *Stockholm* and sinks. Dispute over the Suez Canal results in conflict.

HONORS AND AWARDS

The Lunning Prize goes to Nanna and Jørgen Ditzel and to Timo Sarpaneva.

MAGAZINES

Ville e giardini begins publication in Milan.

TECHNICAL AND SCIENTIFIC ADVANCES

Pampers disposable diapers are introduced. The transatlantic telephone cable is laid.

1956

From left to right:

Palm Room, Biltmore Hotel, New York, by Raymond Loewy Associates

Eames lounge chair and ottoman for Herman Miller

The "PK22" lounge chair by Poul Kjærholm

Frank Lloyd Wright's "Imperial Triangle," a fabric designed for the 1922 Imperial Hotel, Tokyo, is reproduced by F. Schumacher

George Nelson "Marshmallow" sofa for Herman Miller

World House Gallery, New York, by Frederick Kiesler and Armand Bartos

ARCHITECTURE

Construction begins on Le Corbusier's Tokyo Museum of Art. Pier Luigi Nervi's Palazzetto dello Sport is finished in Rome. In Bloomfield, Connecticut, the Connecticut General Life Insurance Co. building by Gordon Bunshaft of Skidmore, Owings, & Merrill is given interiors with modular partitions and workstations; collaborating with SOM on the interior design is the Knoll Planning Unit.

Eero Saarinen designs the Kresge Auditorium and adjacent chapel for M.I.T. in Cambridge, Massachusetts, and also the John Deere Administration Center in Moline, Illinois; it will be finished in 1963. Morris Lapidus designs the Eden Roc hotel in Miami Beach. In Paris, the UNESCO headquarters is being built to the design of Marcel Breuer, Pier Luigi Nervi, and Bernard Zehrfuss.

BOOKS

Sherrill Whiton's *Elements of Interior Design and Decoration* is republished as *Interior Design and Decoration*. George Nelson's essays are collected in *Problems of Design.* Ernest J. McCormick writes *Human Engineering.* Louise Ade Boger and H. Batterson Boger compile *The Dictionary of Antiques and the Decorative Arts.* Alf Boe writes *From Gothic Revival to Functional Form.* Ethel Hall Bjerkoe writes *The Cabinetmakers of America.*

CULTURE AT LARGE

Albert Camus is given the Nobel Prize for literature, Sir Laurence Olivier is given an honorary degree from Oxford, and Eugene O'Neill is given a Pulitzer Prize (posthumously) for *Long Day's Journey into Night.*

DESIGNERS AND INSTALLATIONS

Barbara D'Arcy begins designing a series of highly influential model rooms at Bloomingdale's, New York, work she will continue to direct for more than twenty years. Albert Hadley goes to work for McMillen. William Pahlmann designs the Forum of the Twelve Caesars restaurant in New York's Rockefeller Center. Near Paris, Emilio Terry designs a theater for Charles de Beistegui's Château de Groussay, the design based on a nine-teenth-century theater at Bayreuth. Franco Albini designs interiors for La Rinascente department store, Rome. Carlo Scarpa designs the Olivetti show-room in Venice's St. Mark's Square. Harvey Probber designs his own showroom in New York. Bertha Schaefer designs a New York showroom for M. Singer & Sons. Boris Kroll and Jens Risom design their own areas of the Pritchard & Roberts show-room in Dallas. Alexander Girard designs interiors of a Los Angeles house for film director Billy Wilder. Also in Los Angeles, Henry End and Tom Lee collabo-rate on a redesign of the Coconut Grove restaurant.

Model rooms at Bloomingdale's

EXHIBITIONS

FURNITURE
AND FURNISHINGS

MAGAZINES

PROGRESS IN
THE PROFESSION

TECHNICAL AND
SCIENTIFIC ADVANCES

For the *Interbau* exposition in West Berlin, Hugh Stubbins designs the Congress Hall. Bloomingdale's department store shows more than three hundred pieces of furniture by Paul McCobb in fifteen room settings. Poul Kjærholm's cantilevered chair of wicker on a steel frame wins the grand prize at Milan's tenth Triennale. The work of Antoni Gaudí is shown at New York's Museum of Modern Art.

Gio Ponti designs his "Superleggera" side chair for Cassina. Bruno Munari begins a long association with Danese, the first product from which is a cubic melamine ashtray. The Castiglioni brothers produce the "Mezzadro" stool topped with a tractor seat, an idea based on one of Marcel Duchamp's readymades, and the "Sella" stool with a bicycle seat on a rocking base; they will both be manufactured by Zanotta in the 1970s. Max Bill designs the "Auto-Mat" numberless clock for Junghans. Charlotte Perriand designs furniture for Air France offices in London and Tokyo. Nanna Ditzel designs the egg-shaped wicker "Hammock Chair" for Bonacina. Poul Henningsen designs the "PH Kogelen (Cone)" lamp and the "PH 5 Pendant (Artichoke)" lamp for Louis Poulsen. Poul Kjærholm designs "Armchair II."

Laverne produces the "Invisible" group of see-through plastic furniture. Eero Saarinen designs the "Tulip" pedestal tables and chairs for Knoll. Vladimir Kagan designs the "Sculptra" collection for Grosfeld House. Edward Wormley designs the "Janus" collection for Dunbar. Isamu Noguchi designs hexagonal aluminum tables for Alcoa. Ward Bennett designs a furniture line for Lehigh. Dorothy Liebes designs carpets for Bigelow-Sanford. Paul Goodman designs a bent-plywood chair for his own company, Plycraft; it will sometimes be attributed to Norman Cherner. Danish designers Grethe Meyer and Børge Mogensen design the "Øresund" storage cabinet system. Richard Riemerschmid dies at eighty-nine.

Zodiac begins publication in Milan. The Danish monthly *Mobilia* begins publishing its text in four languages.

The National Society of Interior Designers is founded as a rival to the American Institute of Decorators. The International Council of Societies of Industrial Design is founded; by 1965 it will comprise thirty-seven organizations from twenty-two countries.

Velcro is introduced.

1957

From left to right:

Gio Ponti's "Superleggera" chair

Poul Henningsen's "Artichoke" lamp for Louis Poulsen

Eero Saarinen's pedestal chair for Knoll

SOM's Connecticut General building, Bloomfield, Connecticut

ARCHITECTURE

The Seagram Building, New York, is finished to the designs of Ludwig Mies van der Rohe. Le Corbusier completes the Secretariat building at Chandigarh, India, and Oscar Niemeyer designs the President's Palace at Brasilia. Paul Rudolph, having just completed the Jewett Arts Center at Wellesley College, is named chairman of Yale University's School of Art and Architecture and begins the design of the department's new building; the building will be finished in 1964, and Rudolph will stay at Yale until 1965; other news at Yale is the opening of a hockey rink designed by

Eero Saarinen. Pierre Koenig designs the Case Study House No. 21 in Los Angeles. Alvar Aalto designs a church at Imatra, Finland.

BOOKS

Mario Praz writes *La Casa della Vita*; it will be translated into English as *The House of Life*. Helen Comstock writes *100 Most Beautiful Rooms in America*; among the one hundred are the West Parlor of Mount Vernon, the Upstairs Parlor of Mount Pleasant, Philadelphia, the Maple Room at Winterthur, and the Palladian Room at Gunston Hall, Lorton, Virginia.

CULTURE AT LARGE

Leonard Bernstein's musical *West Side Story* is on Broadway. Samuel Barber's *Vanessa* is at the Metropolitan Opera. Vincente Minnelli's *Gigi* is on the screen. Jasper Johns has his first one-man show in New York.

DESIGNERS AND INSTALLATIONS

Inside New York's Seagram Building, Philip Johnson and William Pahlmann design the Four Seasons restaurant, with table settings by Garth Huxtable. Melanie Kahane designs the Playbill restaurant in the Hotel Manhattan and a house for songwriter and producer Billy Rose. Also in New York, Gordon Bunshaft designs an apartment for himself, Henry End rejuvenates the Hotel Navarro, and Marvin Affrime founds the Space Design Group with Frank Failla as its chief designer. In Dallas, T. H. Robsjohn-Gibbings designs interiors for the Bruno Graf house designed by Edward Durell Stone. In Houston, the AID presents room settings in the new Ludwig Mies van der Rohe–designed wing of the Museum of Fine Arts; among the designers is Edward J. Perrault. Everett Brown designs the Guildhall ballroom complex for the Ambassador West Hotel, Chicago. Ann Hatfield designs the Dorado Beach Hotel in Puerto Rico. Verner Panton designs the Komigen café in Langesø, Denmark. Dorothy Draper designs interiors and furnishings for the International Hotel at New York's Kennedy Airport. In San Francisco, Alexander Girard designs a showroom for Herman Miller in a historicist style that is a precocious forerunner of the postmodern movement soon to come. Eszter Haraszty leaves Knoll to found her own design studio in New York.

Scandinavian design storms the Louvre

EXHIBITIONS

The Exposition Universelle is held in Brussels; its Pan-American Airways Pavilion is by Victor Lundy, and its circular grille-wrapped U.S. Pavilion is by Edward Durell Stone with a mural by Saul Steinberg; a restaurant annex to the Stone building is by Eszter Haraszty. At the Milan fair, the Castiglioni brothers design the Radio Exhibition. In Paris, the Louvre shows *Formes Scandinaves* with exhibition layouts by Finn Juhl. At Heal's in London, *Lucienne Day: Designs at Home and Abroad* shows Day's textiles, wallpapers, and ceramics.

FURNITURE AND FURNISHINGS

Arne Jacobsen designs the "Svanen" ("Swan") chair and sofa and the "Aegget" ("Egg") chair for Fritz Hansen. Donald A. Wallance begins designing hospital furniture for Hard Manufacturing, Buffalo, New York. Ettore Sottsass, Jr., designs Olivetti's "Elea 9003" mainframe computer. George Nelson designs the "Pretzel" chair, and Charles and Ray Eames design the "Aluminum Group," both for Herman Miller.

GOVERNMENT EVENTS

The European Common Market is established.

HONORS AND AWARDS

The Lunning Prize goes to Poul Kjærholm and Signe Persson-Melin.

MAGAZINES

Form, the German magazine of furniture and industrial design, is founded.

TECHNICAL AND SCIENTIFIC ADVANCES

The United States launches its first satellite, *Explorer I*. The Sheraton hotel chain introduces a toll-free reservation number and an electronic reservations system.

1958

From left to right:

The Four Seasons restaurant, New York, by Philip Johnson and William Pahlmann

Le Corbusier's Secretariat building is added to his monumental government complex at Chandigarh, India

Some of Poul Kjærholm's furniture designs

Paul Rudolph

Construction nears completion at the Arrivals Building, Idlewild Airport, near New York, by SOM. The mobile is by Alexander Calder.

Frank Lloyd Wright dies at ninety-two, just as his Guggenheim Museum is being completed. Gio Ponti, Pier Luigi Nervi, and others design the Pirelli tower in Milan. Paolo Portoghesi designs the Casa Baldi and the Casa Papanice, both in Rome. Philip Johnson designs the Roofless Chapel at New Harmony, Indiana. Minoru Yamasaki designs a conference center for Wayne State University, Detroit. Bertram Goldberg designs Marina City in Chicago.

Henry Dreyfuss writes *The Measure of Man: Human Factors in Design*, establishing the field of anthropometry. Anthropologist Edward T. Hall writes *The Silent Language*. Arthur Drexler and Greta Daniel write an *Introduction to Twentieth Century Design*, based on the collection of the Museum of Modern Art. Lois Wagner Green edits *Interiors' Book of Offices*. Louise Ade Boger writes *The Complete Guide to Furniture Styles*.

Vance Packard writes *The Status Seekers*, and William Burroughs writes *Naked Lunch*. Ethel Merman stars in *Gypsy*. Mark Rothko completes a series of nine paintings for New York's Four Seasons restaurant, but they will not be hung.

Designs for Business designs interiors of New York's Corning Glass Building and New York offices for C. J. LaRoche & Co. George Nelson designs interiors for New York University's Loeb Student Center. Michael Greer designs his own New York duplex and the New York townhouse of Mr. and Mrs. Peter I. B. Lavan. Billy Baldwin designs the Round Hill Club, Greenwich, Connecticut. Donald Deskey designs the Marco Polo Club in New York's Waldorf-Astoria Hotel. Angelo Donghia joins Yale Burge Interiors; it will be renamed Burge-Donghia Interiors in 1966. William Pahlmann is design consultant for Restaurant Associates, New York, for which he will design the Zum-Zum chain and other restaurants.

American design conquers Moscow

EXHIBITIONS

In New York, the Metropolitan Museum of Art presents *Form Givers at Mid-Century*. Hans Wegner's furniture is the subject of an exhibition at Georg Jensen, New York. Arne Jacobsen's buildings and furniture designs are shown at the Royal Institute of British Architects gallery, London. *The American National Exhibition* is held in Moscow with George Nelson the principal designer among many.

FURNITURE AND FURNISHINGS

Edward Wormley designs the "A" chair for Dunbar. Jack Lenor Larsen introduces printed velvet. Vladimir Kagan designs the "Capricorn" collection of indoor/outdoor furniture. Herman Miller introduces the "Comprehensive Storage System" by George Nelson. Franco Albini designs the "Tre Pezzi" chair of tubular steel. Ernesto Gismondi founds the Italian lighting company Artemide. Weaver Anni Albers, wife of painter Josef Albers, begins designing textiles for Knoll, a relationship that will last twenty-five years. Billy Baldwin covers his "Slipper Chair" in white cotton trimmed with cobalt blue for Mary Runnells's house, Hobe Sound, Florida. Nicos Zographos designs the "Zographos" (or "Ribbon" or "28") chair.

GOVERNMENT EVENTS

Fidel Castro becomes premier of Cuba.

HONORS AND AWARDS

The S. M. Hexter fabric company begins a series of annual competitions for "Interiors of the Year," a series that will continue through the 1980s; the first jurors include Olga Gueft, editor in chief of *Interiors*, Harry Anderson, publisher of *Interior Design*, and Gilbert Werlé, president of the New York School of Interior Design, and the first winner is Virginia Whitmore Kelly. Architect Edward Durell Stone is made an honorary member of the AID. The Lunning Prize goes to Arne Jon Jutrem and Antti Nurmesniemi. George Nelson is given the Trailblazer Award for Most Creative Design in Postwar Years by the National Home Fashions League.

MAGAZINES

The magazine *Furniture Design* is established; it will later be called *FDM: Furniture Design and Manufacturing*.

TECHNICAL AND SCIENTIFIC ADVANCES

Texas Instruments produces the integrated circuit.

1959

From left to right:

Units from George Nelson's "Comprehensive Storage System" for Herman Miller

Charles and Ray Eames arrive in Moscow with their film *Glimpses of USA*

A retail store application of a George Nelson storage system

William Pahlmann

THE '60s

Over the protests of Philip Johnson and other architects and citizens, McKim, Mead, & White's 1910 Pennsylvania Station in New York, its interior based on the ancient Baths of Caracalla, is demolished in 1963. Its loss, however, will lead to heightened appreciation for historic structures and to the establishment of New York's landmarks preservation law. Yet at the end of the century, important interiors will still not be secure; Alvar Aalto's 1964 Edgar Kaufmann, jr., Conference Rooms in New York, unwanted by their building's new owner, will face an uncertain future. It is the heyday of the Pop movement, and painting, sculpture, and interior design celebrate the disposable and revel in images from Hollywood, advertising, comic books, automobile design, and popular culture in general. Sarah Tomerlin Lee, the recently appointed editor in chief of *House Beautiful*, looks on the bright side, writing in 1965 that "Because we feel that conformity as a deadly blanket over the land," she is dedicating an issue to the individualist. "Individualism," she says, "once the glorious prerogative of wealth, fame, and beauty, is now the reward of the aware." Similarly, Warren Platner, having designed the 1967 Ford Foundation interiors in New York, says, "That sense of place—that experience which makes a particular building matter— comes from a theme, an idea. In the Ford Foundation that idea is democracy." Democracy in action impinges on design as, in 1968, the U.S. Congress passes the Architectural Barriers Act, mandating accessibility to federally owned or federally financed facilities and leading to formation of the Architectural and Transportation Barriers Compliance Board, commonly called the Access Board. And computers begin to make their first appearances in design offices. In 1966, the design firm Saphier, Lerner, & Schindler buys a Xynetics 1000 automated drafting system, and computers are also in use by JFN, a New York space planning firm, and by the Decision Resource Service of Herman Miller.

Verner Panton's 1967 plastic
chair for Vitra

Frank Lloyd Wright remembered in Milan

Wegner designs the leather-upholstered "Bull" chair and ottoman. Marion Dorn, working for Edward Fields Carpets, designs a large oval rug for the Diplomatic Reception Room of the White House.

The Vietnam War begins.

Edgar Kaufmann, jr., establishes the Kaufmann International Design Award; the trophy is designed by Finn Juhl, and the first winners are Charles and Ray Eames.

The Interior Decorator and Contract News is founded; it will later change its name to *The Designer*. *Contract* magazine is also founded; it will later become *Contract Design*.

Herman Miller establishes the Herman Miller Research Corporation, naming Robert Propst its first director.

Textile-grade olefin fibers are introduced. U.S. scientists develop the laser (light amplification by stimulated emission of radiation). The American Heart Association links high death rates to cigarettes. Throughout the decade, lighting efficiency and ideas of desirable lighting levels increase.

1960

From left to right:

Alexander Girard's La Fonda del Sol restaurant, New York

Model room exhibit, Midtown Gallery, New York, by Raymond Loewy Associates

Lobby, SOM's Union Carbide building, New York

Lobby, UNESCO headquarters, Paris, by Breuer, Nervi, and Zehrfuss, finally in use

ARCHITECTURE

Louis Kahn's Richards Medical Research building is finished in Philadelphia. Eero Saarinen's TWA Terminal is built at Idlewild Airport (later to be renamed JFK) near New York. Marcel Breuer and Hamilton Smith's St. John's Abbey church is completed in Collegeville, Minnesota. Pier Luigi Nervi designs an exhibition hall in Turin, Italy. Eero Saarinen dies at fifty-one.

BOOKS

Design for Modern Living is written by Gerd and Ursula Hatje. Ladislav Sutnar writes *Visual Design in Action: Principles, Purposes.* Johannes Itten writes *The Art of Color.* For the American Institute of Decorators, Gertrud Lackschewitz compiles *Interior Design and Decoration: A Bibliography.*

CULTURE AT LARGE

Joseph Heller writes *Catch-22.* Muriel Spark writes *The Prime of Miss Jean Brodie.* Graphic designer Milton Glaser declares "I♥NY."

DESIGNERS AND INSTALLATIONS

Under the leadership of Davis Allen, a team of interior designers at Skidmore, Owings, & Merrill (including Ward Bennett and Richard McKenna) designs interiors for New York's Chase Manhattan Bank headquarters, including an art-filled private office for David Rockefeller. Tom Lee Ltd. designs the Somerset Hotel in Boston. Valerian Rybar designs the cocktail lounge and bar of the Colony Hotel in Palm Beach, Florida. Edward J. Perrault designs interiors for his own house in Houston. Victor Lundy designs interiors for the I. Miller shoe salon, New York. Tony Duquette designs Tony-winning costumes for the Broadway production of *Camelot.* Carlo Scarpa designs the Gavina shop/showroom in Bologna. The first "office landscape" planning experiments are conducted in Quickborn, Germany.

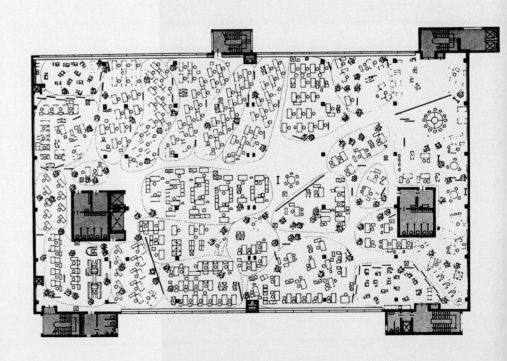

The first Salone del Mobile is held in Milan, an annual furniture show that will continue through the end of the century.

Jack Lenor Larsen introduces stretch upholstery. Nanna Ditzel designs a cane chair and ottoman for Wengler; it will later be reintroduced by Fennkong. Afra and Tobia Scarpa design the "Bastiano" sofa and chair for Gavina; they will later be sold in the United States by Knoll. Florence Knoll designs an oval executive desk on a single steel column. Herman Miller's Textiles & Objects shop opens in New York under the direction of Alexander Girard; it will close in 1963.

John F. Kennedy becomes president.

An interior design competition at the Parsons School of Design is sponsored by the Duke Pini di San Miniato; jurors include the Duchess of Windsor and Salvador Dali, and the winner is Ronald Bricke. Hans Wegner is given the International Design Award of the newly renamed American Institute of Interior Designers. Mario Bellini receives the first of his seven Compasso d'Oro awards. Weaver Anni Albers receives the Gold Medal for Craftsmanship from the American Institute of Architects. The Kaufmann International Design Award is given to architect Walter Gropius. The first Arthur Drexler Award for industrial design is given to Charles and Ray Eames.

The American Institute of Decorators changes its name to the American Institute of Interior Designers, but keeps its acronym of AID. The American Society for Testing Materials (ASTM) changes its name to the American Society for Testing *and* Materials. The Resources Council is formed.

Yuri Gagarin is the first man in space. An early investigation of the possibilities of computer-aided design is J. W. Dawson's article "The Computer in Building Design" in *Architectural and Engineering News*.

1961

Germany spawns "office landscape"

From left to right:

View through roof of model, Pier Luigi Nervi's exhibition hall, Turin, Italy

The Quickborner Team's "office landscape" plan for Buch und Ton, Gütersloh, Germany, dispenses with regimentation

Marcel Breuer and Hamilton Smith's abbey church at St. John's Abbey and University, Collegeville, Minnesota

Alexander Girard's Textiles & Objects retail shop for Herman Miller, New York

Chase Manhattan Bank interior by Davis Allen and others at SOM

ARCHITECTURE

Charles Moore designs a house for himself in Orinda, California. Alvar Aalto's Cultural Center, Wolfsburg, Germany, is finished, as is his Neve Vahr apartment block in Bremen. The U.S. Air Force Academy, Colorado Springs, is designed by Skidmore, Owings, & Merrill. Louis Kahn designs the Assembly Hall at Dacca, Bangladesh. Ralph Rapson begins work on the Cedar-Riverside housing complex in Minneapolis, the first federally funded "New-Town-in-Town"; it will be completed in 1973. Frank Gehry opens his office in Venice, California. Robert Venturi designs a house for his mother in Chestnut Hill, Pennsylvania.

BOOKS

Kate Ellen Rogers writes *The Modern House, U.S.A.: Its Design and Decoration.* Elizabeth Aslin writes *Nineteenth Century English Furniture.* Michael Greer writes *Inside Design.* Richard Neutra writes *World and Dwelling.*

CULTURE AT LARGE

Andy Warhol paints *Marilyn*; Elizabeth Taylor and Richard Burton star in *Cleopatra*; Edward Albee's *Who's Afraid of Virginia Woolf?* is staged with Uta Hagen. Rachel Carson's *Silent Spring* warns against pesticides in the food chain. First Lady Jacqueline Kennedy conducts a televised tour of the White House.

DESIGNERS AND INSTALLATIONS

William N. Breger, a faculty member, designs new 56th Street quarters for the New York School of Interior Design. Albert Hadley leaves McMillen Inc. to join the firm of "Sister" Parish; he will become a partner in 1968. Ward Bennett, with Earl Pope, designs the Rubin apartment on New York's Park Avenue. Florence Knoll designs interiors for Cowles Publications, New York. Elisabeth Draper designs a gymnasium and auditorium for Miss Porter's School in Farmington, Connecticut. Michael Greer designs an apartment for Mr. and Mrs. Harry Anholt in the Park Lane Hotel, New York. Alexander Girard designs an apartment for Hallmark Cards atop the company's headquarters in Kansas City. Franco Albini designs Milan subway interiors.

Also in Milan, Mario Bellini opens a design office. In Athens, Greece, T. H. Robsjohn-Gibbings designs apartment interiors for Aristotle Onassis and for Nicholas Goulandris. In Le Havre, France, Jean Prouvé designs interiors for the Museum and Cultural Center. Charlotte Perriand (with Maria Elisa Costa) designs apartment interiors in Rio de Janeiro.

EXHIBITIONS

The IBM Gallery in New York hosts an exhibition presented by the Parsons School of Design, *Young Designers in New York.* In Milan, Achille and Pier Giacomo Castiglioni design the Montecatini Pavilion. The work of Ilmari Tapiovaara is shown in Stockholm.

Parish and Hadley join forces

FURNITURE AND FURNISHINGS	**G**OVERNMENT EVENTS	**H**ONORS AND AWARDS	**M**AGAZINES	**P**ROGRESS IN THE PROFESSION	**T**ECHNICAL AND SCIENTIFIC ADVANCES

Charles and Ray Eames design "Tandem 2600," single and double rows of seating, for Herman Miller; it will become a standard for airport waiting areas. George Nelson designs the "Catenary" group of seating and tables for Herman Miller. The Castiglioni brothers design the long-armed "Arco" floor lamp for Flos, and Joe Colombo designs the "Colombo" lamp for O-Luce. Gavina begins production of Marcel Breuer's 1924 "Laccio" table and 1925 "Wassily" chair; Breuer calls Dino Gavina "the most emotional and impulsive furniture manufacturer in the world." Charles Pollock designs a leather sling chair for Knoll. Ward Bennett designs the "Sled" chair. Jack Lenor Larsen, after a seven-week tour of Nigeria and South Africa, launches his "African Collection."

The Cuban missile crisis begins and ends.

The Kaufmann International Design Award is given to the Olivetti corporation. After this year, the foundation will give its awards for use in design education, but on a special occasion it will give an award to Germany's Volkswagenwerk.

Abitare is founded in Milan by Piera Peroni.

The Interior Design Educators' Council (IDEC) is founded. The Color Marketing Group is founded; by century's end, its membership will be fifteen hundred color designers "involved in the use of color as it applies to the profitable marketing of goods and services."

John Glenn is the first American to orbit the earth. *Architectural and Engineering News* publishes J. P. Eberhard's "A Computer-Based Building Process: Its Potentials for Architecture." Flexible plastic polypropylene is introduced.

1962

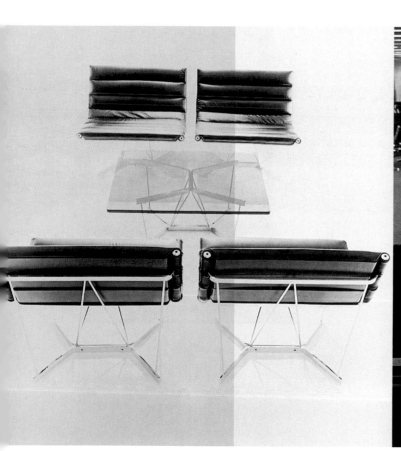

From left to right:

Albert Hadley

Chapel, U.S. Air Force Academy, near Colorado Springs, Colorado, by Walter Netsch of SOM

Image from a Steelcase ad for a stacking chair

George Nelson's "Catenary" seating and table for Herman Miller

Charles and Ray Eames's "Tandem 2600" seating for Herman Miller

ARCHITECTURE

New York's Pennsylvania Station is razed. Marcel Breuer and his partner Herbert Beckhard design the Koerfer house in Switzerland. Hans Scharoun designs the Berlin Philharmonic. Le Corbusier designs the Carpenter Center for the Visual Arts at Harvard University, Cambridge, Massachusetts. Two years after his death, Eero Saarinen's terminal building is completed at Dulles Airport, near Washington. Ralph Rapson designs the Pillsbury house in Wayzata, Minnesota, and the Guthrie Theater in Minneapolis.

Philip Johnson designs a museum for pre-Columbian art at Dumbarton Oaks, Washington, D.C. Edgar Kaufmann, jr., having inherited Fallingwater, donates it with a $500,000 endowment to the Western Pennsylvania Conservancy.

BOOKS

Vogue's Book of Houses, Gardens, People is published with an introduction by Diana Vreeland and photographs by Horst. Victoria Kloss Ball writes *Opportunities in Interior Design and Decoration.* T. H. Robsjohn-Gibbings and Carlton W. Pullin write *Furniture of Classical Greece.*

CULTURE AT LARGE

The Guggenheim Museum's show of Pop art includes work by Andy Warhol, Jasper Johns, and Robert Rauschenberg.

DESIGNERS AND INSTALLATIONS

Franco Albini, his son Marco Albini, Franca Helg, and Antonio Piva begin renovations, additions, and interiors for Genoa's Sant'Agostino Museum; the work will continue for more than twenty years. Piero Fornasetti designs a ballroom in the Time-Life building, New York. The Space Design Group of Atlanta, headed by William Pulgram, designs offices for Kenyon & Eckhardt and for Eastman Kodak, both in New York's Pan-Am Building. Designs for Business, headed by Gerald Luss, designs New York offices for Maritime

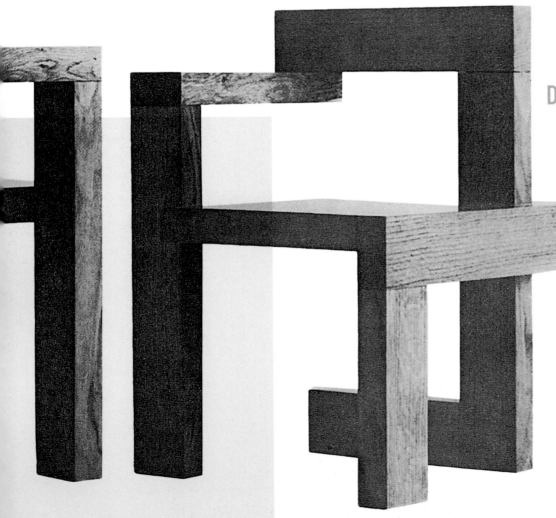

Designer licensing advocated

Overseas Corp. Billy Baldwin designs a St. Regis Hotel suite for Barbara and William S. Paley, the Kenneth Salon, a one-room apartment for himself, and interiors for Tiffany & Co., all in New York. Irving Harper and Philip George found the design firm Harper & George.

An exhibition of Otto Wagner's design is shown in Vienna. The Victoria & Albert, London, presents a retrospective of the art and design of Alphonse Mucha.

George Nelson designs the "Sling Sofa" for Herman Miller. Manuel Canovas founds Les Tissus Manuel Canovas for the manufacture of his fabrics, carpets, and wallpapers. Boris Kroll presents his "Shibui" collection. Joe Colombo designs a "Mini-kitchen" for Boffi and the "4801" plywood chair for Kartell. Vico Magistretti designs "Chair 892" for Cassina, and Marco Zanuso designs the "Lambda" chair for Gavina. Eero Aarnio's fiberglass "Ball" chair for Asko has built-in stereo speakers or—in some versions— a telephone. Robin Day's "Mark II" stacking polypropylene chair for Hille, where he has been design consultant since 1949, is introduced and will sell more than twelve million copies. A textile collection by Dorothy Liebes is introduced by Stroheim & Romann.

John F. Kennedy is assassinated.

The National Society of Interior Designers launches its licensing program, advocating licensing of interior designers, with Louis A. Malamud as its national chairman. The American Institute of Kitchen Dealers is founded; it will become the National Kitchen and Bath Association in 1982.

J. J. Souder and W. E. Clark's "Computer Technology: A New Tool for Planning" is published in the *AIA Journal.*

1963

From left to right:

Gerrit Rietveld's oak chair for the Steltman jewelry shop, The Hague, Netherlands

Steelcase's "Coordinated Filing System"

Armstrong Cork headquarters, Lancaster, Pennsylvania, by SOM

Marcel Breuer's and Herbert Beckhard's Koerfer house, Moscia, Tessin, Switzerland, with Breuer's cut-out plywood furniture

George Nelson's "Sling Sofa" for Herman Miller

ARCHITECTURE

Kenzo Tange designs the Olympic Sports Halls in Tokyo. Alvar Aalto designs the Otaniemi Institute of Technology, Otaniemi, Finland. Ron Herron of the Archigram group conceives his "Walking City." Josep Lluís Sert's Maeght Foundation is built in Saint-Paul-de-Vence, France. Philip Johnson designs the New York State Theater at Lincoln Center.

BOOKS

The first English-language publication of Gaston Bachelard's *The Poetics of Space* appears. Katharine Tweed edits *The Finest Rooms by America's Great Decorators*; included is work by William Pahlmann and Edward Martin, Rose Cumming, Marian Hall and Diane Tate, McMillen Inc., "Sister" Parish, George Stacey, Smyth, Urquhart, & Marckwald, and Michael Taylor; Russell Lynes supplies an introduction. Gordon Russell writes *Looking at Furniture*. Mario Praz's *La Filosofia dell'Arredamento* is published in English as *An Illustrated History of Interior Decoration from Pompeii to Art Nouveau.* Robert Koch wites *Louis C. Tiffany, Rebel in Glass,* the first serious study since Tiffany's death in 1933.

CULTURE AT LARGE

The Beatles appear on *The Ed Sullivan Show.* In discos, popular dances include the watusi, the monkey, and the frug. *Hello, Dolly!* opens on Broadway.

DESIGNERS AND INSTALLATIONS

Terence Conran's first Habitat shop opens in London. Hans Hollein designs the Retti candle shop in Vienna. David T. Williams designs interiors for the Kahala Hilton in Honolulu. Another California decorator show house is established, this one benefiting Pasadena's Junior Philharmonic Committee. Nicos Zographos founds a firm to produce his own furniture designs. Diego Giacometti designs a café-bar as well as chairs and lighting fixtures for the Maeght Foundation in St.-Paul-de-Vence. In New York's newly completed CBS building by Eero Saarinen, Warren Platner designs the Ground Floor restaurant and Florence Knoll designs executive offices.

EXHIBITIONS

At the New York World's Fair, the egg-shaped IBM Pavilion designed by Eero Saarinen contains a nine-screen show by Charles and Ray Eames about brains and computers, the Chrysler Corporation's display is designed by George Nelson, the New York State Pavilion is by Philip Johnson, the Time Capsule Pavilion is by Eliot Noyes, and Dorothy Draper presents the Dorothy Draper Dream House. The *Exhibition of Stained Glass and Mosaics* is seen at London's Victoria & Albert. *Architecture without Architects*, largely based on the investigations of Bernard Rudofsky, is at the Museum of Modern Art, New York, which opens its Philip L. Goodwin Galleries for Architecture and Design.

"Action Office" offers alternative to mahogany desk

FURNITURE AND FURNISHINGS

Fritz Haller begins the design of his modular office furniture system, which will still be on the market at the end of the century. For Herman Miller, George Nelson designs the "Action Office" based on research by Robert Propst into office work habits; it will spawn a long series of office furniture systems. For the French company Airborne, Olivier Mourgue designs the "Djinn" chaise of stretch fabric and urethane on a steel frame. Danish designer Børge Mogensen designs the "Asserbo" chair for Karl Andersson. Bruno Mathhson and Piet Hein design the "Superellipse" table for Dux. British designer Peter Murdoch designs the "Spotty" polka-dot fiberboard child's chair. Italian designer Vico Magistretti designs the "Modello 115" rush-seat chair for Cassina. Ward

Bennett designs the "Landmark" chair for Brickel. Lella and Massimo Vignelli design the "Saratoga" seating group for Poltronova. David Rowland designs a steel-framed stacking chair for General Fireproofing Co. Gerrit Rietveld dies at seventy-six.

GOVERNMENT EVENTS

War escalates in Vietnam. The Palestine Liberation Organization is founded in Egypt.

HONORS AND AWARDS

The New York chapter AID's Elsie de Wolfe Award is given to William Pahlmann. At the Milan Triennale, a gold medal goes to textile designer Jack Lenor Larsen.

MAGAZINES

The English publication *The Studio* magazine, founded in 1893, changes its name to *Studio International*.

TECHNICAL AND SCIENTIFIC ADVANCES

The first word processor is produced. Xerox unveils the fax machine. A conference on "Architecture and the Computer" is held at the Boston Architectural Center.

1964

From left to right:

Poul Kjærholm's new "PK 240" table with his 1955 "PK 1" side chairs

Philip Johnson's New York State Theater, Lincoln Center, New York. The sculpture is by Elie Nadelman.

"Action Office" units for Herman Miller by George Nelson and Robert Propst

ARCHITECTURE

The Mauna Kea Beach Hotel, Hawaii, is designed by Skidmore, Owings, & Merrill, with interiors by SOM's Davis Allen. Louis Kahn's Salk Institute is completed at La Jolla, California. The Sea Ranch condominiums on the Pacific coast are designed by Moore Lyndon Turnbull Whitaker. Ulrich Franzen designs the Alley Theater in Houston. Charles Gwathmey designs a house and studio for his parents on Long Island, and Richard Meier designs a house for his parents in Essex Fells, New Jersey. Also on Long Island, Jack Lenor Larsen designs his own Round House, a composition of three circular elements. Le Corbusier dies while swimming at age seventy-eight.

BOOKS

The Decorator Digest: Chapters in the History of Early American Decoration and Its European Background is edited by Natalie Allen Ramsey. Bernard Rudofsky writes *The Kimono Mind: An Informal Guide to Japan and the Japanese.* Joseph T. Butler writes *American Antiques 1800–1900.* Gaetano Pesce presents his "anti-design" ideas in *Manifesto on Elastic Architecture.*

CULTURE AT LARGE

The Sound of Music, Doctor Zhivago, Red Desert, and *Juliet of the Spirits* are on the big screen. *Bonanza, The Fugitive,* and *Bewitched* are on the small one.

DESIGNERS AND INSTALLATIONS

Florence Knoll retires and is replaced by Robert Cadwallader. Alvar Aalto designs the Edgar Kaufmann, jr., Conference Rooms at the Institute of International Education in New York. Alexander Girard becomes design director for Braniff airlines, producing the company's airport lounges, airplane interiors, graphics, and furniture. In San Francisco, Arthur Gensler establishes a three-person design firm in space above a Greek restaurant. Carleton Varney of Dorothy Draper & Co. designs an apartment for Ethel Merman in New York's Berkshire Hotel. Billy Baldwin tells a *New York Times* reporter, "Cotton is my life," and he designs a New York apartment for S. I. Newhouse Jr. for which he covers his signature "Slipper Chair" in black leather.

Davis Allen takes modern design to the hotel room

EXHIBITIONS

Hans Wegner's furniture is shown at both Georg Jensen, New York, and the Kunstindustrimuseet, Copenhagen. *The Expression of Gio Ponti* is shown at the University of California, Los Angeles.

FURNITURE AND FURNISHINGS

Poul Kjærholm's "PK 24" steel and cane chaise is designed for Fritz Hansen. Ulrich Franzen's "Franzen Floor Lamp" is made by Egli. Vico Magistretti designs the "Eclisse" lamp for Artemide. Joe Columbo's "4867" chair of injection-molded plastic is made by Kartell. Pierre Paulin designs the ribbon-like "Chair 582" for Artifort. Grethe Meyer designs the first of several earthenware collections for Royal Copenhagen Porcelain. Gae Aulenti designs the "Pipistrello" telescoping table lamp for Martinelli Luce and the "Jumbo" coffee table for Knoll. Knoll also produces Warren Platner's wire furniture, Charles Pollock's "Swivel" office chair, and the stacking "Albinson Chair" by Don Albinson, a graduate of the Eames office and currently head of Knoll's design department. Jack Lenor Larsen designs the "Fine

Arts" collection of sheets and towels for J. P. Stevens. Hans Wegner designs a chair with metal legs, wood backrest, and leather-covered seat. The Italian design group Studio DA designs the "Alda" plastic lounge chair for Confort. The "Kasruselli 412" plastic armchair is designed by Yrjo Kukkapura. Cassina begins the production of the "I Maestri" classic modern furniture designs from the 1920s and '30s, including pieces by the team of Le Corbusier, Pierre Jeanneret-Gris, and Charlotte Perriand. Max Clendinning designs the "Maxima" seating group for the English company Race Furniture and another group for Liberty's.

GOVERNMENT EVENTS

Civil rights demonstrations occur in Selma, Alabama. Anti-pollution legislation is proposed.

HONORS AND AWARDS

The New York Chapter American Institute of Decorators scholarship award goes to graduating Pratt student Joseph D'Urso.

TECHNICAL AND SCIENTIFIC ADVANCES

The hotel minibar is introduced.

1965

From left to right:

Poul Kjærholm's adjustable "PK 24" chaise

The Mauna Kea Beach Hotel, Hawaii, designed by Davis Allen of SOM: an open-air lounge and a guest room detail

Hans Wegner's "PP 701" chair with wood back and upholstered leather seat

Wood screen from the Kaufmann Conference Rooms, Institute of International Education, New York, designed by Alvar and Elissa Aalto

ARCHITECTURE

BOOKS

CULTURE AT LARGE

DESIGNERS
AND INSTALLATIONS

EXHIBITIONS

FURNITURE
AND FURNISHINGS

The Whitney Museum by Marcel Breuer and his partner Hamilton Smith opens in New York.

Complexity and Contradiction in Architecture by Robert Venturi is published by the Museum of Modern Art and takes a skeptical view of modernism. *The Dictionary of Interior Design* is compiled by Martin Pegler. *The New Brutalism* is explored by Reyner Banham. Essays by Rudolph Arnheim are collected in *Toward a Psychology of Art.* David Hicks on Decoration is published. Ole Wanscher writes *The Art of Furniture: 5,000 Years of Furniture and Interiors.* Edward T. Hall writes *The Hidden Dimension.* Gyorgy Kepes writes *The Man-Made Object.* Louise Ade Boger writes *Furniture: Past and Present.* Grand Rapids furniture manufacturer Hollis S. Baker writes *Furniture in the Ancient World: Origins and Evolution, 3100–475 B.C.*

To save them from the rising waters of the Aswan High Dam, ancient Egyptian treasures at Abu Simbel are moved to higher ground.

The design studios Archizoom Associati and Superstudio are established in Florence. Gae Aulenti designs the Olivetti showroom in Paris. William Parker McFadden designs the Greenhouse spa in Dallas for Charles of the Ritz and Neiman-Marcus. Raymond Loewy and William Snaith design interiors of the Paris Hilton. Alexander Girard's L'Etoile restaurant and Russel Wright's Shun Lee Dynasty restaurant open in New York. William Haines, formerly an MGM film star, designs interiors for Walter Annenberg's desert estate Sunnylands, and his other clients will include Jack Warner and Carole Lombard. Gracie Mansion, the home of New York's mayor, is redesigned by Ellen Lehman McCluskey and others.

The Pasadena Art Museum shows the furniture designs of Paul Tuttle.

For Knoll, outdoor furniture of woven Dacron mesh edged in vinyl is designed by Richard Schultz; its production will be revived in 1993. Cedric Hartman introduces his classic "1U WV" floor lamp, better known as the "Pharmacy" lamp; it will be widely imitated. Ingo Maurer designs the "Bulb" lamp. Nicos Zographos designs the "CH-66" chair of tubular steel. Bill Stumpf designs the first version of the "Ergon" chair. Chicago industrial designer Henry P. Glass designs the "Cylindra" furniture line based on prefabricated plywood tubes; it is manufactured in Cincinnati. Vico Magistretti designs the "Stadio" table and the "Chimera" lamp, both for Artemide. Finnish designer Yrjö Kukkapuro designs the fiberglass "Chair 414k" for

Robert Venturi advocates *Complexity, Contradiction*

Haimi. Gino Valle, son of an architect and brother of designer Lella Vignelli, designs the "Cifra 3" desk clock for Solari. Anna Castelli Ferrieri becomes design consultant at Kartell, specializing in injection-molded plastics. Marco Zanuso and Richard Sapper design the "Grillo" telephone for Siemens. Roberto Sebastian Matta designs the "Malitte" seating system, produced by Gavina and distributed by Knoll. The Cassina brothers and Piero Busnelli found C&B Italia for the production of contemporary furniture designs; among its first products are the "Quattro Gatti" table and "Amanta" armchair by Mario Bellini. Rud Thygesen and Johnny Sørenson establish a furniture design studio in Denmark.

Protests against U.S. policy in Vietnam intensify.

The annual Rosenthal Studio Prize is established for product designs made in Germany.

The Italian quarterly *Ottagono* begins publication. The September issue of *Architectural Digest*, edited by Peter and Alison Smithson, is devoted to the work of Charles and Ray Eames.

New York designer Louis Tregre begins working on a designer competency examination for the American Institute of Interior Designers (AID). His work will be the basis for the future NCIDQ examination.

Houston surgeon Michael De Bakey implants plastic arteries attached to an artifical heart during a three-and-a-half-hour valve replacement operation.

1966

From left to right:

Whitney Museum, New York, by Marcel Breuer and Hamilton Smith

Ingo Maurer's "Bulb" lamp

Nicos Zographos's "CH-66" chair

Alexander Girard's "Eden" fabric for Herman Miller

Cedric Hartman's "1U WV" floor lamp; it will become a classic.

ARCHITECTURE

Gunnar Birkerts designs the Federal Reserve Bank in Minneapolis. Mario Botta designs a house in Stabio, Switzerland. John Portman designs the atrium-centered Hyatt Regency Hotel in Atlanta; its interiors are by Roland William Jutras. Marcel Breuer and Herbert Beckhard's church of St. Francis de Sales is completed in Muskegon, Michigan. The competition-winning design for a new Boston City Hall is by Kallman, McKinnell, & Knowles. Peter Eisenman founds the Institute for Architecture and Urban Studies in New York and designs House I, Princeton, New Jersey, beginning a series that will culminate in the 1970 Frank house (House VI), Cornwall, Connecticut. Richard Meier designs the Smith house, Darien, Connecticut.

BOOKS

The historical survey *Great Interiors* is edited by Ian Grant with a preface by Cecil Beaton. Gillo Dorfles writes *Kitsch: The World of Bad Taste.* Jack Lenor Larsen and Azalea Thorpe write *Elements of Weaving.*

CULTURE AT LARGE

Gabriel García Márquez writes *One Hundred Years of Solitude.* Mike Nichols films *The Graduate.* Aretha Franklin demands "Respect."

DESIGNERS AND INSTALLATIONS

Warren Platner, head of interior design for the architecture firm of Roche & Dinkeloo, designs interiors of the Ford Foundation Headquarters, New York, with conference room wall-coverings by Sheila Hicks, auditorium seating by Charles and Ray Eames, and examples of his own furniture, which will be produced by Lehigh; Platner will soon have a flourishing firm of his own. Harry Hinson designs interiors for Bonwit Teller Westchester in Scarsdale, New York. Emily Malino is at work on Mount Sinai Hospital, New York. Henry End is designing the Nassau Beach Club and the Balmoral Club, both in Nassau, the Bahamas, as well as interiors of the Plaza Hotel, New York, and the Carlton Tower Hotel, London. Gae Aulenti designs the Olivetti showroom in Buenos Aires. Vico Magistretti begins designing a series of Cerruti stores in Paris, Tokyo, and Vienna. Tom Lee Ltd. designs the Café de l'Auberge, Toronto. Gerald Luss, now of Luss/Kaplan, designs New York offices for the Minskoff development organization. The Quickborner Team from Germany designs the first "office landscape" interior in the United States for the Freon Division of DuPont in Wilmington. In a former New York townhouse, McMillen Inc. creates Celanese House. Paul Rudolph designs townhouse interiors for himself on New York's Beekman Place. Jack Lenor Larsen designs a New York apartment for himself with vaults of stretched fabric. Pierre Moulin and Pierre LeVec open a New York antiques shop called Pierre Deux; it will import traditional toiles de Jouy, which will become very popular; there will eventually be twenty-two Pierre Deux shops.

EXHIBITIONS

Expo '67 is held in Montreal; its features include a giant geodesic dome by R. Buckminster Fuller and Moshe Safdie's Habitat housing complex. The design of Marco Zanuso is shown at the Festival dei Due Mondi, Spoleto, Italy.

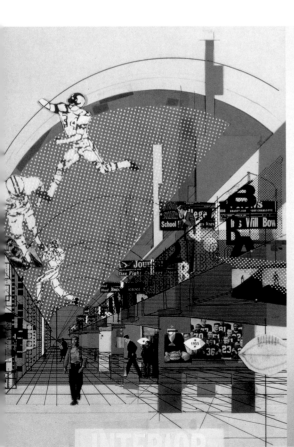

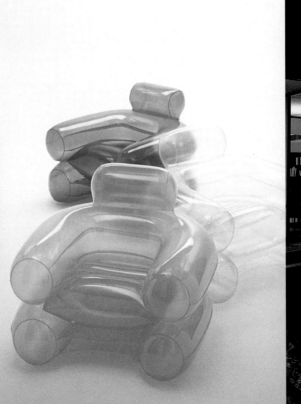

Jørn Utzon designs a furniture line for Fritz Hansen. Arne Jacobsen designs the "Cylindra" line of stainless-steel vessels and utensils for Stelton. Antti Nurmesniemi designs the "001 Chaise Longue" for Vuokko Oy. Verner Panton designs the "Panton" chair, introduced by Vitra, and the "Cubus Collection" of cotton fabric for Mira-X. DePas, D'Urbino, & Lomazzi design the inflatable "Blow" chair for Zanotta and Eero Aarnio designs the "Pastilli" chair; both are made entirely of plastic. Cini Boeri designs the "BoBo" chair for Arflex. Vico Magistretti designs the "Eclisse" table lamp for Artemide. Cesare Leonardi and Franca Stagi

design the "Dondolo" rocking chair. Joe Colombo designs the "Additional System" group of assemble-your-own seating for Sormani. American textile designer Sheila Hicks establishes a studio in Paris called Ateliers des Grands Augustins. Billy Baldwin's "Slipper Chair" reappears in blue and pink tattersall in a house for Kathryn and Gilbert Miller, Mallorca, Spain.

In the Six-Day War, Israel seizes control of neighboring territories. The United Nations arranges a cease-fire.

The Hexter Award goes to Michael de Santis.

The Interior Decorator and Contract News changes its name to *The Designer*. *House and Garden* publishes an article on "Sister" Parish's summer house in Dark Harbor, Maine, starting a trend for the American country look.

The hand-held electronic calculator is introduced.

Toiles de Jouy coexist with inflatable seating

1967

From left to right:

National Collegiate Hall of Fame project by Venturi and Scott Brown

The inflatable "Blow" chair for Zanotta by DePas, D'Urbino, & Lomazzi

Ford Foundation, New York. The architects are Kevin Roche and John Dinkeloo, with Warren Platner in charge of interior design.

Richard Meier's Smith house, Darien, Connecticut

Atrium, Hyatt Regency Atlanta, by John Portman

ARCHITECTURE

Eero Saarinen's Gateway Arch is dedicated in St. Louis, Missouri. I. M. Pei designs the Everson Museum of Art in Syracuse, New York. Paolo Portoghesi designs the Chiesa della Sacra Famiglia in Salerno, Italy. Stanley Tigerman, in a Miesian vein he will soon abandon, proposes an "Instant City." With partners Robert F. Gatje and Mario Jossa and with associated architect Beat Jordi, Marcel Breuer begins the design of the Baldegg Convent in Switzerland; work on the complex will continue until 1972.

BOOKS

Harry Siegel writes *A Guide to Business Principles and Practices for Interior Designers;* it will be revised in 1982. Michael Saphier, whose firm, SLS Environetics, is a leader in office design, writes *Office Planning and Design,* and, for Herman Miller, Robert Propst writes *The Office: A Facility Based on Change.* Designer and author Gordon Russell writes his autobiography, *Designer's Trade.* David Hicks writes *David Hicks on Living—with Taste.*

CULTURE AT LARGE

Popular songs are "Hey Jude" and "Mrs. Robinson." Stanley Kubrick films *2001: A Space Odyssey.* Chuck Close paints his self-portrait.

DESIGNERS AND INSTALLATIONS

English designer David Hicks brings his patterned carpets and fabrics to the United States. Cecil Beaton designs the Raffles Club restaurant in New York, his first commercial interior design. Gerald Luss of Luss/Kaplan designs a duplex for an art collector at New York's UN Plaza. Billy Baldwin designs villa interiors at Skopios, Greece, for Jacqueline and Aristotle Onassis. The Swedish studio A&E Desian is founded by Tom Ahlstrom and Hans Erlich. Niels Diffrient begins a series of airplane interior designs for American Airlines. Warren Platner designs the Georg Jensen Design Center in New York. Joseph Braswell designs interiors for the Bonwit Teller store in Chicago. George Nelson designs the Rosenthal Porcelain Studio showroom in New York. In Paris Charles Sévigny designs an apartment for couturier Hubert de Givenchy.

EXHIBITIONS

The Royal Academy of Art, London, presents *50 Years Bauhaus.* In New York, the first "Designer's Saturday" market event is held in member showrooms; it will become an annual event. *Design Italian Style* is seen at the Hallmark Gallery, New York. In Glasgow, the Scottish Arts Council presents *Charles Rennie Mackintosh, Architecture, Design, and Painting.* In New York, the American Federation of Arts and the Cooper-Hewitt Museum present *Please Be Seated: The Evolution of the Chair, 2000 B.C.–2000 A.D.* Inflatable designs *(Structures gonflables)* are shown at the Musée d'Art Moderne, Paris.

FURNITURE AND FURNISHINGS

American designer Richard Neagle's "Nike" chair for the Italian manufacturer Sormani is an early example of vacuum-formed plastic furniture. Angelo Donghia establishes a fabric and wallcovering company called Vice Versa. Knoll International buys the Italian furniture company Gavina and presents the "In/Out" furniture system by Angelo Mangiarotti. The Finnish textile company Marimekko begins offering its wares worldwide. Joseph D'Urso opens his practice in New York. Ward Bennett designs the "Scissor" chair for Brickel. Paul Mayén designs the "Knock-Down" glass-topped coffeetable for Habitat. Cini Boeri designs the "IV-6" table lamp for Arteluce. Eero Aarnio designs the "Gyro" chair for Asko. John Mascheroni designs the "Tubo" coffeetable for Mascheroni. Piet Hein designs the "Super-Elliptical" table for Fritz Hansen. Adrian and Ditte Heath design the "Chair 194" for France & Son of Denmark. The "Sacco" beanbag chair is designed by Gatti/Paolini/Teodoro for Zanotta. The "Selene" plastic chair is designed by Vico Magistretti for Artemide. The "Action Office II" is designed by Robert Propst for Herman Miller.

GOVERNMENT EVENTS

Martin Luther King, Jr., and Robert Kennedy are assassinated.

HONORS AND AWARDS

R. Buckminster Fuller is awarded the gold medal of the Royal Institute of British Architects. The Braun Prize is instituted for industrial design. As in 1961, the International Design Award of the American Institute of Interior Designers goes to Hans Wegner.

PROGRESS IN THE PROFESSION

Educator Arnold Friedmann authors a landmark report, "A Critical Study of Interior Design Education." IDEC publishes a "Comprehensive Bibliography for Interior Design" edited by Doris Burton, and a series of supplements will follow. The American Society for Testing and Materials publishes standards for resilient floor coverings. The U.S. Congress passes the Architectural Barriers Act.

TECHNICAL AND SCIENTIFIC ADVANCES

There are 78 million television sets in American homes. The Yale School of Architecture holds a conference on computer-aided design, and the proceedings will be published the next year as *Computer Graphics in Architecture and Design* by M. A. Milne.

Arnold Friedmann analyzes design education

1968

From left to right:

Marcel Breuer's Baldegg Convent, near Lucerne, Switzerland

Alan Buchsbaum's Metamorphosis beauty salon, Great Neck, New York

Alexander Girard's "Toostripe" woven textile for Herman Miller

Armi Ratia wearing one of her Marimekko fabrics

"Sacco" beanbag chairs by Gatti/Paolini/Teodoro for Zanotta

ARCHITECTURE

Ludwig Mies van der Rohe dies at age eighty-three, and Walter Gropius dies at age eighty-six. Carlo Scarpa begins the design of the Brion cemetery at San Vito d'Altivole, Italy. In Mexico, Luis Barragán designs the Galvez house. The second Geller house, in Lawrence, New York, is finished by Marcel Breuer and Herbert Beckhard. Richard Meier designs the Saltzman house in East Hampton, New York.

BOOKS

Mario Dal Fabbro writes *Upholstered Furniture*. Hugh Honour writes *Cabinet Makers and Furniture Designers*. Martin Battersby writes *The Decorative Twenties*, which will be reprinted in 1989. Rudolph Arnheim writes *Visual Thinking*. Georges and Rosamund Bernier edit *European Decoration: Creative Contemporary Interiors*. Mario Praz writes *Il gusto neoclassico*; it will be published in English as *On Neo-Classicism*.

CULTURE AT LARGE

Dame Margot Fonteyn celebrates her fiftieth birthday, and Duke Ellington his seventieth. A concert at Woodstock, New York, offers "peace, love, and music" to an audience of 400,000.

DESIGNERS AND INSTALLATIONS

Dorothy Draper dies at age eighty. Gwathmey & Henderson designs the Electric Circus dance club and an apartment for Faye Dunaway, both in New York. Stephen Kiviat and James Rappoport design a New York showroom for their new furniture company, Atelier International. Warren Platner designs interiors for a library in Suffield, Connecticut, and a house in Guilford, Connecticut. William Haines and Ted Graber design interiors for the American ambassador's house in Regent's Park, London. French designer Philippe Starck, at age nineteen, becomes the artistic director of the fashion house Pierre Cardin.

The Italian design group UFO designs the Bamba Issa discotheque at Forte dei Marmi. David Hicks designs the nightclub on the oceanliner *Queen Elizabeth II*. Alan Buchsbaum designs Cado furniture showrooms in Los Angeles, Boston, and Chicago. Robert Bray and Michael Schaible establish their practice in New York.

EXHIBITIONS

The first NEOCON (National Exposition of Contract Furnishings) is held at Chicago's Merchandise Mart, establishing an anual event that will last through the end of the century. At the art galleries of the University of California, Santa Barbara, David Gebhard and Harriette Von Breton organize a show of the work of Kem Weber. The Museum of Modern Art, New York, displays "Wall Hangings."

NEOCON furniture market established in Chicago

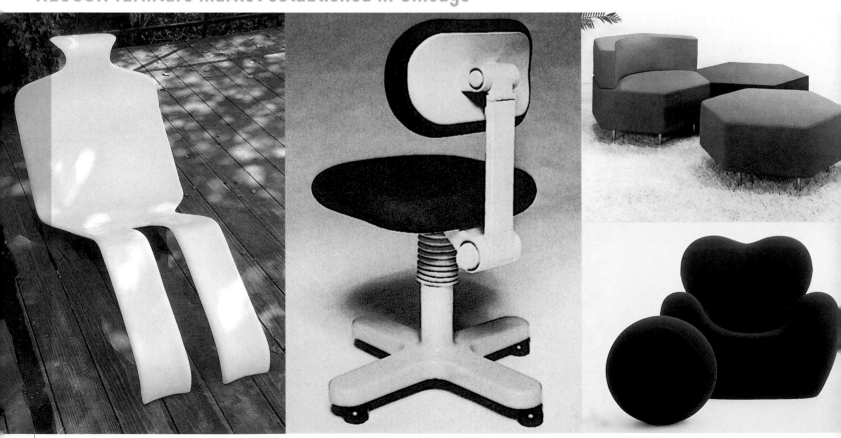

Charles and Ray Eames design the "Soft Pad" group for Herman Miller. Olivier Mourgue designs "Bouloum" chaises for Arconas. Giancarlo Piretti designs the "Plia" plastic folding chair and "Plana" folding armchair for Cassina. Anna Castelli Ferrieri designs the "Round-Up" stacking cylindrical plastic storage units for Kartell. Gaetano Pesce designs the "Up" series of chairs for C&B Italia. Ettore Sottsass Jr. designs the "Synthesis 45" office system for Olivetti. Douglas Ball designs the "S System" steel desk. Harvey Probber designs the "Cubo" and "Hexablock" seating groups. Joe Colombo's "Tube" chair for

Flexform is made of four plastic tubes covered in polyurethane foam and stretch fabric, and Colombo also designs the "Roto-Living" unit for Sormani. Stoppino, Gregotti, and Meneghetti design the "537" table lamps for Arteluce. Vico Magistretti designs the "Selene" plastic chair, and Livio Castiglioni and Gianfranco Frattini design the "Boalum" light snake, both for Artemide.

Fighting escalates in Northern Ireland between Roman Catholics and Protestants.

Metropolitan Home begins publication.

The Institute of Business Designers is incorporated. The American Institute of Kitchen Dealers, founded in 1963, begins its certification of kitchen designers.

Men walk on the moon. The U.S. government establishes Arpanet, a computer network for military sites and universities; by the end of the century it will have evolved into the Internet and will be in use by 200 million people.

1969

From left to right:

Olivier Mourgue's "Bouloum" chaise for Arconas

A chair from Ettore Sottsass, Jr.'s "Synthesis 45" office system for Olivetti

"Hexablock" seating and table elements by Harvey Probber

Gaetano Pesce's "Up" chair and spherical ottoman for C&B Italia

Warren Platner's house for himself in Guilford, Connecticut. The Platner-designed wire furniture is produced by Knoll.

Marcel Breuer

THE '70s

Architecture critic Ada Louise Huxtable, writing in the *New York Times* in 1976, notes that "modern architecture is at a turning point. . . . The theory and practice of modernism are under serious attack." While modern design continues strongly, it is joined by examples of postmodernism such as Charles Moore's 1978 Piazza d'Italia in New Orleans, Philip Johnson's AT&T building, New York, also from 1978, and Michael Graves's series of showrooms for Sunar, beginning in 1979. And in Italy, the "Bel Design" that had prevailed in Italy since the late '50s begins to fade in the early '70s; its underlying optimism is dampened by terrorism and an oil-related economic crisis, and its concept of functional beauty is questioned by groups of design rebels (Radical Design, UFO, Global Tools, Gruppo 9999, Zziggurat, Studio Alchymia, and eventually Memphis). Government influence on interior design continues with the 1970 passage of the Occupational Safety and Health Act, which will lead to the establishment of both NIOSH (the National Institute for Occupational Safety and Health, part of the Department of Health and Human Services) and OSHA (the Occupational Safety and Health Administration, part of the Department of Labor). Professional life is simplified by the 1975 merger of two competing professional organizations, the AID and the NSID, to form the American Society of Interior Designers (ASID). Professionalism is also strengthened by the 1970 formation of the Foundation for Interior Design Education Research (FIDER) and the 1972 National Council for Interior Design Qualification (NCIDQ). In 1973, FIDER will accredit its first five U.S. schools of interior design.

Louis Kahn's 1977 Yale Center
for British Art, New Haven,
with interior design by
Benjamin Baldwin

ARCHITECTURE

The John Hancock tower, Chicago, designed by Bruce Graham of Skidmore, Owings, & Merrill, is the second tallest building in the world. The Mummers' Theater in Oklahoma City is designed by John Johansen. In the Arizona desert, Paolo Soleri begins the construction of Arcosanti. Richard Neutra dies at age seventy-eight. Alvar Aalto's Mt. Angel Benedictine College Library is completed in Oregon. Charles Gwathmey and Robert Siegel establish the Gwathmey Siegel firm. James Wines and others form SITE (Sculpture in the Environment). Architecture critic Ada Louise Huxtable wins the Pulitzer Prize.

BOOKS

Interior Design: An Introduction to Architectural Interiors is written by Arnold Friedmann, John F. Pile, and Forrest Wilson; it will be reprinted in 1976. *David Hicks on Bathrooms* is published. Gilbert Frey writes *The Modern Chair: 1850 to Today*. Ann Ferebee writes *A History of Design from the Victorian Era to the Present*.

CULTURE AT LARGE

Robert Smithson completes his earthwork *Spiral Jetty*. The Dow-Jones industrial average drops to 631. Hospital care costs in the United States climb to $81 per day.

DESIGNERS AND INSTALLATIONS

Piero Fornasetti opens a shop in Milan. Carlo Mollino designs interiors and furniture for the Teatro Regio in Turin. In Paris, Pierre Paulin designs private quarters for President Georges Pompidou in the Élysée Palace. Gae Aulenti designs a New York showroom for Knoll, and showrooms in Turin and Brussels for Fiat. Milton Glaser designs interiors for the Childcraft store, New York. Donghia Associates is formed. Bruce Burdick opens a design studio in Los Angeles; he will move it to San Francisco in 1977.

Jacques Grange opens his own design firm after working with Henri Samuel and antiques dealer Didier Aaron. Dallek (with Stanley Felderman as chief designer) designs the New York headquarters for Fabergé. Davis Allen of Skidmore, Owings, & Merrill designs interiors for the American Can Company, Greenwich, Connecticut. In New York, Billy Baldwin designs a Park Avenue apartment for Diana and T. Reed Vreeland, upholstering his signature "Slipper Chair" in scarlet flowered chintz; according to Baldwin, Vreeland said she wanted the living room to be "a garden in hell," and he "knew what that meant: red." George Beylerian opens the Casa Idea Shop at Bloomingdale's.

EXHIBITIONS

The Modern Chair:1918–1970 is seen at the Whitechapel Art Gallery, London. Edgar Kaufmann jr.'s *The Rise of an American Architecture* is at the Metropolitan Museum of Art, New York, with exhibition design by James Stewart Polshek. The designs of Hector Guimard are seen at the Museum of Modern Art, New York. Expo '70 is held in Osaka; it features a dozen metal fountains designed by Isamu Noguchi and a pneumatic U.S. pavilion designed by Davis & Brody. The Museum of Contemporary Crafts, New York, shows the textile designs of Dorothy Liebes. London's *Daily Telegraph Magazine* sponsors *Experiments in Living*, including Max Clendinning's "Expando-Space" system of movable panels.

OSHA new workplace watchdog

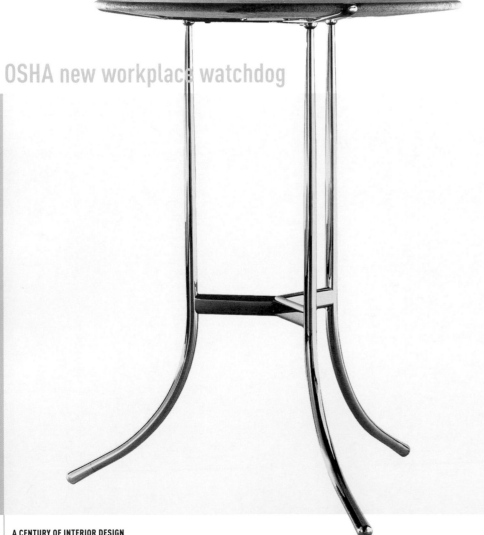

FURNITURE AND FURNISHINGS

Cini Boeri designs the "Serpentone" seating of extendable, flexible foam-rubber for Arflex and the "Lunar" table for Knoll. Giotto Stoppino designs the "Alessia" fiberglass chair for Driade. For Poltronova, Archizoom designs the "Mies" chair, Ettore Sottsass, Jr., designs his "Grey" furniture line, DePas, D'Urbino, & Lomazzi pay homage to DiMaggio with their glove-shaped "Joe" chair. Vico Magistretti designs the "Gaudi" and "Vicario" chairs for Artemide. French designer Marc Held designs the "Culbuto" chair, which will be produced by Knoll. Danish designer Steen Østergaard designs the plastic "Chair 290" for France & Son. Tobia and Afra Scarpa design their "Soriana" armchair for Cassina. For Sormani, Studio DA designs the "DA 35" table/storage unit and Richard Neagle designs the "Mini-Madio" plastic wardrobe. Superstudio designs the grid-dominated "Quaderna" range of tables for Zanotta. Alberto Rosselli designs the "Jumbo" one-piece fiberglass chair for Saporiti. Eero Aarnio designs the "Mustang" chair; when later produced by Stendig, it will be renamed the "Pony." For offices, Otto Zapf designs the "Softline System" for Knoll, and William Pulgram designs the "TRM" ("task response module") for Eppinger. For her husband, John Lennon, Yoko Ono commissions furniture designs from Dakota Jackson. Cedric Hartman designs and manufactures his marble-topped "AE" table.

GOVERNMENT EVENTS

The U.S. Congress passes the Occupational Safety and Health Act (OSHA).

MAGAZINES

Domus magazine is awarded Italy's Compasso d'Oro.

PROGRESS IN THE PROFESSION

The Foundation for Interior Design Education Research (FIDER) is founded to accredit postsecondary interior design education programs in the United States and Canada. The Parsons School of Design merges with the New School for Social Research; its venerable interior design department is dismantled and replaced by an environmental design department, and its valuable archives of decorative arts are junked; the interior design department will be reinstated in 1992. The Educational Foundation of the Home Fashions League is established. In Paris, Jacques Adnet becomes director of the École Nationale Supérieure des Arts Décoratifs.

TECHNICAL AND SCIENTIFIC ADVANCES

In the early '70s, computer-aided drafting and design (CADD) is in use in a large number of architecture and interior design offices.

1970

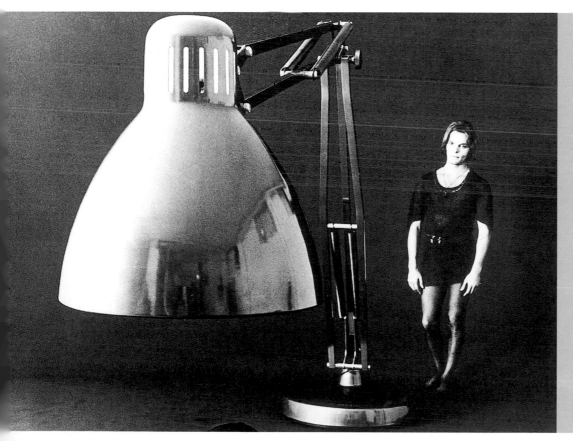

Cedric Hartman's "AE" table

Chapel by Marcel Breuer and his partner Robert Gatje in the ski resort Flaine, Haute Savoie, France

Gaetano Pesce's "Moloch" lamp, a gigantic enlargement of Jacob Jacobsen's 1937 "Luxo" lamp

ARCHITECTURE

Danish architect and furniture designer Arne Jacobsen dies at age sixtynine. Alvar Aalto designs Finlandia Hall in Helsinki. Aldo Rossi designs the San Cataldo cemetery in Modena, Italy. Richard Meier designs the Bronx Developmental Center, New York.

BOOKS

Industrial designer Victor Papanek writes *Design for the Real World*. David Hicks writes *David Hicks on Decoration with Fabrics*. Martin Battersby writes *The Decorative Thirties*; along with his *The Decorative Twenties*, it will be republished in 1989. Gillo Dorfles writes *Marco Zanuso, Designer*.

CULTURE AT LARGE

Fiddler on the Roof becomes the longest-running Broadway musical, breaking the record set by *Hello, Dolly!*

DESIGNERS AND INSTALLATIONS

For the Weyerhauser Corporation in Tacoma, Washington, Skidmore, Owings, & Merrill designs 300,000 square feet of "office landscape" space; the job's chief designer is Charles Pfister, working under design partner Edward C. ("Chuck") Bassett; its custom-designed office system will later be marketed by Knoll as the "Stephens System." Associated Space Design's headquarters for the McDonald's Corporation includes a padded "Think Tank." Designer Tom Lee is killed in an automobile accident, and his firm, Tom Lee Ltd., will be headed by his widow, Sarah Tomerlin Lee, formerly marketing vice president of Lord & Taylor and editor in chief of *House Beautiful*. Joe Colombo dies at forty-one. Billy McCarty designs the Vidal Sassoon salon in London. For Mary Wells and Harding Lawrence, Billy Baldwin designs interiors and furniture for La Fiorentina, St.-Jean Cap Ferrat.

Velvet tabourets coexist with tractor seats

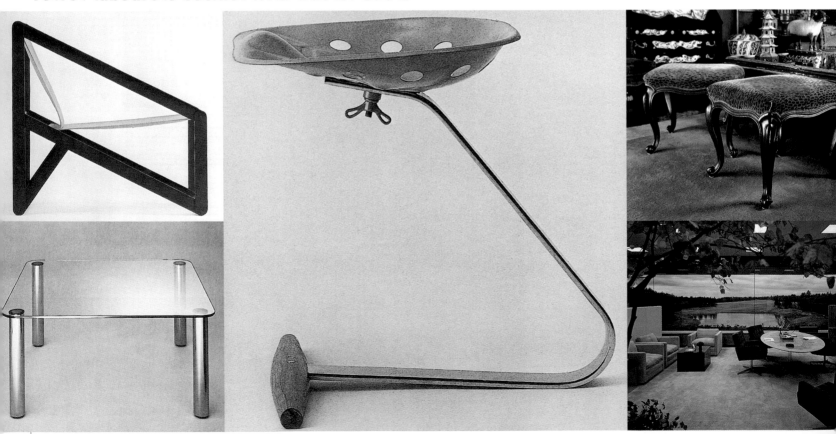

EXHIBITIONS

An exhibition of *Art Nouveau* is seen at the Virginia Museum in Richmond. *Guimard, Horta, Van de Velde* is seen in Paris. The *Visiona* exhibition for the German manufacturer Bayer includes work by Verner Panton, Joe Colombo, and Olivier Mourgue.

FURNITURE AND FURNISHINGS

Ward Bennett designs the "University" chair, produced by Brickel for use in the L. B. Johnson Library (by Skidmore, Owings, & Merrill) at the University of Texas in Austin. A variation, the 1978 "University Chair 1550," will also be produced by Brickel. The "Toio" lamp designed by the Castiglioni brothers is based on an automobile headlight. Giotto Stoppino designs stacking tables for Kartell. Gaetano Pesce designs the "Platone" folding desk chair for Castelli. Bruno Munari designs the "Lipari" ashtray for Danese. Zanotta produces tubular-steel furniture designed by Giuseppe Terragni in the 1930s. Cassina begins production of Gerrit Rietveld's 1917 "Red Blue" and 1934 "ZigZag" chairs. Pierre Paulin designs the "Endless Sofa" for Alpha.

GOVERNMENT EVENTS

India and Pakistan are at war.

HONORS AND AWARDS

Textile designer Boris Kroll receives an honorary doctorate from the Philadelphia College of Textiles.

PROGRESS IN THE PROFESSION

The American Society for Testing and Materials publishes standards for the production of leather.

TECHNICAL AND SCIENTIFIC ADVANCES

Intel Corporation announces the "computer on a chip" or microprocessor. The United States launches the Apollo 14 moon mission.

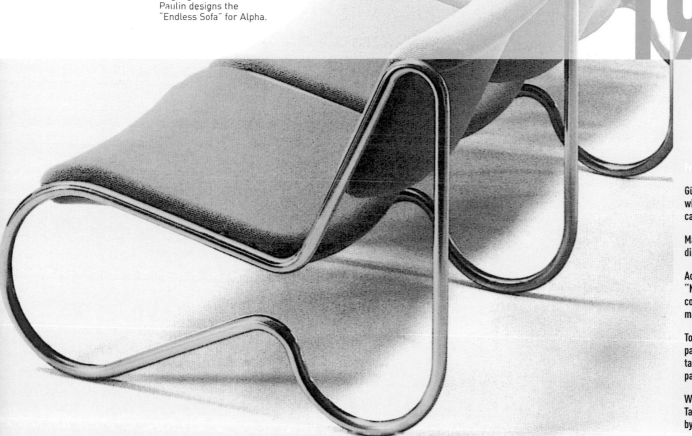

1971

From left to right:

Günter Silz's "London" chair with a folding beech frame and canvas sling

Marco Zanuso's "253 Marcuso" dining table for Zanotta

Achille Castiglioni's "Mezzadro" tractor-seat stool, conceived in 1957 and finally manufactured by Zanotta

Tony Duquette's version of a pair of Louis XV mahogany tabourets, upholstered in painted faux ocelot velvet

Weyerhauser headquarters, Tacoma, Washington, designed by Charles Pfister of SOM

Chrome-plated seating by Arne Jacobsen for Fritz Hansen

Louis Kahn's Exeter Library is completed in Exeter, New Hampshire, as is his Kimbell Art Museum in Fort Worth, Texas. The twin 110-story towers of Minoru Yamasaki's World Trade Center open in New York; they will stand for only twenty-nine years. Kisho Kurokawa designs the Nakagin Capsule Building in Tokyo. Gio Ponti designs the Denver Art Museum, his only work in the United States. Herman Hertzberger designs the Centraal Beheer insurance company offices in Apeldoorn, the Netherlands.

Olivier Marc writes *Psychanalyse de la maison;* it will be translated in 1977 as *Psychology of the House.* Norma Skurka writes *Underground Interiors: Designing for Alternative Life Styles,* showing work by Paul Rudolph, Alan Buchsbaum, Gamal El Zoghby, Seymour Avigdor, Charles Moore, Olivier Mourgue, Hugh Hardy, C. Ray Smith, and others. Robert Venturi, Denise Scott Brown, and Steven Izenour write *Learning from Las Vegas.*

Leonard Bernstein composes his *Mass* for the opening of the Edward Durell Stone–designed Kennedy Center in Washington. *Grease* is on Broadway, and *The Godfather* on the movie screen.

The Bacardi International headquarters, Bermuda, is designed by Maria Bergson. A New York office for Mercedes-Benz is designed by Hans Krieks. The Gunwyn Ventures offices, Princeton, New Jersey, are designed by Michael Graves. In interiors for the house of Maité and Don Plácido Arango y Arias in Madrid, Billy Baldwin reinterprets his "Slipper Chair" in apricot cotton; Baldwin also designs a Washington, D.C., house for Deeda and William McCormick Blair, Jr. Warren Platner designs the Kent Memorial Library in Suffield, Connecticut. Barbara D'Arcy becomes director of store design for the Bloomingdale's chain. John Saladino opens his office in New York. Sarah Tomerlin Lee of Tom Lee Ltd. completes the Rye Town Hilton Inn in Port Chester, New York.

Gehry makes chairs of cardboard

EXHIBITIONS

Italy: The New Domestic Landscape at the Museum of Modern Art, New York, is curated by Emilio Ambasz; Gaetano Pesce contributes an environment called *Habitat for Two People in an Age of Great Contaminations*. Farther uptown, the Metropolitan Museum of Art presents for the first time a one-man show honoring a living architect, Marcel Breuer, and opens a reconstruction of the living room of Frank Lloyd Wright's 1914 Little house, built in Wayzata, Minnesota. The Fine Arts Society, London, presents a retrospective exhibition of designer and author Christopher Dresser (1834–1904). The Louvre, Paris, shows the furniture designs of Knoll.

FURNITURE AND FURNISHINGS

Frank Gehry designs his "Easy Edges" furniture made of corrugated cardboard for Cheru Enterprises; it will soon be manufactured by Vitra; with slight modifications, it will be reissued in 1982 as "Rough Edges"; and Vitra will revive the design in 1993. Angelo Donghia designs the "Madison" armchair and side chair. Jack Lenor Larsen begins a textile program for Braniff Airlines. Mario Bellini designs "Le Bambole" upholstered seating for C&B Italia. Bruno Munari designs hanging shelves for Robots. Norwegian designer Peter Opsvik designs the "Tripp-trapp" chair for Stokke Fabrikker. Richard Sapper designs the "Tizio" lamp for Artemide. Antonia Astori designs the "Oikos 1" modular furniture system for her own company, Driade; it is one of a series of such systems she will devise. John Saladino designs the "Saladino" table lamp with a clear glass cylindrical base.

GOVERNMENT EVENTS

District of Columbia police arrest five men inside the Democratic National Headquarters in the Watergate complex. An international convention bans germ warfare.

PROGRESS IN THE PROFESSION

Professional organizations consider the possibility of making competency examinations prerequisites to membership; the idea leads to the formation of the National Council for Interior Design Qualification (NCIDQ). The U.S. Congress passes the Consumer Products Safety Act. The American Society for Testing and Materials publishes standards for occupational health and safety, for environmental acoustics, and for security systems and equipment.

TECHNICAL AND SCIENTIFIC ADVANCES

Apollo astronauts are on the moon, and a Soviet spacecraft lands on Venus.

1972

From left to right:

Louis Kahn's Kimbell Art Museum, Fort Worth, Texas

"Le Bambole" seating by Mario Bellini for C&B Italia

John Saladino's "Saladino" lamp

Part of Gaetano Pesce's *Habitat for Two People in an Age of Great Contaminations* at the Museum of Modern Art, New York

Frank Gehry's "Easy Edges" seating of corrugated cardboard

ARCHITECTURE

Richard Meier's Douglas house is built in Harbor Springs, Michigan. The John Hancock tower, Boston, is designed by Harry Cobb of I. M. Pei & Partners.

BOOKS

Billy Baldwin, seventy years old, writes *Billy Baldwin Decorates* and announces his retirement. Fiorenzo Cattaneo edits *Roomscapes: The Decorative Art of Renzo Mongiardino*. Jack Lenor Larsen and Mildred Constantine write *Beyond Craft: The Art Fabric*. *Five Architects* is published, showing the work of Peter Eisenman, Michael Graves, John Hejduk, Charles Gwathmey, and Richard Meier.

CULTURE AT LARGE

Peter Shaffer's *Equus* is on Broadway; Erica Jong writes *Fear of Flying*. Federal Express begins operations.

DESIGNERS AND INSTALLATIONS

In Chicago, the Leo Burnet offices are designed by Maria Bergson. In New York, the Kips Bay Boys' Club presents its first Decorator Showhouse, which will become the country's premier annual show house; those designing rooms this first year include Mario Buatta, Stair & Co., David Barrett, Burgin International (Thomas Britt and Robert Coufos), McMillen Inc. (Mark Hampton and Alexandra Stoddard), and Ellen Lehman McCluskey. McCluskey also designs executive and dining suites for McGraw-Hill, New York. David Easton and Michael La Rocca establish Easton & La Rocca. Gwathmey Siegel designs Pearl's restaurant in New York.

Architect Stephen Kiviat and textile artist Susan Kimber design their own New York apartment. In Vienna, Hans Hollein designs the Schullin jewelry shop, and, in Florence, he inserts a museum of modern art into the Strozzi Palace. In San Francisco, John Dickinson converts a nineteenth-century fire station into his own quarters. Deborah Sussman designs a series of stores for Standard Shoes.

Kips Bay show house instituted in New York

EXHIBITIONS

The Royal Institute of British Architects presents an exhibition of the work of designer Eileen Gray; it will be followed by another Gray show at London's Victoria & Albert in 1979. The Fine Arts Society, London, shows *The Arts and Crafts Movement: Artists, Craftsmen, and Designers 1890–1930*. A one-man show of the work of Charles Eames is at the Museum of Modern Art, New York, as are *Another Chance for Housing: Low-Rise Alternatives* and an exhibition of the tapestries of Helena Hernmarck.

FURNITURE AND FURNISHINGS

Italian furniture manufacturers Piero and Franco Busnelli buy out Cesare Cassina, and C&B Italia changes its name to B&B Italia. Gae Aulenti designs the "Gaetano" glass table for Zanotta. Angelo Mangiarotti designs the "Eros" marble table for Skipper. Vico Magistretti designs the "Maralunga" chair and sofa for Cassina. Knoll's "Zapf" office system is designed by Otto Zapf.

GOVERNMENT EVENTS

A cease-fire agreement is signed in Vietnam, but some fighting continues.

MAGAZINES

Architecture Plus, edited by Peter Blake, begins publication.

PROGRESS IN THE PROFESSION

The Foundation for Interior Design Education Research (FIDER) awards its first five accreditations to interior design schools, those at the University of Cincinnati, the University of Georgia, the University of Texas at Austin, Virginia Commonwealth University, and the University of Missouri, Columbia. Nine furniture companies join to found the Business and Institutional Furniture Manufacturers' Association (BIFMA).

TECHNICAL AND SCIENTIFIC ADVANCES

Television pictures of the planet Jupiter are transmitted to Earth.

1973

From left to right:

Banca di Roma, Chicago, by Robert Kleinschmidt and others of SOM

Douglas house, Harbor Springs, Michigan, by Richard Meier

The "Maralunga" chair for Cassina by Vico Magistretti

Sybil's Bar at the New York Hilton by Sarah Tomerlin Lee of Tom Lee Ltd.

Charles Rennie Mackintosh's "Argyle" chair of 1897 is reproduced by Cassina and shown at the Milan Triennale

Harry Seidler's own office, Sydney, Australia, with tapoo try by Josef Albers

Architect Louis Kahn dies at age seventy-three in a train station in New York as his Institute of Management is being finished in Ahmadabad, India. Edward Larrabee Barnes designs the Walker Art Center in Minneapolis. Arata Isozaki designs the Gunma Prefectural Museum of Modern Art in Takasaki, Japan. Robert A. M. Stern designs the Lang house, Washington, Connecticut. Charles Moore designs the Pyramid House for himself in Centerbrook, Connecticut. The 110-story Sears Tower, designed by Skidmore, Owings, & Merrill, is built in Chicago; for its lobby, silk banners are commissioned from Jack Lenor Larsen; it has elevator speeds of eighteen hundred feet per minute.

Charles Moore, Donlyn Lyndon, and Gerald Allen write *The Place of Houses.* Peter Blake writes *Form Follows Fiasco.* Dan Klein writes the *All Colour Book of Art Deco.* Clement Meadmore writes *The Modern Chair: Classics in Production.* Billy Baldwin writes *Billy Baldwin Remembers.*

Dancer Mikhail Baryshnikov of the Kirov Ballet defects to the West. Terra-cotta warriors are unearthed near Xian, China; over six thousand will be found by the end of the century. Raymond Loewy designs the Soviet automobile "Moskwitch." Tom Stoppard writes the play *Travesties.*

MoMA honors Charles Rennie Mackintosh

DESIGNERS AND INSTALLATIONS

Warren Platner designs the American Restaurant in Kansas City and the Steelcase showroom in Chicago. Massimo and Lella Vignelli design interiors for the Minneapolis Institute of Fine Arts. The second Kips Bay Decorator Showhouse in New York presents rooms by Robert Metzger, Richard Ridge, Trask & Clark, Diane Russell, and others. Ettore Sottsass, Jr., and Adam Tihany collaborate on the design section of the Milan Triennale.

EXHIBITIONS

Furniture of Charles Rennie Mackintosh opens at the Museum of Modern Art, New York.

FURNITURE AND FURNISHINGS

Don Chadwick designs modular seating for Herman Miller. Archizoom designs the "AEO" armchair for Cassina. Nicos Zographos forms a company to produce his own furniture designs. Italian lighting manufacturers Arteluce and Flos merge. DePas, D'Urbino, & Lomazzi design the "Sciangai" folding clothes stand for Zanotta; it will win the Compasso d'Oro.

GOVERNMENT EVENTS

As a result of the Watergate scandal, Richard M. Nixon is the first American president to resign. India detonates an atomic bomb.

PROGRESS IN THE PROFESSION

The National Council for Interior Design Qualification (NCIDQ) is incorporated in the state of Delaware, and its examination is developed with the help of the Psychological Corporation and Educational Testing Service. The NCIDQ's first president is Louis Tregre. FIDER accredits four more schools of interior design: the University of Florida, the University of Manitoba, the University of Oregon, and Kansas State University.

TECHNICAL AND SCIENTIFIC ADVANCES

Merchandise prices begin to be transmitted by bar codes. Computers are supplied with LSI (large-scale integrated) chips.

1974

From left to right:

"The Home," part of the exhibition *Signs of Life: Symbols in the American City,* Smithsonian Institution, Washington, D.C., by Venturi and Scott Brown

Institute of Management, Ahmadabad, India, by Louis Kahn

Brant house, Greenwich, Connecticut, by Venturi and Scott Brown

Don Chadwick's "Limbo" modular seating for Herman Miller

ARCHITECTURE

Norman Foster designs an office building for Willis Faber & Dumas in Ipswich, Suffolk. James Wines of SITE designs the Best Products store in Houston. Josep Lluis Sert's Fundación Joan Miró is completed in Barcelona. Alvar Aalto's Finlandia Hall Concert and Convention Center is completed in Helsinki.

BOOKS

Jack Lenor Larsen and Jeanne Weeks write *Fabrics for Interiors*.

CULTURE AT LARGE

Stephen Spielberg's *Jaws* sets box-office records. *A Chorus Line* is the hit of Broadway. The highest-rated TV program is *All in the Family*.

DESIGNERS AND INSTALLATIONS

For the Aid Association for the Lutherans headquarters in Appleton, Wisconsin (building design by William Pedersen of Kohn Pedersen Fox), George Nelson designs the interiors; his custom furniture system for the building will be marketed by Storwal as "Nelson Workspaces." In Paris, Davis Allen of Skidmore, Owings, & Merrill designs a suite in the Tour Fiat for brothers Gianni and Umberto Agnelli. In New York, Denning & Fourcade design an apartment for Diane Von Furstenberg, Kenneth Walker of Walker/Grad designs the Miller residence using lots of Mylar,

Joseph D'Urso designs an apartment for Reed Evins, Paul Rudolph revises the interiors of a Beekman Place townhouse for himself, and Alan Buchsbaum designs his own loft and furniture. Luis Rey is named vice-president of McMillen Inc. For the Kips Bay Decorator Showhouse, designers include Mallory-Tillis (Stephen Mallory and James Tillis), Arthur E. Smith Inc., David Barrett, Donghia Associates, Kevin McNamara, and Richard Lowell Neas.

EXHIBITIONS

At the Museum of Modern Art, New York, Arthur Drexler curates *The Architecture of the École des Beaux-Arts*. The Architectural League of New York organizes an Eileen Gray exhibition; it will travel to Los Angeles, Princeton, and Boston. An exhibition designed by Charles and Ray Eames for the American Bicentennial Commission, *The World of Franklin and Jefferson*, begins touring. The Renwick Gallery, Washington, D.C., pays homage to the Herman Miller and Knoll furniture companies in *A Modern Consciousness: D. J. DePree, Florence Knoll*, and the Walker Art Center, Minneapolis, shows *Nelson, Eames, Girard, Propst: The Design Process at Herman Miller*.

AID + NSID = ASID

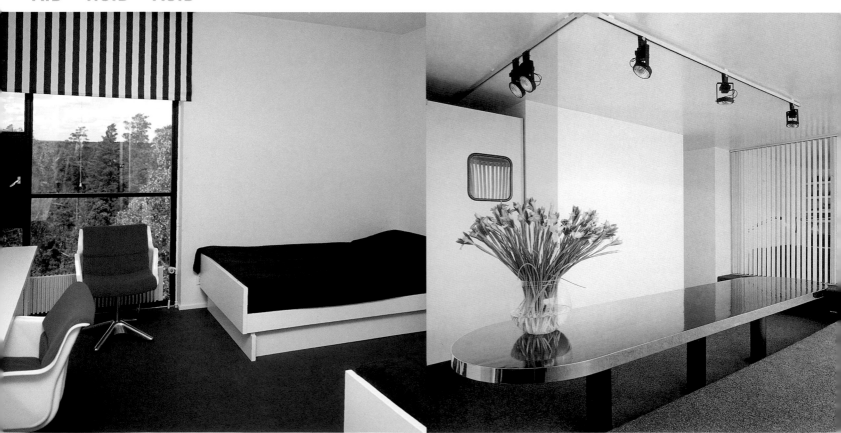

FURNITURE AND FURNISHINGS

Robert De Fuccio designs the "Triangle" chair for Stow/Davis. Billy Baldwin designs tables and upholstered furniture for Luten Clarey Stern. Hans Wegner designs the "701" chair for PP Møbler. Mario Bellini designs the "Area 50" table lamps for Artemide. Gae Aulenti designs the "Patroclo" table lamp for Artemide and the "Aulenti Collection" for Knoll. Gaetano Pesce designs the "Sit Down" suite of armchairs for Cassina. Harvey Probber modifies his "Cubo" seating group with an angled back cushion. The Austrian group Haus-Rucker-Co. designs the "Quart" series of modular storage furniture for Elst. Wedgwood is acquired by Waterford Glass, the two companies operating as Waterford Wedgwood. Charles Pfister designs a range of clear glass bowls and ashtrays; made by Vistosi in Murano, they are sold by Knoll.

GOVERNMENT EVENTS

The Suez Canal, closed since the Israeli-Arab War of 1967, is reopened.

HONORS AND AWARDS

Painter and designer Sonia Delaunay is made an officer of the French Legion of Honor.

MAGAZINES

The *Journal of Interior Design Education and Research* is first published by the Interior Design Educators Council.

PROGRESS IN THE PROFESSION

The American Society of Interior Designers (ASID) is formed by the merger of the 8,000-member American Institute of Interior Designers (AID) and the 5,400-member National Society of Interior Designers (NSID). The National Council for Interior Design Qualification (NCIDQ) publishes a booklet, "Guidelines for the Statutory Licensing of Interior Designers." FIDER accredits eight more schools of interior design, bringing the total number to seventeen; by the end of the century there will be 137 FIDER-accredited schools in the United States and Canada.

TECHNICAL AND SCIENTIFIC ADVANCES

The Altair 8800 is the first personal computer.

1975

From left to right:

Timo Penttilä's guest room for the City Institute, Espoo, Finland

The Reed Evins apartment, New York, designed by Joseph D'Urso

"Parish Magnolia," a glazed cotton chintz designed by "Sister" Parish for F. Schumacher

Harvey Probber's "Rake-Back Cubo" seating group

Gaetano Pesce's "Sit Down" armchair for Cassina

ARCHITECTURE

Finnish architect and furniture designer Alvar Aalto dies at age seventy-eight. In Paris, Centre Pompidou is completed to the competition-winning designs of Renzo Piano and Richard Rogers. Mario Botta designs a striped house at Ligornetto, Switzerland. Ricardo Legorreta designs the Camino Real Baja hotel in Cabo San Lucas, Mexico. Paolo Portoghesi designs a mosque and center for Islamic culture in Rome.

BOOKS

James Nuckolls writes *Interior Lighting for Environmental Designers*. Harry Siegel writes *This Business of Interior Design*, which will later be revised as *Business Guide for Interior Designers*. Ralph Caplan writes *The Design of Herman Miller*.

CULTURE AT LARGE

Philip Glass and Robert Wilson's opera *Einstein on the Beach* premieres in Avignon, France. Sarah Caldwell is the first woman to conduct the Metropolitan Opera. Christo installs *Running Fence* across twenty-five miles of California land near the coast.

DESIGNERS AND INSTALLATIONS

Warren Platner's Windows on the World restaurant opens atop the north tower of the World Trade Center in New York; it will be the cover story for both *Interiors* and *Interior Design*; Platner's observation deck opens atop the other tower. Also in New York, Philip Johnson and John Burgee provide a new interior for Lincoln Center's Avery Fisher Hall, Gwathmey Siegel designs the Shezan restaurant, Paul Mayén designs an apartment for Edgar Kaufmann, jr., and Angelo Donghia designs a showroom for his own firm and remodels a coach house. Robert Bray and Michael Schaible design the First National Bank of Hialeah, Florida. In Paris, Philippe Starck begins the design of two nightclubs, La Main Bleue and Les Bains-Douches. Mark Hampton, at thirty-six, opens his New York office after working for David Hicks, for Parish-Hadley, and for McMillen Inc. The Studio Alchymia design collaborative is founded in Milan. Outside Venice, Afra and Tobia Scarpa design their own country house. In Vienna, Hans Hollein begins work on a central office and three branches of the Austrian Travel Agency. Kips Bay Decorator Showhouse participants include Robert Metzger, Parish-Hadley, Rubén de Saavedra, Mario Buatta, John Saladino, Noel Jeffrey, Ellen Lehman McCluskey, and Richard Lowell Neas. The annual Westweek furniture exposition is instituted at the Pacific Design Center, Los Angeles.

EXHIBITIONS

The Cooper-Hewitt, National Design Museum, New York, newly established as the Smithsonian Institution's branch for the study of the decorative arts, opens in new quarters, the former Andrew Carnegie mansion, in New York, restored by Hardy Holzman Pfeiffer. The opening exhibition, *Man TransForms*, is conceived by Austrian architect Hans Hollein. At the Museum of Modern Art, New York, curator Emilio Ambasz shows the work of Luis Barragán. The Princeton University Art Museum shows *The Arts and Crafts Movement in America, 1876–1916*.

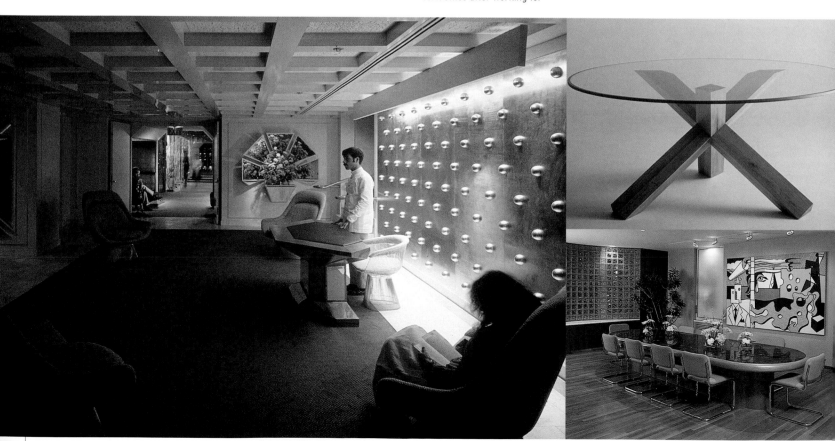

FURNITURE AND FURNISHINGS

Mario Bellini designs the "Cab" chair for Cassina; it will be sold in the United States through Atelier International; also for Cassina, he designs the "La Rotonda" table on intersecting wood legs. Billy Baldwin designs fabrics and wallcoverings for Woodson Wallpapers. A molded-plywood chair is designed by Peter Danko. Bruno Mathsson designs the "Ingrid" chair and the "Sonja" sectional sofa for Dux. Gretchen Bellinger, formerly with SOM, Knoll, and V'Soske, opens her own fabric company and produces "Transportation Cloth." Darcy Bonner designs a "Wearable Chair" that is strapped to the user's legs.

GOVERNMENT EVENTS

The United States and the USSR sign a disarmament treaty.

HONORS AND AWARDS

The ASID presents a "Salute to Women in Design" and gives its Thomas Jefferson Award to Lisa Taylor, director of the Cooper-Hewitt, National Design Museum.

MAGAZINES

With the membership of more than fifty furniture manufacturers, BIFMA begins publishing a newsletter.

PROGRESS IN THE PROFESSION

Led by Atlanta architect and interior designer William Pulgram, a joint committee of the ASID and the AIA works to prepare a series of jointly approved documents for interiors work. New York designer Hans Krieks holds master classes for professional designers. The Incorporated Institute of British Decorators and Interior Designers changes its name to the British Institute of Interior Design.

TECHNICAL AND SCIENTIFIC ADVANCES

Steve Jobs and Steve Wozniak found Apple Computers.

Cooper-Hewitt moves uptown

1976

From left to right:

Windows on the World restaurant in New York's World Trade Center, designed by Warren Platner

Mario Bellini's "La Rotonda" table for Cassina

Dining room, New York apartment, by Gwathmey Siegel

Mario Bellini's "Cab" chair for Cassina, with leather cover over steel frame

Mario Buatta, "Prince of Chintz," designs for the Kips Bay Decorator Showhouse, New York.

ARCHITECTURE

Louis Kahn's Yale Center for British Art, New Haven, Connecticut, has interiors by Benjamin Baldwin. A ski house at Vail, Colorado, by Venturi, Rauch, and Scott Brown is furnished with Gustav Stickley mission oak pieces. Tadao Ando designs the Wall House in Hyogo, Japan. Stanley Tigerman designs the "Daisy House" in Porter, Indiana. Gwathmey Siegel designs the Taft house in Cincinnati. Harry Weese designs the stations of the Washington, D.C., Metro system. Harry Seidler designs the Australian embassy in Paris. Luis Barragán's Gilardi house is completed in Mexico City.

BOOKS

John Fleming and Hugh Honour publish a *Dictionary of the Decorative Arts*; George Nelson writes *How to See: Visual Adventures in a World God Never Made*. William J. Mitchell writes *Computer-Aided Architectural Design*. William M. C. Lam writes *Perception and Lighting as Formgivers for Architecture*. C. Ray Smith writes *Supermannerism*. Rudolph Arnheim writes *The Dynamics of Architectural Form*. Carleton Varney writes *Carleton Varney Decorates from A to Z: An Encyclopedia of Home Decoration*. Bernard Rudofsky writes *The Prodigious Builders: Notes toward a Natural History of Architecture*. Renato De Fusco writes *Le Corbusier, Designer: Furniture, 1929*. Victor Papanek and Jim Hennessey write *How Things Don't Work*.

CULTURE AT LARGE

Moviegoers watch Stephen Spielberg's *Close Encounters of the Third Kind*, Woody Allen's *Annie Hall*, and George Lucas's *Star Wars*.

DESIGNERS AND INSTALLATIONS

In California, John Dickinson is forging a distinctive style of spare furnishings, pale colors, large scale, and rustic textures. In New York, Massimo and Lella Vignelli design interiors for St. Peter's Lutheran Church. In the concourse beneath the plaza of New York's World Trade Center, a complex of restaurants is designed by Harper & George, with graphics by Milton Glaser. In Chicago, Warren Platner designs Water Tower Place. For Calvin Klein in New York, Joseph D'Urso designs both a minimalist apartment and a minimalist showroom. Susana Torre designs the Torczyner & Wiseman law offices in New York, displaying the firm's collection of Magritte paintings. Sarah Tomerlin Lee of Tom Lee Ltd. is given the commission for interior design of the fifty-one-story Helmsley Palace Hotel, New York, a new structure attached to the historic Villard Houses; it will be completed in 1981. Marvin B. Affrime, principal of the Space Design group, designs the Johns-Manville World Headquarters interiors near Denver. Ruben de Saavedra designs a New York townhouse for Peter and Adela Holzer. Juan Montoya designs a Manhattan apartment for himself. Designing rooms for the Kips Bay Decorator Showhouse are Mario Buatta, Richard Ridge, Kevin McNamara, Mallory-Tillis, Richard Lowell Neas, and McMillen Inc. In Copenhagen, Poul Kjærholm designs the dining room in the Royal Copenhagen Porcelain concert hall. In Barcelona, Jorge Pensi and others form the Grupo Berenquer.

Supermannerism arrives with a Pop

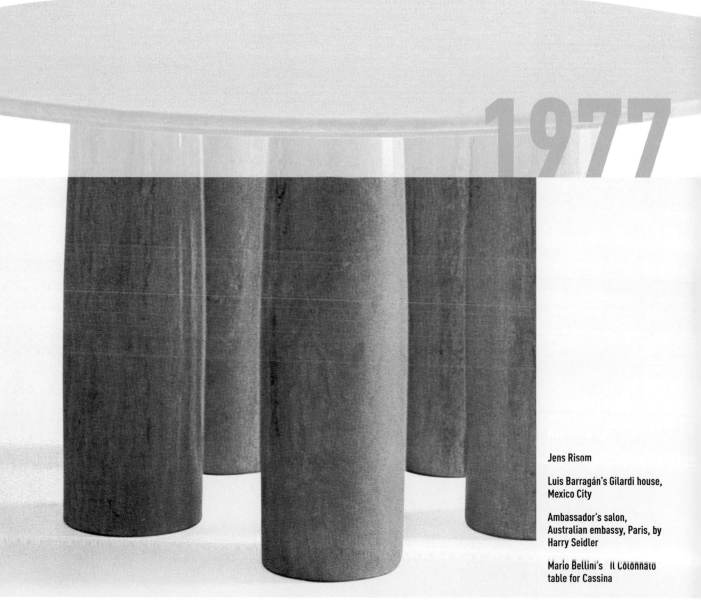

EXHIBITIONS

Arne Jacobsen retrospective exhibitions are seen in Amsterdam and Paris. Adler & Sullivan's trading room for the Chicago Stock Exchange, built in 1894 and demolished in 1972, is reconstructed at the Art Institute of Chicago. In Barcelona, Javier Mariscal organizes the *Grand Hotel* exhibition. In Milan, Michele De Lucchi and Ettore Sottsass, Jr., curate *Italian Design of the Fifties*.

FURNITURE AND FURNISHINGS

Vico Magistretti designs the "Atollo" table lamp for O-Luce and the "Nuvola Rossa" folding bookcase for Cassina. Cini Boeri designs the "Gradual System" sofa for Knoll. Jens Risom and Alan Burr design a range of folding-leg tables for Howe. Mario Bellini designs the "Il Colonnato" table on columnar marble legs for Cassina. King & Miranda (Perry King and Santiago Miranda) design the "Donald" table lamp for Arteluce.

GOVERNMENT EVENTS

United States–Vietnam peace talks begin.

HONORS AND AWARDS

George Nelson and Emilio Ambasz receive the gold medals from the Institute of Business Designers. Architect Paul Rudolph and educator Stanley Barrows receive the New York ASID chapter's Elsie de Wolfe Award. Florence Knoll receives the ASID's Total Design Award.

MAGAZINES

Interiors divides itself into two magazines, *Contract Interiors* and *Residential Interiors*. *Residential Interiors* will soon cease publication, however, and in 1978 *Contract Interiors* will revert to the title *Interiors*. In Italy, designer and critic Alessandro Mendini founds *Modo*.

TECHNICAL AND SCIENTIFIC ADVANCES

First mass production of desktop computers. Bill Gates and Paul Allen found Microsoft.

1977

Jens Risom

Luis Barragán's Gilardi house, Mexico City

Ambassador's salon, Australian embassy, Paris, by Harry Seidler

Mario Bellini's "Il Colonnato" table for Cassina

ARCHITECTURE

Norman Foster designs the Sainsbury Centre for the Arts, University of East Anglia, near Norwich, England. I. M. Pei & Partners design the East Wing of the National Gallery of Art, Washington, D.C. Frank Gehry's drastic remodeling of a house for himself in Santa Monica is built; he also designs the Loyola University Law School in Los Angeles, but it will not be completed until 1991. Arquitectonica designs the "Pink House" in Miami Shores, Florida. Seven years after his death, Arne Jacobsen's National Bank of Denmark is finished in Copenhagen. Two years after his death, Alvar Aalto's Riola Parish Church is finished near Bologna. Just before his death this year at age seventy-two, Carlo Scarpa's Banca Popolare is finished in Verona; just after, his Brion Cemetery is finished at San Vito d'Altivole.

BOOKS

Joan Kron and Suzanne Slesin chronicle a trend in *High-Tech: The Industrial Style and Source Book for the Home.* Peter Thornton writes *Seventeenth-Century Interior Decoration in England, France, and Holland.* Peter Bradford and Barbara Prete write *Chair.* Richard B. Fisher writes *Syrie Maugham.* John Pile writes *Open Office Planning,* and Michael Saphier writes *Planning the New Office.*

CULTURE AT LARGE

The Metropolitan Opera transmits its first live telecast, with Renato Scotto and Luciano Pavarotti in *La Bohème.*

DESIGNERS AND INSTALLATIONS

Charles Eames dies at age seventy-one. Adam Tihany opens his own office in New York. Bromley Jacobsen designs the Abitare store, New York. Ward Bennett designs a Los Angeles showroom for Brickel Associates. The Space Design Group designs offices for International Paper, New York. Alan Buchsbaum designs New York clothing stores for Charivari. For Washington's Federal Design Assembly, evocative "environments" are designed by Charles Moore of Moore Ruble Yudell, Stanley Tigerman, and Susana Torre. Robin Jacobsen designs Girard's disco in Baltimore. Richard Meier inserts the Aye Simon Reading Room into Wright's Guggenheim Museum. Kips Bay Decorator Showhouse designers include Robert Metzger, Rubén de Saavedra, Mel Dwork, Parish-Hadley, Anthony Hail, Melanie Kahane, Carleton Varney, Susan Zises, Gary Crain, Mark Hampton, Rita Falkner, and Tom O'Toole. Powell/Kleinschmidt design the Knoll showroom, Chicago. In Copenhagen, Poul Kjærholm designs the Kanalen restaurant. In Basel, Verner Panton designs interiors for himself.

EXHIBITIONS

The Larsen Influence, a retrospective of the textile designs of Jack Lenor Larsen, is seen at New York's Fashion Institute of Technology. Larsen and Edward Fields are both named honorary fellows of the ASID. *The Splendors of Dresden* is seen at the National Gallery of Art, Washington, D.C.; it will travel to the Metropolitan Museum of Art, New York, and to San Francisco's Palace of the Legion of Honor. The Cooper-Hewitt, National Design Museum, New York, shows *Ornament in the Twentieth Century* and *Vienna Moderne: 1898–1918.* The Philadelphia College of Textiles shows *Art in Science,* focusing on the environmental use of fabrics demonstrated in experimental works by Aleksandra Kasuba, Les Levine, and Alexander Messinger. The Santa Barbara Museum of Art surveys the work of designer Paul Tuttle.

FURNITURE AND FURNISHINGS

Alessandro Mendini spoofs design history with his "Poltrona di Proust" for Alchymia. John Dickinson designs a twenty-two-piece furniture collection for Macy's San Francisco. Ernesto Gismondi designs the "Sintesi" adjustable table lamp for Artemide. Anni Albers designs fabric and Douglas Ball designs the "Race" office system for Sunar; in 1979, Ball will become Sunar's director of design. Gretchen Bellinger introduces "Corde du Roi." Niels Diffrient designs an executive office chair for Knoll.

GOVERNMENT EVENTS

A Middle East peace plan is outlined at a Camp David summit meeting.

HONORS AND AWARDS

The ASID's Thomas Jefferson Award is given to Clement E. Conger, curator of the White House. The New York chapter ASID's Elsie de Wolfe Award is given to I. M. Pei. Charlotte Perriand receives the gold medal of the Académie d'Architecture, Paris.

MAGAZINES

Interior Design institutes an annual listing of "Interior Design Giants" based on their dollar volume of work. First of the seventy-five firms listed is SLS Environetics Inc., with a staff of 158 and a volume of $51 million.

PROGRESS IN THE PROFESSION

The AIA and the ASID present the results of their collaborative efforts to produce joint contract documents. For Steelcase, Louis Harris & Associates conducts a poll of office workers and office designers, resulting in "The Steelcase National Study of Office Environments: Do They Work?"

TECHNICAL AND SCIENTIFIC ADVANCES

The first commercial network of cellular telephones is formed.

1978

Steelcase studies offices, asks "Do They Work?"

From left to right:

Frank Gehry's office interiors for the law firm Berger, Kahn, Shafton, and Moss in West Los Angeles

I. M. Pei, winning the Elsie de Wolfe Award

Verner Panton, designing his own house in Basel, Switzerland

Richard Meier's Aye Simon Reading Room, built within Frank Lloyd Wright's Guggenheim Museum, New York

ARCHITECTURE

The annual Pritzker Architecture Prize is inaugurated, its first recipient being Philip Johnson. Richard Meier designs the Atheneum in New Harmony, Indiana.

BOOKS

Published are: *Modern Furniture* by John F. Pile; *George Nelson on Design* by George Nelson; *David Hicks: Living with Design* by David Hicks with Nicholas Jenkins; *Eileen Gray: Designer* by Stewart Johnson; *The Extraordinary Work of Süe et Mare* by Raymond Foulk; *Furniture: A Concise History* by Edward Lucie-Smith; *The Sense of Order: A Study in the Psychology of Decorative Art* by E. H. Gombrich; and *The Decorative Designs of Frank Lloyd Wright* by David A. Hanks, which will be reprinted in a larger format twenty years later.

CULTURE AT LARGE

Beverly Sills retires from singing and becomes music director of the New York City Opera. William Styron writes *Sophie's Choice*. Woody Allen films *Manhattan*.

DESIGNERS AND INSTALLATIONS

Michael Graves begins a series of eight showroom designs for the furniture company Sunar. Benjamin Baldwin completes his design for a house for himself in Sarasota, Florida, and Billy Baldwin designs one for himself on Nantucket Island. Tod Williams designs New York offices for the investment banking firm B.E.A. Emilio Ambasz designs offices for Banque Bruxelles Lambert in Milan. Eva Jiricna designs her first in a series of Joseph shops in London. Kips Bay Decorator Showhouse rooms are designed by Richard Ridge, Noel Jeffrey, Juan Montoya, Samuel Botero, and Georgina Fairholme. Van Day Truex dies at age seventy-five and is succeeded as design director of Tiffany & Co. by Walter Hoving.

EXHIBITIONS

An exhibition at the Hayward Gallery, London, reviews design of the '30s. Also in London, Eileen Gray is the subject of an exhibition at the Victoria & Albert.

FURNITURE AND FURNISHINGS

Antonio Citterio and Paolo Nava design the "Diesis" sofa for B&B Italia. Emilio Ambasz and Giancarlo Piretti design the "Vertebra" seating line for Open Ark; it will be sold by Cassina, and in 1981, it will be awarded the Compasso d'Oro. David Rowland designs the "Sof-Tech" chair with vinyl-coated steel springs for Thonet. Robert Heritage designs the "Tipster" stacking/linking chair for Race. In Paris, designer Andrée Putman founds Écart International, a furniture company for the re-edition of 1930s designs by Jean-Michel Frank, Eileen Gray, Robert Mallet-Stevens, René Herbst, Pierre Chareau, and others. Bill Stumpf and Don Chadwick produce the first version of their "Equa" flexible plastic chair for Herman Miller; its development will last five years.

Sunar showrooms spread pox of postmodernism

Also for Herman Miller, Chadwick designs the "C-Forms" desk system. Michele De Lucchi and Ettore Sottsass, Jr., are design consultants to Olivetti for its "Synthesis" office system. Giandomenico Belotti's "Spaghetti" chair strung with PVC is produced by Alias and will be imported to the United States by ICF. Enzo Mari designs the "Delfina" chair for Driade and "Elementale" tiles for Gabbianelli. Castigliani's "Metafora 1" table, designed by Massimo and Lella Vignelli, is a glass top resting on a cube, a sphere, a cylinder, and a pyramid; the Vignellis also design the "Acorn" and "Rotonda" chairs for Sunar. Angelo Donghia opens a new showroom in Miami.

GOVERNMENT EVENTS

Control of the Panama Canal passes from the United States to Panama.

HONORS AND AWARDS

ASID institutes its Designer of Distinction award, and the first recipient is William Pahlmann. Professor Arnold Friedmann of the University of Massachusetts, Amherst, receives a Design Project Fellowship from the National Endowment for the Arts.

MAGAZINES

Winterthur Portfolio is founded, as is the English magazine *Design Studies*. The Italian magazine *Abitare* institutes a U.S. supplement called *Abitare in America*, but it will publish only four issues.

PROGRESS IN THE PROFESSION

The International Society of Interior Designers (ISID) is founded in Los Angeles. The Parsons School of Design, New York, merges with the Otis Art Institute, Los Angeles. In France, the ministry of industry establishes VIA (Valorisation de l'Innovation dans l'Ameublement) to promote modern furniture design.

TECHNICAL AND SCIENTIFIC ADVANCES

Post-It Notes make their first appearance. The global volume of plastics production exceeds the volume of steel production, and the "Plastics Age" begins.

1979

Antonio Citterio and Paolo Nava's "Diesis" sofa for B&B Italia

Richard Meier's Atheneum at New Harmony, Indiana

Anna Castelli Ferrieri's stool for Kartell

Another view of Meier's Atheneum

THE '80s

Challenges to modernism continue. In 1980, Alessandro Mendini's "Kandissi" chair for Studio Alchymia and his *Banal Object* exhibition at the Venice Biennale are manifestations of the "anti-design" attitude now prevalent in Italian design. The following year's debut of the Memphis group will strengthen the trend, at least temporarily. A different, more animalistic sort of "anti-design" is seen in Paris, where painter Gérard Garouste and designers Elizabeth Garouste and Mattia Bonetti design Le Privilège restaurant in 1981 and show their *objets primitifs* and *objets barbares* in a Louis XVI setting at the interior design firm House of Jansen. Computerization also continues. *Interior Design* magazine reports in 1983 that "about one third" of its one hundred "Interior Design Giants" (the firms reporting the largest volumes of work) now "have some sort of sophisticated CADD (Computer Aided Drafting and Design) system." An attempt to encourage interior design professional organizations to work in concert comes in 1983, when *Interior Design* invites the groups' leaders to meet for a day of discussion. Present at the meeting are: Jay Hines, ASID student president; Lyman Johnson, chair of the FIDER Board of Trustees; Sandra Ragan, vice president of IBD; Stacy Simmons, chair of the AIA Interiors Committee; Louis Tregre, chair of the NCIDQ; Ronald Veitch, president of the IDEC; and William Richards Whaley, president of the ASID. The leaders' meetings will become a regular event and will eventually grow into larger meetings called "issues forums." Pulling the profession together in a more entertaining way is the establishment in 1985, at the suggestion of *Interior Design* publisher Lester Dundes, of a hall of fame dinner honoring designers and benefiting the Foundation for Interior Design Education Research. The event will be held annually at the Waldorf-Astoria ballroom through the end of the century.

Andrée Putman's 1985 Paris office for French minister of culture Jack Lang

ARCHITECTURE

The second winner of the Pritzker prize is Luis Barragán of Mexico. Helmut Jahn's State of Illinois building is built in Chicago, and Michael Graves's Portland Public Services Building is designed for Portland, Oregon. In Eureka Springs, Arkansas, Fay Jones designs the Thorncrown Chapel.

BOOKS

Edgar de N. Mayhew and Minor Myers, Jr., write *A Documentary History of American Interiors from the Colonial Era to 1915.* Textile designer Edmund Rossbach writes *The Art of Paisley.* Marian Page writes *Furniture Designs by Architects.* Philippe Garner writes *Twentieth-Century Furniture* and *The Contemporary Decorative Arts from 1940 to the Present Day.* Erica Brown writes *Interior Views: Design at Its Best.* Van Day Truex's *Interiors: Character and Color* is published posthumously.

CULTURE AT LARGE

The Metropolitan Museum of Art, New York, presents an exhibition of the paintings of Clyfford Still; Still dies a few months later. Ted Turner establishes the Cable News Network. A Pablo Picasso retrospective is at New York's Museum of Modern Art.

DESIGNERS AND INSTALLATIONS

The former oceanliner *France* is rechristened the SS *Norway* and is given one of Angelo Donghia's last designs. Louis M. S. Beal designs interiors for the American Academy of Arts and Sciences, Cambridge, Massachusetts, by Kallmann, McKinnell, & Wood. Designers for the Kips Bay Decorator Showhouse include Rubén de Saavedra, Robert Metzger, Gary Crain, and Keith Irvine & Thomas Fleming. Piero Fornasetti opens his "Themes and Variations" shop/studio in London. Naomi Leff opens her own office in New York. Gae Aulenti begins her renovation of Paris's Gare d'Orsay, to be completed in 1987. In Milan, Ettore Sottsass, Jr., and others form Sottsass Associati. Andrée Putman begins designing a series of four U.S. boutiques for Karl Lagerfeld and fifteen for Yves Saint Laurent. Michael

Taylor designs a New York showroom for Ralph Lauren Western Wear, and John Saladino designs a New York showroom for Thonet. Antti Nurmesniemi begins a restoration of Eliel Saarinen's 1914 Helsinki Railway Terminus. Robert Hutchinson transforms an 1880 Victorian house in San Francisco for modern use, and Joseph D'Urso does the same for a 1930s house in Los Angeles. Adam Tihany designs a New York apartment for himself. Sarah Tomerlin Lee of Tom Lee Ltd. designs the Parker Meridien Hotel, New York. Phyllis Lambert and Gene Summers, with designer Marcia Johnson, renovate the 1923 Los Angeles Biltmore, using furniture by Ludwig Mies van der Rohe and art by Jim Dine.

EXHIBITIONS

For the Cooper-Hewitt, National Design Museum, New York, Bernard Rudofsky curates *Now I Lay Me Down to Eat,* examining the dining posture of the Romans and other matters. The furniture designs of Vladimir Kagan are seen in *Three Decades of Design* at New York's Fashion Institute of Technology. The Cranbrook Academy of Art shows the work of a graduate, Niels Diffrient. The Parsons School of Design presents a retrospective of twenty years of work by Massimo and Lella Vignelli. The Victoria & Albert's Eileen Gray exhibition comes to New York's Museum of Modern Art. The *Stile floreale* design of Eugenio Quarti is shown in Milan.

John Saladino designer of the year

Gaetano Pesce's "Manhattan Sunrise" sofa for Castelli imitates a Manhattan skyline; for Cassina, Pesce designs the "Sansone" tables and the "Dalila" armchairs. Peter Danko designs a one-piece molded-plywood armchair for Thonet. Poul Kjærholm dies at age fifty-one, his last design an armchair with a frame of steam-bent wood. Achille Castiglioni designs the "Gibigiana" lamp for Flos, and Gae Aulenti designs the "Parola" lamp for Fontana Arte. Ingo Maurer designs "Bulb Bulb," a lighting fixture larger than his 1966 "Bulb." Toshiyuki Kita designs the "Wink" chairs and chaises for Cassina; Antti Nurmesniemi designs the "004" chairs for Vuokko; Peter Opsvik designs the "Variable" rocking chair for Stokke; Bruce Burdick designs the "Burdick Group" for Herman Miller; Gae Aulenti designs a glass coffeetable with wheels for Fontane Arte, Milan. DePas, D'Urbino, & Lomazzi design the "Grand'Italia" sofa for Zanotta. Spanish designer Oscar Tusquets Blanca designs the "Hypóstila" shelving for Ediciones de Diseño. French designer Martin Szekely designs the "Coin" collection in wood and aluminum for Skina and the "Cornette" chair in black carbon steel for Galerie Néotù, Paris. Pierre Paulin designs the "Dangari" polypropylene outdoor stacking chair for Stamp. Joseph D'Urso designs the "D'Urso Collection" for Knoll.

Diplomatic ties are established between the United States and China.

Emilio Ambasz's "Logotec" lighting wins the American National Industrial Design Award. *Interiors* magazine names its first Designer of the Year: John Saladino. Bill Stumpf is named Designer of the 1970s by *Industrial Design* magazine. The ASID names Everett Brown its Designer of Distinction.

A directory of U.S. design firms (including interior design, graphic design, and product design) is published by Wefler & Associates, Chicago; it lists seven hundred firms.

In Washington State, Mount St. Helens erupts. American space shuttles bring new discoveries about Saturn's moons and the surfaces of Mars and Venus.

1980

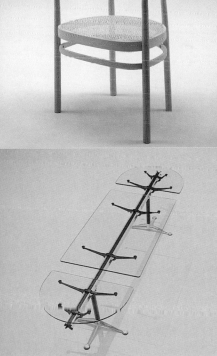

From left to right:

The Eileen Gray exhibition at the Museum of Modern Art, New York

The atrium of Helmut Jahn's State of Illinois building, Chicago

Lobby, Parker Meridien Hotel, New York, by Sarah Tomerlin Lee of Tom Lee Ltd.

Poul Kjærholm's armchair with a frame of steam-bent wood and a seat of woven cane

Glass-topped table elements from the "Burdick Group" for Herman Miller

ARCHITECTURE

Marcel Breuer dies at age seventy-nine. The Pritzker prize is given to James Stirling of Great Britain. Norman Foster designs the Hong Kong and Shanghai Bank headquarters in Hong Kong; it will be finished five years later. Tadao Ando designs the Koshino house near Kobe, Japan. Mario Botta designs a cylindrical house at Stabio, Switzerland.

BOOKS

Victoria Kloss Ball's *Architecture and Interior Design* is published in two volumes. Christopher Wilk writes *Marcel Breuer: Furniture and Interiors.* David Hanks writes *Innovative Furniture in America.* William Turner advises *How to Work with an Interior Designer.* Eric Larrabee writes and Massimo Vignelli designs *Knoll Design.*

CULTURE AT LARGE

Umberto Eco's *The Name of the Rose* is an international best-seller. Claes Oldenburg's thirty-eight-foot *Flashlight* is erected at the University of Nevada in Reno.

DESIGNERS AND INSTALLATIONS

Benjamin Baldwin, with the help of Roger Ferri, designs the interiors of the Americana Hotel in Fort Worth, Texas. Coop Himmelblau designs the Roter Engle (Red Angel) Music Bar in Vienna. Designing rooms for the Kips Bay Decorator Showhouse are Ellen Lehmann McCluskey, Georgina Fairholme, Angelo Donghia, John F. Saladino, and Noel Jeffrey. Ted Graber, a former partner of the late William Haines, redesigns the family quarters of the White House for Ronald and Nancy Reagan. Krueck and Olsen design a Chicago showroom for Thonet. Charles Pfister opens his own office in San Francisco.

EXHIBITIONS

In Paris, the Musée des Arts Décoratifs presents an exhibition of the work of Jack Lenor Larsen; the accompanying catalog, written by François Mathey, Mildred Constantine, and others, is *Jack Lenor Larsen: 30 Years of Creative Textiles.* The Fashion Institute of Technology, New York, shows *Boris Kroll—Tapestries and Textiles.*

FURNITURE AND FURNISHINGS

The "Memphis" movement is first introduced at this year's Salone del Mobile, and it will continue until 1988; first introductions include the "Lido" sofa by Michele De Lucchi, the "Hilton" teacart by Javier Mariscal, and—all by Ettore Sottsass, Jr.—the "Carlton" bookcase, "Mandarin" table, and "Casablanca" and "Beverly" cabinets. Vico Magistretti designs the blanket-draped "Sinbad" armchair for Cassina. Angelo Mangiarotti designs the "Asolo" granite table for Skipper. Giotto Stoppino and Ludovico Acerbis design the "Madison" shelving system for Acerbis. Marco Zanini designs the "Dublin" sofa. John Saladino designs the "Pavilion" sofa, the "Papyrus" chair, and the "Sectioned Column" table.

Paris draped in Larsen fabric

Gretchen Bellinger introduces her "Isadora" pleated silk. King & Miranda design the "Airmail" chair for Marcatré. Peter Opsvik designs the "Balans Variable" ergonomic stool for Stokke Fabrikker. French artist François Bauchet designs a lacquered wood piece called "It's Also a Chair." In London, Robin Day designs the "Hadrian" seating line for the lobbies of the new Barbican Centre; it will be marketed by Hille.

There is an assassination attempt against Pope John Paul II at St. Peter's.

Emilio Ambasz's "Vertebra" seating wins the Compasso d'Oro. *Interiors* magazine's second annual Designer of the Year is Michael Graves. The ASID's third Designer of Distinction is Barbara D'Arcy. The Parsons School of Design gives an honorary doctorate to Jack Lenor Larsen.

Beginning publication are *The World of Interiors* in England, and *Form and Function* in Finland.

The American Society of Furniture Designers is founded "to advance and improve the profession of furniture design."

First successful surgery on an unborn baby is performed.

1981

From left to right:

Ettore Sottsass, Jr.'s "Carlton" bookcase/room divider, part of the "Memphis" collection

Charles Pfister

Krueck and Olsen's Thonet showroom in Chicago's Merchandise Mart

Vico Magistretti's "Sinbad" chairs for Cassina

Ellen Lehmann McCluskey's room at the Kips Bay Decorator Showhouse, New York

ARCHITECTURE

The Vietnam Veterans' Memorial in Washington, D.C. is designed by Maya Lin. Kevin Roche is awarded the Pritzker Prize. The Atlantis apartment building is designed in Miami by Arquitectonica. Renzo Piano is commissioned to design the Menil Collection museum in Houston. The Haj Terminal at the King Abdul Aziz International Airport in Jeddah, Saudi Arabia, is designed by Skidmore, Owings, & Merrill.

BOOKS

FIDER publishes *The Study of Two-, Three-, and Four-Year Interior Design Programs in the United States and Canada* by Kate E. Rogers and others. Erica Brown (no relation to Eleanor McMillen Brown) writes a book celebrating *Sixty Years of Interior Design: The World of McMillen*. Werner Blaser writes *Mies van der Rohe: Furniture and Interiors*, and Eduard F. Sekler writes *Josef Hoffmann*. Philippe Garner writes *The Encyclopedia of Decorative Arts, 1890–1940*. Barbaralee Diamonstein writes *Interior Design: The New Freedom*; her subjects are Ward Bennett, Robert Bray and Michael Schaible, Mario Buatta, Angelo Donghia, Joseph D'Urso, Mark Hampton, Sarah Tomerlin Lee, Warren Platner, John Saladino, Robert A. M. Stern, and Massimo and Lella Vignelli.

CULTURE AT LARGE

Alice Walker writes *The Color Purple*. Michael Jackson's album *Thriller* is a superhit.

DESIGNERS AND INSTALLATIONS

California designer John Dickinson dies at age sixty-two. Vignelli Associates designs the Hauserman showroom in Los Angeles with fluorescent-light artwork by sculptor Dan Flavin. In Paris, Philippe Starck designs the president's apartment and offices in the Élysée Palace, and other rooms there are designed by Ronald-Cécil Sportes and Jean-Michel Wilmotte. In London, Eva Jiricna designs the restaurant Le Caprice and does interior design studies for Richard Rogers's Lloyd's of London project, including the design of the Captain's Room restaurant. In Hong Kong, Joseph D'Urso designs the I Club. In Paris, Gae Aulenti designs interiors for the Musée d'Art Moderne. In Chicago's Merchandise Mart, Arata Isozaki designs a showroom for E. F. Hauserman and Robert A. M. Stern designs one for Shaw-Walker. Bromley Jacobsen designs the Allied Fibers showroom in Atlanta. George Ranalli renovates the Callender School in Newport, Rhode Island. In New York, Piero Sartogo and Michael Schwarting design interiors for the Italian Trade Center, and Alan Buchsbaum designs an apartment for Diane Keaton. Sarah Tomerlin Lee of Tom Lee Ltd. designs interiors for I. M. Pei's Warwick Post Oak hotel in Houston. Skidmore, Owings, & Merrill designs the Kuwait Chancery in Washington, with Michael McCarthy the partner in charge, Paul Vieyra the senior designer, and Davis Allen the interior designer. Designers for Kips Bay's tenth-anniversary Decorator Showhouse include Mariette Himes Gomez, Zajac & Callahan, and Richard L. Ridge.

EXHIBITIONS

Italian Re-Evolution is at the La Jolla Museum of Art, California. *Scandinavian Modern: 1880–1980* is at the Cooper-Hewitt, National Design Museum, New York. *At Home in Manhattan: Modern Decorative Arts, 1925 to the Depression* is at the Yale University Art Gallery, New Haven, Connecticut. *Design since 1945*, with exhibition design by George Nelson, is at the Philadelphia Museum of Art. *Art and Industry* is at the Boilerhouse Project of the Victoria & Albert, London. Alexander Girard designs the installation of his own collection in the Museum of International Folk Art, Santa Fe, New Mexico.

Carlos Riart designs a rocking chair for Casas; it will be sold in the United States through Knoll. Philippe Starck designs the "Pratfall" and "Costes" chairs for Driade. For Castelli, Charles Pollock designs the "Penelope" chair. Mario Botta's "Prima" side chair, "Seconda" armchair, and "Terzo" table are all produced by Alias and available in the United States through ICF. Svein Gusrud designs the "Balans Activ" chair for Busse. The "Icarus" office furniture line by Ettore Sottsass, Jr., and Michele De Lucchi is designed for Olivetti, and Paolo Piva's "Alanda" glass table for B&B Italia. John Saladino designs the "Corolla" chair, and Harvey Probber the "Oval Arm" seating group. Frank Gehry designs his first "Fish" light for Formica ColorCore plastic laminate.

Great Britain and Argentina are at war over the Falkland Islands.

Orlando Diaz-Azcuy is the *Interiors* magazine Designer of the Year. Edward Wormley is the ASID Designer of Distinction. The Decorators Club gives its medal of honor to Sarah Tomerlin Lee.

Facilities Design and Management magazine begins publication.

The Domus Academy is founded in Milan, with Andrea Branzi its first director. The American Institute of Kitchen Dealers changes its name to the National Kitchen and Bath Association. Alabama is the first state to pass an interior designer certification law, requiring passage of the NCIDQ exam in order to use the title "interior designer."

The first cordless telephone is produced.

Designer certification a reality

1982

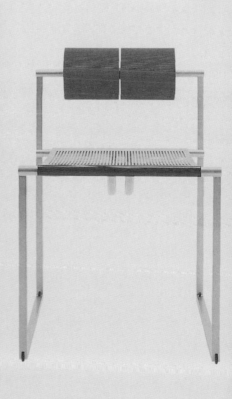

From left to right:

The Kuwait Chancery, Washington, D.C., by Michael McCarthy, Paul Vieyra, and Davis Allen of SOM

Paolo Piva's "Alanda" table for B&B Italia

"Oval Arm" seating by Harvey Probber

Mario Botta's "Prima" chair for ICF

ARCHITECTURE

On adjacent blocks of Manhattan's Madison Avenue, Philip Johnson designs the AT&T building and Edward Larrabee Barnes the IBM building. In Venice, California, Frank Gehry designs the Norton house. The Pritzker prize goes to I. M. Pei. Gordon Bunshaft of Skidmore, Owings, & Merrill designs the National Commercial Bank in Jeddah, Saudi Arabia. Zaha Hadid wins a competition for the design of the Peak, a private club and residential complex in Hong Kong. Richard Meier designs the High Museum, Atlanta.

BOOKS

The Interior Design Educators Council publishes *Interior Design as a Profession*. Victor Papanek writes *Design for Human Scale*. Charles McCorquodale writes *A History of Interior Decoration*. Andrew Loebelson advises *How to Profit in Contract Design*. Barbara Radice chronicles the work of *Memphis*. John Pile and Norman Diekman write *Drawing Interior Architecture*. Robert Judson Clark and others edit *Design in America: The Cranbrook Vision, 1925–1953*. Sherman Emery writes *Styled for Living*. Carleton Varney writes his *ABC's of Decorating*, covering subjects from "acanthus" and "accessories" to "zoological designs" and "zwiebmuster."

CULTURE AT LARGE

Rudolf Nureyev becomes director of the Paris Opera Ballet. Paul Taylor choreographs *Sunset*. Mark Helprin writes *Winter's Tale*. *A Chorus Line* becomes the longest-running Broadway show.

DESIGNERS AND INSTALLATIONS

Billy Baldwin dies at age eighty. John Saladino designs a Christian Science reading room in Greenwich, Connecticut. In Chicago, Krueck and Olsen design "The Painted Apartment." Sarah Tomerlin Lee of Tom Lee Ltd. designs the Sheraton Russell hotel, New York. Contributing room designs to the Kips Bay Decorator Showhouse are Melvin Dwork, Scruggs-Myers, Braswell-Willoughby, and Michael de Santis. De Santis also designs executive offices for Petra in Tulsa, Oklahoma.

EXHIBITIONS

The work of Ernö Goldfinger is shown at the Architectural Association, London. The work of Gerrit Rietveld is shown at the Central Museum, Utrecht. The textile designs of Angelo Testa are seen in Chicago. *Carlo Scarpa et le musée de Vérone* is seen in Paris. The Victoria & Albert, London, exhibits *Taste*.

FURNITURE AND FURNISHINGS

Brian Kane designs the "Rubber" chair for Metropolitan; Davis Allen of Skidmore, Owings, & Merrill designs the "Andover" chair for Stendig; Charles Pfister's concrete wall sconce is introduced by Boyd Lighting. Beylerian offers the "Bistro Table" designed by Anna Castelli Ferrieri and manufactured by Kartell. Cini Boeri designs the "Pacific" sofa and loveseat and the "Malibu" table, all for Arflex. Gae Aulenti designs the "Cardine" table for Zanotta. Andrée Putman designs the "Entrepôts Lainé" collection for Tectona. Massimo Morozzi designs the "Tangram" table for Cassina. Pierre Sala designs the "Clairefontaine" desk for his own company, Furnitur. Aldo Rossi designs the "Cabina dell'Elba"

Professional leaders meet

wardrobe for Molteni. Giotto Stoppino and Ludovico Acerbis design the "Menhir" group of marble tables for Acerbis. Vico Magistretti designs the "Veranda 3" sofa for Cassina. Arata Isozaki designs the curvaceous "Monroe" chair, produced by Tendo Mekko. Oscar Tusquets Blanca designs the "Varius" armchair for Casas. Toshiyuki Kita designs the "Kick" table for Cassina. Alessi hires eleven architects and designers to create coffee and tea services; they are: Charles Jencks, Michael Graves, Hans Hollein, Richard Meier, Alessandro Mendini, Paolo Portoghesi, Aldo Rossi, Stanley Tigerman, Oscar Tusquets Blanca, Robert Venturi, and Kasumasa Yamashita. Jean-Michel Wilmotte designs the "Cylindre" chair. For Memphis,

Michele De Lucchi designs the "First" chair, Ettore Sottsass, Jr., designs the "City" and "Park Lane" tables and the "Schizzo" and "Lettraset" fabrics, and Nathalie du Pasquier designs the "Royal" chaise longue.

Interiors names Joseph Rosen its Designer of the Year. The ASID names Edward J. Perrault its Designer of Distinction. The International Association of Lighting Designers begins its annual Awards for Excellence in Lighting Design. Charlotte Perriand is named a chevalier of the French Legion of Honor.

Design Book Review is first published, as is *Design Issues. American Institute of Architects Journal* is renamed *Architecture. House and Garden* is redesigned and repositioned.

Interior Design calls for an all-day meeting of leaders of various interior design professional organizations; such meetings will become regular events. Connecticut is the second state to certify interior designers.

The HIV virus is identified.

1983

From left to right:

Bench from the "Entrepôts Lainé" collection by Andrée Putman for Tectona

Davis Allen in his "Andover" chair for Stendig

Chicago apartment by Krueck and Olsen

Massimo Morozzi's "Tangram" table for Cassina

Richard Meier's High Museum, Atlanta

ARCHITECTURE

Richard Meier is the winner of the sixth annual Pritzker prize and designs a decorative arts museum in Frankfurt, West Germany. James Stirling's *Neue Staatsgalerie* is opened in Stuttgart. SITE designs a "deconstructed" outlet for Best Products in Milwaukee.

BOOKS

Jim Morgan writes *Marketing for the Small Design Firm*. NCIDQ publishes *The Interior Design Practice: Qualifying Factors of Competent Practice* by D. Hardy and others. William L. Pulgram and Richard E. Stonis write *Designing the Automated Office*. Michael Brill and others publish volume one of *Using Office Design to Increase Productivity*; volume two will be published the following year. Peter Thronton writes *Authentic Décor*. Isabelle Anscombe writes *A Woman's Touch: Women in Design from 1860 to the Present Day*. British furniture designer and manufacturer Jack Pritchard, who founded Isokon in 1931, writes the autobiographical *View from a Long Chair*. Edie Cohen and Sherman Emery write *Dining by Design*.

CULTURE AT LARGE

Eudora Welty writes a memoir, *One Writer's Beginnings*. Czech novelist Milan Kundera writes *The Unbearable Lightness of Being*.

DESIGNERS AND INSTALLATIONS

Mark Hampton is at work on the restoration of the interiors of Gracie Mansion, the residence of the mayor of New York, and on Blair House in Washington, D.C. Philippe Starck designs Café Costes in Paris. Andrée Putman designs Restaurant CAPC at the Centre d'Art Plastique Contemporain in Bordeaux. Geoffrey Bennison designs an apartment for himself in the Mayfair section of London. Charles Pfister designs Square One restaurant in San Francisco. SITE designs a New York clothing showroom for WilliWear. Alan Buchsbaum designs New York apartments for Ellen Barkin and Bette Midler. Ettore Sottsass, Jr., designs the Grace Designs furniture showroom in Dallas. Bromley Jacobsen designs a showroom for Allied Fibers in Dallas. Michael Graves designs a New York boutique for Diane Von Furstenberg. Angelo Donghia, in the last year of his life, designs the Intercontinental Hotel in New Orleans. Kips Bay Decorator Showhouse designers include Bromley Jacobsen, Samuel Botero, Sandra Nunnerly, and Dexter Design. The first "Design New York" market is sponsored by the Resources Council Inc. Swid Powell presents its first tableware collection with designs by Gwathmey Siegel, Richard Meier, Robert A. M. Stern, Stanley Tigerman and Margaret McCurry, Arata Isozaki, and Laurinda Spear. Jean-Michel Wilmotte designs an office for the French ambassador in Washington, D.C.

EXHIBITIONS

Design in America: The Cranbrook Vision, 1925–1950 opens at the Metropolitan Museum of Art, New York. The work of Carlo Scarpa is seen in a Venice exhibition designed by Mario Botta. The Musée des Arts Décoratifs, Montreal, shows the work of Gaetano Pesce and assembles the traveling exhibition *Eva Zeisel: Designer for Industry*.

DIFFA fights AIDS

FURNITURE AND FURNISHINGS

Niels Diffrient designs his "Helena" and "Jefferson" chairs for Sunar Hauserman, a recent affiliation of Sunar Furniture and Hauserman Movable Walls. Herman Miller introduces its "Ethospace" office panel system designed by Bill Stumpf and Don Chadwick. Knoll introduces a line of bent-plywood furniture by Robert Venturi—nine chairs, a sofa, and three tables—that parody Sheraton, Queen Anne, and other historical styles. Davis Allen designs the "Bridgehampton" tables and chairs for Stendig. Alan Buchsbaum begins a series of rug designs for V'Soske. Jean-Michel Wilmotte designs the "Élysée" stool. Hans Hollein designs the "Mitzi" sofa for Poltronova. Ferdinand Alexander Porsche designs the "IP48S" aluminum and leather lounge chair for Inter Profil, Munich. Hans Wegner designs a rocking chair with a woven rope back for PP Møbler ApS. Gae Aulenti designs the "Sanmarco" table for Zanotta. Vico Magistretti designs the "Idomeneo" lamp for O-Luce. Emilio Ambasz and Giancarlo Piretti design low-voltage lighting for Erco. Ingo Maurer designs the "Ya Ya Ho" low-voltage lighting system on suspended cables. Diego Giacometti designs furniture and lighting for the Picasso Museum, Paris.

HONORS AND AWARDS

Interiors chooses Raul de Armas of Skidmore, Owings, & Merrill as its Designer of the Year. The ASID names Michael Taylor its Designer of Distinction.

MAGAZINES

Industrial Design changes its name to *International Design*, but is chiefly identified as *I.D.*, confusing some readers of *Interior Design*. *The Designer* changes its name to *The Designer/Specifier*. On *Interior Design*'s annual listing of "Giants," Gensler & Associates moves into first place (as determined by volume of work) and stays there through the end of the century. Mark Hampton begins writing a monthly decorating column for *House and Garden*.

PROGRESS IN THE PROFESSION

IDEC updates its 1968 "Comprehensive Bibliography for Interior Design"; the new version is edited by Betty McKee Treanor and John Garstka. Lousiana is the third state requiring interior designer certification. The Design Industries Foundation for AIDS (DIFFA) is established by Larry Pond of Stendig furniture, Patricia Green of Groundworks fabrics, and others in the interior design field; it will broaden to include members from the fields of architecture, graphics, and fashion, and its name will be changed to Design Industries Foundation *Fighting* AIDS.

TECHNICAL AND SCIENTIFIC ADVANCES

Sony and Philips introduce the CD-ROM. Hewlett-Packard introduces the desktop laser printer.

1984

From left to right:

Bill Stumpf and Don Chadwick's "Ethospace" system for Herman Miller

Gae Aulenti's "Sanmarco" table for Zanotta

Andrée Putman's Restaurant CAPC, Bordeaux

WilliWear showroom, New York, by SITE

Scott Bromley

Robert Venturi's "Sheraton" chair for Knoll

ARCHITECTURE

Hans Hollein of Austria is awarded the Pritzker prize. Bart Prince builds a house for himself in Albuquerque. Near Sydney, Australia, Glenn Murcutt designs the Berowra Waters Inn. Tod Williams and Billie Tsien design a house in Southport, New York. Richard Gluckman designs the Dia Art Foundation in New York. Michael Graves's proposed addition to Marcel Breuer's 1966 Whitney Museum stirs protest.

BOOKS

Billy Baldwin: An Autobiography (as told to Michael Gardine) is published posthumously; one chapter heading quotes his mentor Ruby Ross Wood: "Billy is small, but his sting is deep." Also published is *High Style: Twentieth Century American Design* by David Gebhard, Esther McCoy, and others. John Pile and Norman Diekman write *Sketching Interior Architecture.* Joseph T. Butler writes a *Field Guide to American Antique Furniture.* Herman Miller publishes *The Negotiable Environment: People, White-Collar Work, and the Office. The International Design Yearbook* is edited by Robert A.M. Stern; a new edition, with a new editor each year, will be published through the end of the century.

CULTURE AT LARGE

Paul Taylor choreographs *Last Look* and *Roses.* Madonna records the album *Like a Virgin.* In Paris, Christo wraps the Pont Neuf in nylon fabric.

DESIGNERS AND INSTALLATIONS

Powell/Kleinschmidt designs the Northwestern University Law School, and partner Donald Powell designs his own apartment in Ludwig Mies van der Rohe's 860 Lake Shore Drive, Chicago. SITE designs interiors for the Laurie Mallet house in New York. Steven Holl designs the New York shop/show-room for the Pace Collection. Tigerman Fugman McCurry designs the Herman Miller show-room in Chicago. Cini Boeri designs the Knoll show-room in Milan. Joseph D'Urso designs the Esprit clothing store in Los Angeles, and Ettore Sottsass, Jr., and Aldo Cibic design Esprit showrooms in Hamburg, Düsseldorf, and Zurich. Charles Pfister designs headquarters for Deutsche Bank in Frankfurt, West Germany, and the Grand Hotel in Washington, D.C. Also in Washington, Allan Greenberg renovates offices and reception rooms for the U.S. Department of State. Hardy, Holzman, Pfeiffer designs a New York bookstore for Rizzoli. Bromley Jacobsen designs the Cohen Brothers realty office in New York. On New York's Madison Avenue, Naomi Leff converts the 1898 Rhinelander château into a flagship store for Ralph Lauren, the first of her dozen stores for the same client. Kevin Walz designs the Ricci II shoe store in New York. Alan Buchsbaum designs three New York shops for Ecco Shoes and a New York apartment for Billy Joel and Christie Brinkley. Adam Tihany designs the Alo-Alo restaurant in New York, as well as Le Papillon night-club in Boston. Donghia Associates designs the Natori clothing showroom in New York. Kips Bay Decorator Showhouse designers include Mario Buatta, Tom O'Toole, Barbara Ostrom, and Juan-Pablo Molyneux. In Los Angeles, Gensler Associates designs a show-room for Steelcase. In Paris, Andrée Putman designs an office for French minister of culture Jack Lang, and in New York, with Arata Isozaki, the Palladium nightclub and, with Haigh Space Design, Morgan's, the first of the city's "designer boutique" hotels. Warren Platner designs guest rooms and the Wildflower restaurant for a ski resort in Vail, Colorado. In Atlanta, Michael Graves designs the Carlos Museum of Art and Archaeology for Emory University, and Henry Jova of Jova, Daniels, Busby designs his own house. In Japan, Nigel Coates designs the Metropole Café, Tokyo, and the Hotel Marittimo, Otaru.

Lester Dundes institutes *Interior Design* Magazine Hall of Fame

EXHIBITIONS

An exhibition of chairs, *La Chaise: Objet du Design ou d'architecture*, is seen at the Centre de Création et de Diffusion, Montreal. The work of Paolo Portoghesi is seen in Modena, Italy. The furniture designs of Charlotte Perriand are seen at the Musée des Arts Décoratifs, Paris.

FURNITURE AND FURNISHINGS

The "Serenissimo" table is designed for Acerbis International by Lella and Massimo Vignelli and David Law. The "Wintour" table is designed for Écart by Alan Buchsbaum. Kirk White designs a collection of upholstered pieces for Lee Jofa Furniture. Gretchen Bellinger introduces her "Diva" silks, as well as "Ausable" eelskin. Enzo Mari designs the "Tonietta" chair for Zanotta. Alberto Meda and Paolo Rizzatto design the "Berenice" lamp for Luceplan. Ron Arad designs the "Rover" chair and the "Well-Tempered Chair" for Vitra. Orlando Diaz-Azcuy designs an extensive seating line for Hickory Business Furniture. Alvaro Siza designs the "Flamingo" halogen lamp for Ediciones de Diseño. Gae Aulenti designs the "Jumbo" table for Knoll.

HONORS AND AWARDS

The *Interiors* magazine Designer of the Year is Francisco Kripacz. The ASID's Designer of Distinction is Norman DeHaan. At the suggestion of Lester Dundes, publisher of *Interior Design*, an event benefiting the Foundation for Interior Design Education Research initiates the Interior Design Magazine Hall of Fame; charter members are: Davis B. Allen, Benjamin Baldwin, Florence Knoll Bassett, Mario Buatta, Barbara D'Arcy, Henry End, M. Arthur Gensler, Jr., Richard Himmel, Melanie Kahane, Lawrence Lerner, "Sister" Parish, Warren Platner, John Saladino, Michael Taylor, and Kenneth Walker; special awards go to Paige Rense, editor in chief of *Architectural Digest*, and to recently deceased Angelo Donghia.

MAGAZINES

Professional Office Design magazine is founded. *Blueprint* magazine (London) names Philippe Starck "the world's hottest designer."

PROGRESS IN THE PROFESSION

The Foundation for Interior Design Education Research establishes "Standards and Guidelines for the Accreditation of Post-Professional Master's Degree Programs." The Association for Contract Textiles is formed and will publish performance guidelines for the specifying of fabrics.

TECHNICAL AND SCIENTIFIC ADVANCES

Optical fibers are used to link computers. Microsoft introduces Windows.

1985

From left to right:

Gretchen Bellinger's "Diva" fabric of silk satin, sprinkled with what seem to be rhinestones and small pearls

Apartment at 860 Lake Shore Drive, Chicago, designed for himself by Donald Powell of Powell/Kleinschmidt

Interior Design magazine's legendary publisher Lester Dundes

Arthur Gensler, principal of the most sucessful interior design firm of the century's final quarter

Hong Kong Club, Hong Kong, by Harry Seidler

Tadao Ando designs the Mount Rokko wedding chapel in Kobe, Japan. Richard Rogers's headquarters for Lloyd's of London is built. Rafael Moneo designs the National Museum of Roman Art in Merida, Spain. The Pritzker prize goes to Germany's Gottfried Boehm.

Allen Tate and C. Ray Smith collaborate on *Interior Design in the Twentieth Century*. Penny Sparke writes *Twentieth Century Design: Furniture*. Sivon Reznikoff writes *Interior Graphic and Design Standards*. Edgar Kaufmann, jr., writes *Fallingwater: A Frank Lloyd Wright Country House*.

For the lobby of New York's Equitable building, Roy Lichtenstein paints *Mural with Blue Brushstroke*. James Ivory films *A Room with a View*. Vladmir Horowitz gives his first Moscow recital since 1925.

George Nelson dies at age seventy-eight, and Raymond Loewy dies at age ninety-three. Robert Currie designs a showroom for Luten Clarey Stern in New York, and Lee Stout designs a showroom for Knoll in Brussels. Charles Pfister designs headquarters for Shell in The Hague. In Venice, Gae Aulenti converts the Palazzo Grassi into a museum. Alan Buchsbaum designs interiors and furniture for the Nevele Hotel, Ellenville, New York. Gwathmey Siegel designs the Knoll showroom in Chicago. Andrée Putman designs Karl Lagerfeld stores in Paris and New York and a model apartment in New York's Metropolitan Tower. Vignelli Associates designs its own offices in New York. Scott Bromley and Robin Jacobsen of Bromley Jacobsen design their own loft apartment in New York. Owen, Springer, & Mandolfo design the Charles Jourdan Monsieur shop, New York. Clodagh designs executive offices for the American Can Co. New York. Also in New York, Skidmore, Owings, & Merrill designs the Palio restaurant; Raul de Armas is the design partner in charge and Paul Vieyra the senior designer; it employs a mural by Sandro Chia, chair designs by Davis Allen, and graphics and tableware by Vignelli Associates. The Kips Bay Decorator Showhouse, held this year in the former Cass Gilbert townhouse, includes a kitchen design by Florence Perchuk, and an oval sitting room by Kevin McNamara.Following the death of Angelo Donghia at fifty, John Hutton is made design director of Donghia Furniture and Textiles.

The Walker Art Center in Minneapolis shows *The Architecture of Frank Gehry*. The Metropolitan Museum of Art, New York, presents *In Pursuit of Beauty: Americans and the Aesthetic Movement*. The Museum of Modern Art, New York, celebrates the centennial of the birth of Ludwig Mies van der Rohe and recalls *Vienna 1900*. The Brooklyn Museum reviews *The Machine Age*. The Art Gallery at Harbourfront, Toronto, presents *Seduced and Abandoned: Modern Furniture Design in Canada, the First Fifty Years*. The seventeenth Milan Triennale presents *Il Progetto Domestico: The House of Man,* directed by Mario Bellini; contributing designers include George Ranalli, Clino Trini Castelli, John Hejduk, Peter Eisenman, Rochard Sapper, Cini Boeri, Aldo Rossi, and Bellini himself.

MoMA celebrates Mies centennial

FURNITURE AND FURNISHINGS

Knoll introduces the "Handkerchief" chair by Lella and Massimo Vignelli. There is a proliferation of new panel-based office systems, including the "Nomos" system by Norman Foster for Tecno and the "9-to-5" system by Richard Sapper for Castelli. Mario Bellini designs the "Eclipse" spotlight for Erco. John Saladino designs the "Façade Collection" for Baker Furniture. Antonio Citterio and Terry Dwan design the "Sity" modular seating system for B&B Italia. Jean-Michel Wilmotte designs an out door chair for the park of the Palais Royale, Paris. Hans Wegner designs the "Circle" chair. Jasper Morrison designs the "Thinking Man's Chair" for Cappellini. Shiro Kuramata's "How High the Moon," an armchair of expanded metal mesh, is manufactured by Vitra.

GOVERNMENT EVENTS

An accident occurs at a nuclear plant at Chernobyl, Russia.

HONORS AND AWARDS

Charles Pfister is the *Interiors* magazine Designer of the Year. Rita St. Clair is the ASID's Designer of Distinction. Jacques Grange is named a Chevalier of Arts and Letters by the French government. New members of the Interior Design Magazine Hall of Fame are: Marvin B. Affrime, Ward Bennett, Joseph Braswell, Joseph D'Urso, Albert Hadley, Mark Hampton, Howard Hirsch, Sarah Tomerlin Lee, Charles Pfister, Jay Spectre, and Sally Walsh; special honors go to Equitable CEO Benjamin Holloway and Kips Bay Showhouse publicist and coordinator Diantha Nype.

MAGAZINES

Architectural Lighting magazine is established. In Italy, Mario Bellini founds the magazine *Album*.

PROGRESS IN THE PROFESSION

The Home Fashions League begins to admit men as members.

TECHNICAL AND SCIENTIFIC ADVANCES

The U.S. space shuttle *Challenger* explodes seconds after takeoff, killing the crew of seven. Nicotine chewing gum is developed in Sweden.

1986

From left to right:

Antonio Citterio and Terry Dwan's "Sity" seating system for B&B Italia

The "Nomos" office system by Norman Foster for Tecno

Sarah Tomerlin Lee

The Palio restaurant, New York, by Raul de Armas and Paul Vieyra of SOM

The Vignelli office, New York

Hans Wegner's "Circle" chair for PP Møbler

ARCHITECTURE

Kenzo Tange of Japan is awarded the Pritzker prize. Jean Nouvel designs the Institut du Monde Arabe in Paris. Frank Gehry's Winton Guest House in Wayzata, Minnesota, designed in 1982, is completed, as is his Fish Dance restaurant at Kobe, Japan. Hans Hollein begins work on the Museum of Modern Art, Frankfurt; it will be finished in 1991.

BOOKS

FIDER publishes *A Study of Two-Year Para-Professional Interior Design Programs* by Joy Dohr and others. C. Ray Smith writes *Interior Design in Twentieth Century America: A History.* Miriam Stimpson writes *Modern Furniture Classics.* Lance Knobel writes *Office Furniture.* Andrea Branzi writes *Domestic Animals,* revealing that a sofa can be a pet. Sarah Rossbach writes *Interior Design with Feng Shui.* David Hicks's *Style and Design* is published.

CULTURE AT LARGE

Tom Wolfe's *The Bonfire of the Vanities* is a best-seller. Anselm Kiefer's paintings are seen at the Art Institute of Chicago and other museums.

DESIGNERS AND INSTALLATIONS

Alan Buchsbaum dies of AIDS at age fifty-two. In Marrakesh, the venerable Mamounia Hotel is renovated by French designer André Paccard. In London, Ron Arad designs new quarters for One Off, the design studio and workshop he cofounded in 1981, John Pawson designs the Saatchi house, and Eva Jiricna designs the Legends nightclub. In Paris, Garouste and Bonetti design the Géopoly restaurant, offices for Hachette, and interiors and furniture for Christian Lacroix's fashion salon. Andrée Putman renovates Le Corbusier's 1916 Villa Schwob in La Chaux-de-Fonds, Switzerland, designs interiors for Ebel's watch company in London and Basel, and designs regional government offices in Bordeaux, France.

Lynn Wilson redesigns the Biltmore Hotel in Coral Gables, Florida. In Chicago's Merchandise Mart, Tigerman Fugman McCurry designs a new showroom for Formica, Mark Kapka designs one for Metropolitan, and Eva Maddox designs one for Architectural Wall Systems. Powell/Kleinschmidt designs interiors for the Chicago Mercantile Exchange and for the firm's own office in Chicago. In New York, Chicago, and Miami, Massimo and Lella Vignelli design showrooms for Artemide. Orlando Diaz-Azcuy designs the OUI showroom and offices for a surgeon, both in San Francisco. John Saladino designs his own New York showroom and offices for NutraSweet in Deerfield, Illinois. Clodagh designs her own New York apart-

ment, and Juan Montoya designs his own New York office. Afra and Tobia Scarpa design the Benetton corporate headquarters in New York. Charles Pfister redesigns New York's "21" Club. Steven Holl designs the Giada women's clothing store and an apartment in Museum Towers, both in New York. Seen at the Kips Bay Decorator Showhouse are rooms by Juan Montoya, Ronald Bricke, George Constant, and Bilhuber Inc. French designer Marie-Christine Dorner, settled in Tokyo, designs shops and a café for Komatsu; she will return to Paris in 1987. Marc Held designs interiors for the oceanliner *Wind Star.* Tadao Ando designs the Mon Petit Café in Kyoto, Japan. Philippe Starck designs Restaurants Castel in Paris, Dijon, and Nice,

D.C. passes practice act for designers

EXHIBITIONS

FURNITURE
AND FURNISHINGS

HONORS AND AWARDS

PROGRESS IN
THE PROFESSION

the Hôtel Costes in Paris, the Manin restaurant in Tokyo, and the Bathmann store in Zurich. Swanke Hayden Connell designs New York offices for Dow Jones & Co. Mario Botta's first built work in the United States is the ICF showroom, Long Island City, New York. Sarah Tomerlin Lee of Tom Lee, Ltd.; devises new interiors for the 1901 Willard Hotel, Washington, D.C.

Mario Bellini: Designer is at the Museum of Modern Art, New York. The Boston Museum of Art originates a traveling exhibition, *"The Art That Is Life": The Arts and Crafts Movement in America, 1875–1920*. Paris's Centre Georges Pompidou shows *Les Avante-Gardes de la fin du 20ème siècle*. Also in Paris, the textile designs of Manuel Canovas are seen at the Musée de la Mode. New York's Cooper-Hewitt, National Design Museum presents a retrospective of the work of Joseph Urban.

Cini Boeri and Tomu Katayagi design the all-glass "Ghost" chair for Fiam. Michele De Lucchi designs the "Tolomeo" desk lamp for Artemide. Gaetano Pesce designs the duvet-lined "I Feltri" chair for Cassina. Alberto Meda designs the "Light Light" chair for Alias. Aldo Rossi designs the "Milano" side chair for Molteni. Pascal Mourgue, younger brother of Olivier Mourgue, designs the "Atlantique" furniture line for Artelano. Gianfranco Frattini designs the "Bull" sofa and chairs for Cassina. Piers Gough designs a bent-metal chaise longue for Aram Designs. Jay Spectre designs the "Neo-Deco" furniture line for Century.

Paul Haigh designs the "Enigma" chair for Bernhardt. Charles Pfister designs an executive office furniture line for Baker. Robert Kleinschmidt of Powell/Kleinschmidt designs seating and tables for Sunar. John Saladino designs the "Tube Lamp" and the "Tripod" pull-up table.

Emilio Ambasz is given Britain's International Interior Design Award. Additions to the Interior Design Magazine Hall of Fame are: Neville Lewis, Andrée Putman, Jack Dunbar, Steve Chase, Margo Grant, Anthony Hail, Bruce Gregga, Ethel Smith, William Pulgram, and William Hodgins; special honorees are ARCO executive Robert O. Anderson and illustrator Jeremiah Goodman. The *Interiors* magazine Designer of the Year program honors Kohn Pedersen Fox Conway. Chosen by the ASID as Designer of Distinction is James Merrick Smith.

FIDER gives its first accreditation of a two-year master's degree program in interior design to the University of Tennessee at Knoxville. NCIDQ begins an interior design job analysis; it will be completed the following year and will be the basis for revisions in the NCIDQ examination. The British Institute of Interior Design merges with the Chartered Society of Designers. The District of Columbia is the fourth U.S. jurisdiction to pass a licensing act and the first to pass a practice act (requiring a license to practice as an interior designer, not merely to use the title).

1987

From left to right:

Willard Hotel renovation, Washington, D.C., by Sarah Tomerlin Lee of Tom Lee Ltd.

Orlando Diaz-Azcuy with his fabric collection for HBF

Benetton headquarters, New York, by Afra and Tobia Scarpa

Gaetano Pesce's "I Feltri" chairs for Cassina

John Saladino's "Tube Lamp"

Mario Botta's ICF showroom, New York, with a display of Alvar Aalto furniture

ARCHITECTURE

Luis Barragán dies. In Paris, I. M. Pei's additions to the Louvre include a glass pyramid in the courtyard, and Gae Aulenti remodels the interior of the Gare d'Orsay. Romaldo Giurgola's design for Australia's Parliament House is built in Canberra. Arquitectonica designs the Banco de Credito in Lima, Peru. Steven Holl designs a vacation house on Martha's Vineyard, Massachusetts. The Pritzker prize is shared by Gordon Bunshaft and Oscar Niemeyer.

BOOKS

Interior Design by John F. Pile is published. Carleton Varney honors his mentor in *The Draper Touch: The High Life and High Style of Dorothy Draper.* Stephen Calloway writes *Twentieth-Century Decoration.* Mel Byars compiles *The Design Encyclopedia.* Pauline Metcalf writes *Ogden Codman and the Decoration of Houses.*

CULTURE AT LARGE

Colombian author Gabriel García Marquéz writes *Love in the Time of Cholera.* Wendy Wasserstein's *The Heidi Chronicles* is produced; it will win a Pulitzer Prize and a Tony Award.

DESIGNERS AND INSTALLATIONS

Ray Eames dies at age seventy-six. Philippe Starck designs interiors for the Royalton Hotel, New York. Morphosis designs the Vecta showroom at the Pacific Design Center, Los Angeles. Tod Williams and Billie Tsien design a downtown Manhattan branch for the Whitney Museum and a private pool house on Long Island. Naomi Leff designs a New York prototype for Saks Fifth Avenue Private Label boutiques. Manhattan executive offices for Merrill Lynch are designed by Carolyn Iu of Skidmore, Owings, & Merrill, who leaves SOM to form a partnership with Neville Lewis. Mario Buatta designs rooms for Blair House in Washington, D.C. Capital Bank, Miami, is designed by Don Brinkmann of Gensler & Associates. The Kips Bay Decorators Showcase includes designs by Robert Currie, Noel Jeffrey, John Saladino, and Siskin-Valls. In Tel Aviv, Ron Arad begins work on the foyer interiors of the new opera house designed by Yacov Richter; they will be completed in 1994. In Paris, Marie-Christine Dorner designs the La Villa hotel, Andrée Putman designs the Carita salon, and Philippe Starck designs the discotheque La Cigale. Nigel Coates designs the Katharine Hamnett shops in London and Glasgow and the Jigsaw shops in London and Bristol. Andrée Putman designs shops and offices for Ebel in Paris and New York. Eva Jiricna designs the Vitra shop in Weil-am-Rhein, Germany. Renzo Mongiardino and others redecorate the Roman villa of couturier Valentino.

EXHIBITIONS

The Museum of Modern Art, New York, stages *Design for Independent Living,* a manifestation of growing concerns for "universal design" usable by the aged, the sick, and the disabled. *Architects Inside: From Mies to Memphis* is at the International Design Center New York. John Saladino designs a New York exhibition space for the Italian Tile Commission. At the Museum of Modern Art, New York, an exhibition honors Alvar Aalto, and Philip Johnson and Mark Wigley stage *Deconstructivist Architecture. Design Français* is at the Centre Georges Pompidou, Paris. *Faces of Swedish Design* is at the IBM Gallery, New York. A centenary exhibition of the furniture of Gerrit Rietveld opens in New York and will travel to Chicago, Illinois, and Dayton, Ohio.

Accessible design at MoMA

FURNITURE AND FURNISHINGS

Shiro Kuramata designs a chair of clear plastic with imbedded flowers; he calls it "Miss Blanche." Mark Hampton begins an association with Hickory Chair; the Mark Hampton Collection will eventually grow to more than 250 pieces. Franco Scalamandré, founder of Scalamandré Silks, dies at ninety. Massimo Iosa-Ghini's "Numero Uno" chair is made by Moroso. Jasper Morrison designs a plywood chair for Vitra and a plywood desk for Galerie Néotù. Paul Haigh designs the "Sinistra" chair for Bernhardt. Philippe Starck designs the "Ara" table lamp for Flos. Jean-Michel Wilmotte designs the "La Fontaine" chair and the "Palmer" chest. John Hutton designs the "San Marco" sofa and "Luciano" club chair for Donghia.

GOVERNMENT EVENTS

A truce is called in the Iran-Iraq War. The Soviets withdraw from Afghanistan.

HONORS AND AWARDS

Carol Groh is the *Interiors* magazine Designer of the Year. Louis Tregre is the ASID's Designer of Distinction. In its fourth year, the Interior Design Magazine Hall of Fame welcomes Kalef Alaton, Orlando Diaz-Azcuy, Billy W. Francis, Charles Gwathmey and Robert Siegel, David Hicks, Edith Hills, Juan Montoya, Frank Nicholson, Andre Staffelbach, and Lella and Massimo Vignelli; special honors go to educator Stanley Barrows and long-time *Interiors* editor in chief Olga Gueft.

MAGAZINES

The Journal of Design History begins publication, as does *Design Times*.

PROGRESS IN THE PROFESSION

Florida passes interior designer licensing legislation. The Home Fashions League changes its name to the International Furnishings and Design Association.

TECHNICAL AND SCIENTIFIC ADVANCES

Automatic teller machines revolutionize banking and bank design.

1988

From left to right:

Pedestrian tunnel, United Airlines Terminal, O'Hare Airport, Chicago, by Helmut Jahn of Murphy/Jahn

Mario Buatta's parlor for Blair House, Washington, D.C

Barbara Beckmann's "African Stripe" fabric

Philippe Starck

Executive office, Capital Bank Miami, by Don Brinkmann of Gensler

Frank Gehry is the year's recipient of the Pritzker prize, and his Vitra Design Museum opens in Weil-am-Rhein, Germany. Also for the Vitra campus of buildings, Zaha Hadid designs a fire station. Peter Shelton and Lee Mindel design a house in Alpine, New Jersey. Tadao Ando designs the Church of the Light in Osaka, Japan; he will also contribute a building design to the Vitra complex.

William Rupp and Arnold Friedmann write *Construction Materials for Interior Design. Eames Design: The Office of Charles and Ray Eames, 1941–1978* by Ray Eames and John and Marilyn Neuhart is published. *Mark Hampton on Decorating* is published. FIDER publishes *The History and Philosophy of the FIDER Standards and Guidelines* by Ronald M. Veitch, and the NCIDQ publishes the *NCIDQ Examination Guide.* Steelcase publishes *Mondo Materialis: Materials and Ideas for the Future. New Households, New Housing,* edited by Karen A. Frank and Sherry Ahrentzen, focuses on collective housing, housing for single-parent households, and single-room-occupancy housing. Chester Jones writes *Colefax & Fowler: The Best in English Interior Decoration.*

Popular television programs include *The Cosby Show, Roseanne,* and *Cheers.* A Helen Frankenthaler retrospective opens at the Museum of Modern Art, New York.

Hardy Holzman Pfeiffer renovates Rockefeller Center's Rainbow Room, and Milton Glaser designs its tableware and a private dining room. Powell/Kleinschmidt designs executive dining areas for the First National Bank of Chicago, and partner Robert Kleinschmidt designs his own apartment in Ludwig Mies van der Rohe's 880 Lake Shore Drive, Chicago. Philippe Starck designs the Nani Nani Café, Tokyo. Eva Jiricna designs the Joseph shop, Sloane Street, London. Andrée Putman designs interiors for the Au Bon Marché department store in Paris. Jean-Michel Wilmotte designs interiors beneath I. M. Pei's pyramid at the Louvre. In Chicago's Merchandise Mart, Massimo Vignelli and David Law design the KI showroom. Charles Pfister designs the Paris showroom for Knoll International and his own apartment on San Francisco's Nob Hill; his Square One restaurant in San Francisco is enlarged and redesigned by Andrew Belschner and Joseph Vincent. Carleton Varney of Dorothy Draper & Co. "refreshes" the Greenbrier hotel, White Sulphur Springs, West Virginia. Sarah Tomerlin Lee of Tom Lee Ltd. designs the Hotel Atop the Bellevue in Philadelphia. Designing rooms for the Kips Bay Decorator Showhouse are Stephen Sills, Parish-Hadley, and Rubén de Saavedra.

EXHIBITIONS

Seen at the Cooper-Hewitt, National Design Museum, New York, is *L'Art de Vivre: Decorative Arts and Design in France, 1789–1989*. At the Victoria & Albert, London, is *Scandinavian Ceramics and Glass in the Twentieth Century*.

FURNITURE AND FURNISHINGS

Ron Arad designs the "Schizo" chair of wood and the "Big Easy" series of vinyl. Jhane Barnes is designing textiles for Knoll. Boris Kroll produces the "Island Cloth" collection. Nanna Ditzel's "Bench for Two" is produced by Frederica Stølefabrik. Philippe Starck designs the "Lucifair" lighting sconce for Flos. Oscar Tusquets Blanca designs the "Vortice" table for Carlos Jané. Wolf Prix designs the "Vodol" armchair for Vitra. Vitra also revives "La Chaise," designed by Charles and Ray Eames in 1948. John Hutton designs a stacking chair for Donghia based on the Greek *klismos*; called the "Academy" chair, it will be renamed the "Anziano" chair.

GOVERNMENT EVENTS

The Berlin Wall comes down. An oil tanker spills over a million barrels of oil in the Gulf of Alaska.

HONORS AND AWARDS

New members of the Interior Design Magazine Hall of Fame are: Mel Hamilton, Sally Sirkin Lewis, Robert Currie, Rita St. Clair, Richard Carlson, Betty Sherrill, Donald Powell and Robert Kleinschmidt, and Jacques Grange; special honors go to former editor Sherman Emery and photographer Jaime Ardiles-Arce. The *Interiors* magazine Designer of the Year is Scott Strasser. The ASID Designer of Distinction is Joseph Braswell.

MAGAZINES

Professional Office Design ceases independent publication and becomes part of *The Designer/Specifier*.

TECHNICAL AND SCIENTIFIC ADVANCES

The three families of particles thought to make up all matter are isolated at the CERN laboratories near Geneva.

FIDER and NCIDQ publish guidelines

1989

From left to right:

John Hutton's "Academy" stacking chair for Donghia

Vitra Design Museum, Birsfelden, Germany, by Frank Gehry

Donald Powell

Robert Kleinschmidt

Apartment at 880 Lake Shore Drive, Chicago, designed for himself by Robert Kleinschmidt of Powell/Kleinschmidt

THE CLOSE OF THE CENTURY

The century's last decade sees professional talent and public attention focused on museum design. Frank Gehry's Guggenheim Bilbao and Richard Meier's Getty, both finished in 1997, make the biggest headlines, but there are dozens of others built or planned. Yoshio Taniguchi wins the competition for the expansion of New York's Museum of Modern Art, and in San Francisco alone, Herzog & de Meuron are designing the new de Young Museum, Gae Aulenti the new Asian Art Museum, Ricardo Legoretta the Mexican Museum, and Daniel Libeskind the Jewish Museum. New concepts to consider in office design include flexible schedules, "telecommuting" from home, and the temporary assignment of space to "mobile" workers; the Switzer Group's 1994 IBM facility in Crawford, New Jersey, for example, accommodates 800 employees in only 180 workstations. The long-sought unification of competing interior design professional organizations comes close to a reality in 1995 as the Institute of Business Designers, the International Society of Interior Designers, and the Council of Federal Interior Designers, with the alliance of the Interior Design Educators' Council, join to form the International Interior Design Association; not joining, however, is the largest group of all, the American Society of Interior Designers, leaving the profession at the end of the century still without unity. The mandate of the 1968 Architectural Barriers Act is greatly broadened by the 1991 Americans with Disabilities Act, requiring universally accessible design in public and commercial interiors. Finally, the 1995 discovery of cave paintings at Chauvet, France, puts things in perspective: if these are considered the oldest known examples of interior design, the profession is at least thirty thousand years old.

The 1994 "Aeron" chair by Bill Stumph and Chadwick for Herman Miller

Kenzo Tange's twin-towered City Hall is built in Tokyo. Italy's Aldo Rossi wins the Pritzker prize. Peter Eisenman's Wexner Center for the Visual Arts is built in Columbus, Ohio.

Davis Allen: Forty Years of Interior Design at Skidmore, Owings, & Merrill is written by Maeve Slavin. Jonathan M. Woodham writes *Twentieth-Century Ornament.* The Interior Design Educators' Council publishes its *Interior Design Career Guide.* Anne Massey writes *Interior Design of the Twentieth Century.* Esbjørn Hiort writes *Finn Juhl: Furniture, Architecture, Applied Art.* John Pile compiles *The Dictionary of 20th-Century Design.*

The decade-long cleaning of Michelangelo's Sistine Chapel paintings is completed. A. S. Byatt's novel *Possession* wins England's Booker Prize. A Cincinnati exhibition of photographs by Robert Mapplethorpe is charged with obscenity.

The Paramount Hotel, New York, is designed by Philippe Starck with Haigh Space Architects, and Starck also designs the Teatriz restaurant in Madrid. Eva Jiricna designs nine Joan & David shoe shop interiors in the United States. In the Kips Bay Decorator Showhouse are a drawing room by Michael de Santis, a library by Susan Zises Green, a sitting room by Bunny Williams, and a sixth-floor apartment by Vicente Wolf. In Paris, Jacques Grange designs a boutique for couturier Yves Saint Laurent. In Boston, Adam Tihany designs the Biba restaurant and, in New York, Remi. Andrée Putman designs interiors for Le Lac hotel near Tokyo and for Hotel Im Wasserturm in Cologne. In Fukuoka, Japan, Il Palazzo hotel is designed by Aldo Rossi and Morris Adjmi with interiors by Gaetano Pesce, Ettore Sottsass, Jr., Shiro Kuramata, and Shigeru Uchida. In the Napa Valley of California, Thomas Bartlett designs a house for an art collector. In Groningen, the Netherlands, the Groningen Museum is designed by Alessandro Mendini, Michele De Lucchi, Philippe Starck, and painter Frank Stella. Charles Pfister, in the last year of his life, designs a lodge at Lake Tahoe, in California.

The Decorative Arts Collection of the Metropolitan Museum of Art, New York, presents *Design 1890–1990*, curated by R. Craig Miller; it also presents an exhibition of American picture frames, most shown with nothing in them. The first in a series of International Contemporary Furniture Fairs is held at the Javits Center in New York; they will continue through the decade. At the Salon du Meuble, Paris, the twig furniture designed by Garouste and Bonetti and produced by Lou Fagotin is introduced. There is no Salone del Mobile in Milan this year, as dates are shifted from September to April. The Institut Français de Cologne shows the furniture designs of Pucci De Rossi.

New York and California license designers

FURNITURE AND FURNISHINGS

Herman Miller introduces the "Relay System" by Geoff Hollington. In England, Candia Lutyens establishes a firm to reproduce the furniture designs of her grandfather, Edwin Lutyens. Philippe Starck designs the three-legged "WW" stool. The Centro Studi Alessi opens in Milan. Mario Buatta, the "Prince of Chintz," designs a furniture collection for John Widdicomb. Rodolph introduces the "Checkered Past" fabric collection. Oscar Tusquets Blanca designs the "Ali Baba" divan for Casas. Another Spanish furniture manufacturer, Santa & Cole, begins its "Classic Spanish" line reproducing designs by José Antonio Ciderch and Josep Maria Jujol. Charles Pfister's collection for Baker is dedicated to T. H. Robsjohn-Gibbings.

GOVERNMENT EVENTS

South Africa's Nelson Mandela is released from prison after twenty-seven years; in 1994, he will be elected president of South Africa.

HONORS AND AWARDS

The ASID names Sarah Tomerlin Lee its Designer of Distinction. *Interiors* names Karen Daroff its Designer of the Year. New inductees into the Interior Design Magazine Hall of Fame are: Louis M. S. Beal, Maria Bergson, Robert Bray and Michael Schaible, Thomas Britt, Frank O. Gehry, Philippe Starck, Stanley Tigerman and Margaret McCurry, Carleton Varney, and Tod Williams and Billie Tsien; special honorees are Lester Dundes, Ian Schrager, and Ruth K Lynford.

MAGAZINES

Contract magazine changes its name to *Contract Design. Interiors and Sources* is founded.

PROGRESS IN THE PROFESSION

Legislation for interior designer certification is passed in California, New York, and Virginia. NCIDQ implements an appeals process for its examination.

TECHNICAL AND SCIENTIFIC ADVANCES

The Hubble space telescope is put into orbit. Compact screw-in fluorescent lamps are on the market.

1990

From left to right:

Thomas Bartlett's house for art collector Sally Dommerich in the Napa Valley, California

Mario Buatta shows his furniture collection for John Widdicomb at B. Altman & Co., New York

The stair of Eva Jiricna's Joan & David shop, New York

The lobby stair of Philippe Starck's Paramount Hotel, New York

ARCHITECTURE

Robert Venturi is awarded the Pritzker prize, and he and Denise Scott Brown add the Sainsbury Wing to London's National Gallery. Antoine Predock designs Hotel Santa Fe for Euro Disney, Marne-la-Vallée, France, joining Michael Graves's Hotel New York in the same complex.

BOOKS

Joseph De Chiara, Julius Panero, and Martin Zelnik compile *Time-Saver Standards for Interior Design and Space Planning*. Peter Thornton writes *The Italian Renaissance Interior*. Jay Spectre and his protégé Geoffrey Bradfield write *Point of View: Design by Jay Spectre*. Martin Pawley writes *Eva Jiricna: Design in Exile*. Patrick Mauriés writes *Fornasetti: Designer of Dreams*. Peter Lloyd Jones writes *Taste Today*.

CULTURE AT LARGE

Christo plants 1,340 blue umbrellas in Japan and 1,760 yellow ones in California. *Murphy Brown* and *Roseanne* are hit television series.

DESIGNERS AND INSTALLATIONS

Naomi Leff designs an executive conference center in Beaver Creek, Colorado, Gucci stores in San Diego and Las Vegas, Salvatore Ferragamo stores in several cities, a New York prototype for the A/X Armani Exchange stores, and Washington, D.C. corporate offices for Burlington Northern railroad. Sarah Tomerlin Lee of Tom Lee Ltd. designs the Doral Park Avenue Hotel in New York. Christian Liaigre designs the Montalembert hotel in Paris. Tadao Ando designs a gallery for Japanese screens at the Art Institute of Chicago. Ron Arad designs a furniture showroom and architect's office in London. Cini Boeri designs the Aldo Citterio silver shop in Milan. Nigel Coates designs interiors for the Taxim restaurant in Istanbul. Mario Bellini designs a Tokyo showroom for Cassina within a building by Tadao Ando.

Bausman & Gill design offices for Warner Bros. and for Electra in New York. Robert Metzger, Billy Francis, and Udstad-Dandridge Associates design for the Kips Bay Decorator Showhouse. San Francisco's 1909 Palace Hotel reopens after refurbishment by Stanford Hughes and others at Skidmore, Owings, & Merrill, after which Hughes leaves to form Brayton and Hughes with Richard Brayton. Also in San Francisco, Babey Moulton is founded by Pamela Babey and David Moulton. Eva Maddox designs the DuPont Resource Center in Chicago's Merchandise Mart.

EXHIBITIONS

A retrospective exhibition of the work of Louis I. Kahn opens in Philadelphia before beginning an extensive international tour. The Château Dufresne, Montreal, prepares a traveling exhibition, *What Modern Was*. The Salone del Mobile, Milan, shows *Mobili Italiani 1961–1991*. The furniture designs of Wendell Castle are seen at the American Craft Museum, New York, and at the Peter Joseph Gallery, New York, where his "Angel Chair" is introduced. Gallery 91 at 91 Grand Street, New York, celebrates 1991 with *91 Objects by 91 Designers*.

Philippe Starck designs the "Miss Sissi" table lamp. Douglas Ball designs a range of folding tables for Vecta. Aldo Rossi, Richard Meier, Stanley Tigerman, and Venturi Scott Brown design fabric collections for DesignTex. Peter Eisenman designs a fabric collection for Knoll. DePas, D'Urbino, & Lomazzi design the "Octopus" folding coatrack for Zerodisegno. Pucci De Rossi's "Divola" chair is shown at the International Contemporary Furniture Fair, New York. Nanna Ditzel designs the "Butterfly" chair for Frederica Stølefabrik. Knoll introduces Frank Gehry's furniture of woven wooden strips. Dakota Jackson introduces his own "Vikter" furniture line. Garouste and Bonetti's rough wood and bamboo furniture is produced in signed limited editions by Lou Fagotin.

The Americans with Disabilities Act is passed, to become effective in January 1992, mandating barrier-free design in public and commercial interiors. War begins in the Persian Gulf. The Soviet Union dissolves.

Joining the Interior Design Magazine Hall of Fame are: Don Brinkmann, Scott Bromley, Michael Graves, Naomi Leff, Robert Metzger, and Adam Tihany; special honorees are Philip E. Kelley of Chicago's Merchandise Mart, set designer Santo Loquasto, and the Winterthur Museum and Gardens, in Delaware. *Interiors* magazine chooses Gregory Landahl as Designer of the Year, and the ASID names John Saladino its Designer of Distinction.

Designers World is founded for readers in the American South and Southwest.

Interior designer certification is legislated in Maryland and Tennessee. The ASID moves its headquarters from New York to Washington, D.C.

Digitool Corporation develops a sonic tapeless measuring tool.

Americans with Disabilities Act mandates accessibility

1991

From left to right:

New York offices for Warner Bros. by Bausman & Gill

The 1909 Garden Court of San Francisco's Sheraton Palace Hotel, restored by Stanford Hughes of SOM

DuPont Resource Center, Chicago, by Eva Maddox. The glass-topped table is an element of Herman Miller's "Burdick System"; the wire chairs were designed by Harry Bertoia for Knoll.

The restaurant of the Doral Park hotel, New York, by Sarah Tomerlin Lee of Tom Lee Ltd.

Frank Gehry's woven wood furniture for Knoll

ARCHITECTURE

The Pritzker prize goes to Alvaro Siza of Portugal. Santiago Calatrava's Alamillo Bridge is built in Seville, Spain. Gwathmey Siegel designs a controversial addition to Frank Lloyd Wright's Guggenheim Museum.

BOOKS

American Society of Interior Designers Professional Practice Manual is edited by Jo Ann Asher Thompson, Ph.D. Mark Hampton writes *Legendary Decorators of the Twentieth Century,* illustrating it with his own watercolors; his twenty-two chosen legends are: Elsie de Wolfe, Elsie Cobb Wilson, Ruby Ross Wood, Rose Cumming, Marian Hall, Eleanor Brown of McMillen, Frances Elkins, Jean-Michel Frank, Syrie Maugham, Billy Baldwin, Dorothy Draper, William Pahlmann, John Fowler, Stéphane Boudin, George Stacey, "Sister" Parish, Albert Hadley, Geoffrey Bennison, Madeleine Castaing, Renzo Mongiardino, David Hicks, and Michael Taylor. Joy Monice Malnar and Frank Vodvarka write *The Interior Dimension.*

CULTURE AT LARGE

The Voyage by Philip Glass has its premiere at the Metropolitan Opera. The New York Philharmonic is celebrating its 150th anniversary. A three-hundred-painting Henri Matisse retrospective is at New York's Museum of Modern Art.

DESIGNERS AND INSTALLATIONS

Orlando Diaz-Azcuy designs his own office/studio on San Francisco's Maiden Lane. James Northcutt designs interiors for the Peninsula Hotel, Beverly Hills. Steven Holl designs New York offices for the D. E. Shaw investment firm, and Debra Lehman-Smith designs Washington, D.C., offices for the Ross, Dixon, & Masback law firm. Powell/Kleinschmidt designs the Kent College of Law at the Illinois Institute of Technology. Andrée Putman designs a showroom and office for Écart in Paris. Elyse Lacher designs a showroom for Cy Mann in New York. Shelton, Mindel designs the Ralph Lauren corporate headquarters in New York.

Naomi Leff designs a Milan prototype for Giorgio Armani in-store shops, and Yabu Pushelberg designs a department store in Taiwan. Gensler designs offices for Klein Tools, Chicago. David Rockwell, and Jay Haverson design the Vong restaurant in New York, and John Pawson designs the Wagamama restaurant in London. Lembo Bohn designs the Angelo Pietro restaurant in Kyushu, Japan, and is also included in the Kips Bay Decorator Showhouse, as are Clodagh, Juan Montoya, and Arthur E. Smith Inc.

EXHIBITIONS

Frank Lloyd Wright's 1935 office interior for Edgar Kaufmann is reconstructed and put on exhibition at London's Victoria & Albert.

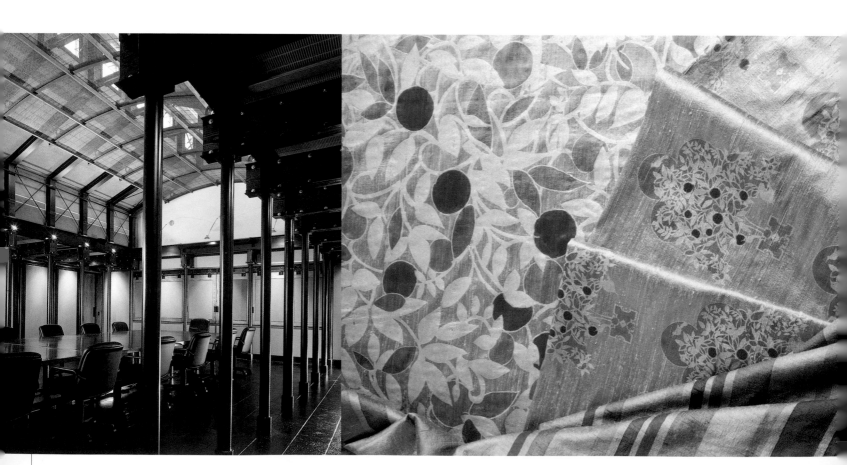

FURNITURE AND FURNISHINGS	**G**OVERNMENT EVENTS	**H**ONORS AND AWARDS	**M**AGAZINES	**P**ROGRESS IN THE PROFESSION	**T**ECHNICAL AND SCIENTIFIC ADVANCES

The "Granducale" furniture collection by Ludovico Acerbis for Acerbis is an homage to the minimalist art of Kasimir Malevich. Achille Castiglioni designs the "Brera" pendant lamp for Flos. Knoll introduces the "Stephens" desk system designed by Bill Stephens, and Brickel introduces "Collegeville" seating designed by Timothy deFiebre. Brunschwig & Fils introduces "Brigham" mohair velvet, and Pollack introduces "Calypso" cotton damask. Christian Liaigre designs the "Remember" lamp for Manufactor.

The Czech and Slovak republics are separated.

Interiors names Gary Lee and Mel Hamilton as Designers of the Year. Richard Himmel is the ASID Designer of Distinction. Owen & Mandolfo's Beverly Hills shop for Davidoff of Geneva wins the Best of Competition award from *Interior Design* and the Institute of Business Designers. The Interior Design Magazine Hall of Fame inducts: Hugh Hardy, Malcolm Holzman, and Norman Pfeiffer of Hardy Holzman Pfeiffer, Eva Maddox, Peter Marino, David Easton, Kevin McNamara, James Northcutt, and Denise Scott Brown and Robert Venturi; special honors go to lighting designer Howard Brandston and the Hedrich-Blessing stable of photographers.

The Designer/Specifier ceases publication. *Environmental Building News* begins publication.

The IBD College of Fellows calls for the unification of interior design professional organizations.

At the world's first Earth Summit, held in Rio, 143 nations agree to reduce their emissions of greenhouse gasses.

ASID prescribes professional practice

1992

From left to right:

Conference room of Klein Tools offices, Chicago, by Gensler & Associates

Fabric designs by Barbara Beckmann: "Citrus Grove," "Petit Orange Trees," and "Citrus Stripe"

Reading room of the I.I.T.—Kent College of Law, Chicago, by Powell/Kleinschmidt

Fabric designs by Mark Pollack for Pollack: "Cadence," "Ribcord," and "Maestro"

ARCHITECTURE

James I. Freed of I. M. Pei & Partners designs the United States Holocaust Memorial Museum in Washington, D.C.; its exhibitions are designed by Ralph Appelbaum. Tadao Ando designs the Vitra Conference Pavilion in Weil-am-Rhein, Germany. Fumihiko Maki of Japan is given the Pritzker prize.

BOOKS

John Kurtich and Garret Eakin write *Interior Architecture*. Carol Soucek King writes *Empowered Spaces: Architects and Designers at Home and at Work*. Barbara Radice writes *Ettore Sottsass: A Critical Biography*. Fiorenzo Cattaneo edits *Roomscapes: The Decorative Architecture of Renzo Mongiardino*. *Lucienne Day: A Career in Design* is published. Guy Julier writes *The Thames & Hudson Encyclopaedia of 20th Century Design*.

CULTURE AT LARGE

Playwright Tony Kushner's *Angels in America: A Gay Fantasia on National Themes* opens on Broadway; it will win the Pulitzer Prize. Michael Graves designs his "Mickey Mouse" teapot and opens a retail shop in Princeton, New Jersey.

DESIGNERS AND INSTALLATIONS

Babey Moulton converts a fifteenth-century monastery in Milan into the Four Seasons Milano hotel. Ron Arad designs the Belgo restaurant and bar in London. Nigel Coates designs the Nautilus and La Fôret restaurants at Schipol Airport, Amsterdam. Brayton and Hughes redesign the interiors of the Royal Hawaiian Hotel, Honolulu. Kaki Hockersmith redesigns the family living quarters in the White House. Peter Marino designs store interiors for Barney's New York on Madison Avenue and in Yokohama, Japan. Stephen Holl and Vito Acconci design the Storefront for Art & Architecture, New York. Anthony Antine designs suites for The Point on Upper Saranac Lake and also designs interiors for his own house in Fort Lee, New Jersey. Swanke Hayden Connell designs New York headquarters for entertainment and media giant Bertelsmann. Among Kips Bay Decorator Showhouse designers are the Cooper Group, Stedila Design, and Geoffrey Bradfield of Jay Spectre Inc. The New York architecture firm Beyer Blinder Belle buys Tom Lee Ltd. its chief asset being Sarah Tomerlin Lee. Elisabeth Draper dies at age ninety-three, and Benjamin Baldwin dies at eighty. In New York, Owen & Mandolfo design an art-filled SoHo branch for Chase Manhattan Bank.

EXHIBITIONS

Toward Modern Design: Revival and Reform in Applied Arts, 1850–1920 is seen at the Cooper-Hewitt, National Design Museum, as is *Mechanical Brides: Women and Machines from Home to Office*. The American Craft Museum, New York, shows *The Ideal Home, 1900–1920*. The work of Marco Zanuso and Richard Sapper is shown at the Museum of Modern Art, New York; and the Guggenheim SoHo displays *Industrial Elegance,* sponsored by Steelcase. At New York's D&D Building, the Decorative Fabrics Association and *Interior Design* magazine present *Material Beginnings: Illusion, Inspiration, and Realization.* In Washington, D.C., *The Age of the Baroque in Portugal* opens at the National Gallery of Art, and American wicker furniture from 1850 to 1930 is

Harvard honors Eileen Gray

seen at the Renwick Gallery. *Citizen Office* is seen at the Vitra Design Museum, Weil-am-Rhein, Germany, with office designs by Ettore Sottsass, Jr., Andrea Branzi, and Michele De Lucchi. The Centre Georges Pompidou, Paris, presents one-man exhibitions of the work of Tadao Ando and Gerrit Rietveld. *Eileen Gray: An Architecture for All Senses* is seen at the Harvard Graduate School of Design, Cambridge, Massachusetts; it will travel to Columbia University and to the Deutsches Architektur Museum in Frankfurt.

Gae Aulenti's "Tour" table for Fontana Arte has a glass top on four large wheels. Ron Arad's "Metaply" collection for the Aleph division of Driade is made of walnut plywood. Nanna Ditzel designs the "Trinidad" chair. Shelton, Mindel design rugs for V'Soske, a commission that will be repeated in 1996. François Bauchet designs a line of chairs for Galerie Néotù.

New York's World Trade Center is bombed.

New members of the Interior Design Magazine Hall of Fame are: François Catroux, Melvin Dwork, Ronald Krueck, Gary Lee, MAC II (Mica Ertegun and Chessy Rayner), Robert A. M. Stern, Lou Switzer, and Trisha Wilson; special honorees are *Interior Design* creative director Alberto Paolo Gavasci and *House Beautiful* editor Louis Oliver Gropp. Trisha Wilson is further honored as the ASID's 1993 Designer of Distinction. Juliette Lamb is *Interiors* magazine's Designer of the Year.

Journal of Interior Design Education and Research changes its name to *Journal of Interior Design. Studies in the Decorative Arts* is first published by the Bard Graduate Center for Studies in the Decorative Arts. The scholarly journal *American Furniture* is first published. *Designers West* ceases publication.

Philips Lighting introduces "Earth Light" compact fluorescents.

1993

From left to right:

Guest room at The Point, Saranac Lake, New York, by Anthony Antine

Bertelsmann headquarters, New York, by Swanke Hayden Connell

Giorgio Armani shop, Boston, by Naomi Leff

Vitra Conference Pavilion, Birsfelden, Germany, by Tadao Ando

ARCHITECTURE

Renzo Piano designs the Kansai International Airport in Osaka, Japan. In Paris, Frank Gehry designs the American Center and Jean Nouvel designs the Cartier Foundation building. Christian de Portzamparc of France receives the Pritzker prize.

BOOKS

Ronald M. Veitch writes *Detailing Fundamentals for Interior Design.* Eva Wilson surveys *8,000 Years of Ornament.* George Beylerian writes *Chairmania.*

CULTURE AT LARGE

Stephen Spielberg's *Schindler's List* is on the screen. A concert features the "Three Tenors"—José Carreras, Placido Domingo, and Luciano Pavarotti. Jacqueline Kennedy Onassis dies. Snoop Doggy Dogg records "(Who Am I) What's My Name?"

DESIGNERS AND INSTALLATIONS

Powell/Kleinschmidt designs the GATX corporate headquarers in Chicago. Peter Marino designs store interiors for Barney's New York in Beverly Hills. Ron Arad designs the Michelle Mabelle shop on Milan's via della Spiga. Andrée Putman designs an apartment for herself in Paris. Eva Jiricna designs the Joan & David shop on New Bond Street, London. George Ranalli remodels the public interiors of the Fashion Center Building, New York. Fabric designer Gretchen Bellinger designs her own house on Long Lake, New York. Stephen Sills and James Huniford design a New York showroom for Nan Swid Design. Room designers for the Kips Bay Decorators Showcase include Anthony Antine, Billy Francis, and Katherine Stephens. The Switzer Group designs an "alternative office" for an IBM facility in Crawford, New Jersey.

EXHIBITIONS

The Cooper-Hewitt, National Design Museum, New York, presents *Good Offices and Beyond: The Evolution of the Workplace* and *Packaging the New: Design and the American Consumer.* The Denver Art Museum shows *Masterworks: Italian Design, 1960–1994.* At New York's Gallery 91, *Design Legacies* honors designers and architects who have died of AIDS; the show is sponsored by DIFFA, Design Pride '94, and the Elsie de Wolfe Foundation.

Professional organizations unify (most of them)

FURNITURE AND FURNISHINGS

Bill Stumpf and Don Chadwick design the "Aeron" ergonomic chair for Herman Miller. Parish-Hadley introduces its own furniture line, designed by David McMahon and manufactured by Baker. Ron Arad designs the "Bookworm" bookshelf. Antonio Citterio and G. Oliver Löw design the "Mobil" plastic storage cart for Kartell. A furniture collection by Shelton, Mindel is produced by Jack Lenor Larsen.

GOVERNMENT EVENTS

In free elections in South Africa, Nelson Mandela is elected president. NATO forces battle in Bosnia.

HONORS AND AWARDS

The annual expansion of the Interior Design Magazine Hall of Fame includes Neil Frankel, Antony Harbour, Mariette Himes Gomez, Carolyn Iu, Stephen Mallory, Patrick McConnell, and Kevin Walz; given special awards are educator Arnold Friedmann and American Academy in Rome president Adele Chatfield-Taylor. The *Interiors* magazine Designer of the Year is Lauren Rottet. The ASID Designer of Distinction is Charles D. Gandy. The Institute of Business Designers initiates a Lifetime Achievement Award and gives it to Ward Bennett.

MAGAZINES

Perspective is first published by the newly formed International Interior Design Association.

PROGRESS IN THE PROFESSION

The Council of Federal Interior Designers, the Institute of Business Designers, and the International Society of Interior Designers vote to merge as a single entity. The new organization will be named the International Interior Design Association. In addition, the Interior Design Educators Council will be allied with the new IIDA in ways that permit collaboration. The American Society of Interior Designers, however, will decide against joining the newly formed organization. The Organization of Black Designers holds its first national conference.

TECHNICAL AND SCIENTIFIC ADVANCES

The Channel Tunnel is opened between England and mainland Europe. Conclusive evidence supports the existence of black holes in space.

1994

From left to right:

Anne Klein Collection boutique, Saks Fifth Avenue, New York, by Shelton, Mindel

Interior Design Magazine Hall of Fame member Carolyn Iu

George Ranalli's bronze reception desk for the lobby of the Fashion Center, New York

Andrée Putman's own apartment, Paris; the chaise is a Le Corbusier design.

A bedroom in Gretchen Bellinger's "camp" in the Adirondack Mountains

At a ceremony at the Palace of Versailles, Japan's Tadao Ando receives the Pritzker prize. Mario Botta's Museum of Modern Art opens in San Francisco.

Benjamin Baldwin: An Autobiography in Design is published. John Pile's 1988 *Interior Design* is republished with a new chapter on the requirements of the Americans with Disabilities Act. Also published is *Parish-Hadley, Sixty Years of American Design* by Albert Hadley, Christopher Petkanas, and the late "Sister" Parish.

Athlete O. J. Simpson is tried for murder and acquitted. *Babe* is on the screen, and Tom Stoppard's *Arcadia* is on the stage.

Double honors to Debra Lehman-Smith

DESIGNERS
AND INSTALLATIONS

EXHIBITIONS

FURNITURE
AND FURNISHINGS

GOVERNMENT EVENTS

HONORS AND AWARDS

Powell/Kleinschmidt designs the Paul Stuart men's store in Chicago. Richard Gluckman designs New York quarters for the Andy Warhol Foundation. The Kips Bay Decorator Showhouse designers include Thomas Britt ("A Sitting Room for Stanley Barrows"), Clodagh ("A Room of One's Own"), Richard L. Ridge ("Le Salon de Chasse"), and Nancy Mullan ("The Swedish Suite"). John Pawson designs the Calvin Klein shop on New York's Madison Avenue. *Scholastic* magazine's New York offices are designed by Hardy Holzman Pfeiffer. Philippe Starck gives new interiors to the Mondrian hotel, West Hollywood,

California. Eva Jiricna designs exhibition space in a 1792 room of Sir John Soane's house in London. Andrée Putman designs interiors for the Sheraton hotel at Roissy, France. Shelton, Mindel begins the design of a thirty-store retail program for Anne Klein. Jon Nathanson and Linda Jacobs, both formerly of ISI, design offices for international bond traders on the forty-sixth floor of New York's Met Life (formerly Pan-Am) building. Owen & Mandolfo design a New York office for the Belgian Consul General.

In New York, the American Craft Museum shows *Craft in the Machine Age, 1920–1945,* the Cooper-Hewitt, National Design Museum shows *Kitsch to Corbusier: Wallpaper from the 1950s,* and the Metropolitan Museum of Art shows *The Herter Brothers: Furniture and Interiors for a Gilded Age.* In Montreal, the Canadian Centre for Architecture shows *Scenes of the World to Come: European Architecture and the American Challenge.* In London, the Design Museum shows the work of Charlotte Perriand.

Richard Hamnum designs the "Huxley Series" for McGuire. For Cassina, Philippe Starck designs a bed and Paolo Rizzatto designs the "Dakota" chair. In the field of fabric, Quadrille presents the "Cortis Collection," Clodagh designs "Corrib" for DesignTex, and Mark Pollack designs a residential collection for Pollack Associates. John Hutton designs the "Klismos" chair for Donghia.

Croatians and Serbs are at war in Bosnia. Israeli prime minister Yitzhak Rabin is assassinated by a Jewish extremist. The Oklahoma City bombing by anti-government extremists leaves more than 150 dead.

Interiors names Debra Lehman-Smith the 1995 Designer of the Year, and she is also elected to the Interior Design Magazine Hall of Fame. Other electees are Frank Israel, Rose Tarlow, and Bunny Williams, with a special award going to display designer Gene Moore. Andre Staffelbach is the ASID Designer of Distinction.

1995

From left to right:

Scholastic magazine offices, New York, by Hardy Holzman Pfeiffer

Greece-inspired "Klismos" chair by John Hutton for Donghia

Paul Stuart store, Chicago, by Powell/Kleinschmidt

The Yellow Giraffe restaurant, São Paulo, Brazil, by Arthur de Mattos Casas

Tadao Ando designs the Museum of Literature in Himeji, Japan. Rafael Viñoly designs the Tokyo International Forum. The Pritzker prize goes to Spain's Rafael Moneo. In Glasgow, Charles Rennie Mackintosh's House for an Art Lover, designed in 1901, is finally built.

Michael Snodin and Maurice Howard publish *Ornament: A Social History since 1450*. Robert Becker publishes *Nancy Lancaster: Her Life, Her World, Her Art*. Mel Byars writes *50 Chairs*.

Madonna appears in *Evita*. A Jasper Johns retrospective is at the Museum of Modern Art, New York.

In San Francisco, Brayton and Hughes design offices and showroom space for Boyd Lighting, and Naomi Leff designs the Giorgio Armani store. Leff also designs a house in Telluride, Colorado, for actors Tom Cruise and Nicole Kidman; for the same clients, she will design two other houses and the interior of a jet. In Chicago, Powell/Kleinschmidt designs offices for LaSalle Partners. Philippe Starck redesigns Miami Beach's Delano hotel and designs the Felix restaurant in Hong Kong's Peninsula hotel. Nigel Coates designs interiors and furniture for the Bargo bar and restaurant, Glasgow. Andrée Putman designs sets for the film *The Pillow Book* and redesigns Morgan's hotel, New York. In Italy, Michele De Lucchi develops a store design program for Mandarina Duck, manufacturers of bags and accessories. And in New York, Hardy Holzman Pfeiffer redesigns the Windows on the World restaurant, and Gaetano Pesce designs offices for Chiat Day. Designing for the Kips Bay Decorator Showhouse are Celeste Cooper for Repertoire, Samuel Botero, and Barbara Hauben-Ross (formerly a partner in Dexter Design).

Retrospectives for Gaetano Pesce and British Arts and Crafts

EXHIBITIONS

The Centre Georges Pompidou, Paris, exhibits the work of Gaetano Pesce. The Bard Graduate Center, New York, presents a retrospective of the designs of Josef Frank. The Dallas Museum of Art shows *Hot Cars, High Fashion, Cool Stuff: Designs of the Twentieth Century.* The centenary of the death of William Morris brings renewed attention to his work and to the British Arts and Crafts movment, including an exhibition at London's Victoria & Albert.

FURNITURE AND FURNISHINGS

Achille Castiglioni designs the "Fucsia" hanging lamp for Flos. Ilkka Suppanen designs the "Flying Carpet" sofa for Cappellini. Björn Dahlström designs the "BD 5" chair and footstool for CBI. Jonas Bohlin designs the "Liv" table. Jacques Grange designs a line of furniture for Widdicomb. Jhane Barnes designs "Honeycomb" upholstery fabric for Knoll. Philippe Starck designs the "Romeo Moon" pendant light for Flos. Ron Arad designs "Reinventing the Wheel" aluminum shelving for Baroni & Associati and the "Boat Eye" marble and aluminum table for Bigelli Marmi. Alberto Meda designs the "Longframe" aluminum chaise for Alias.

HONORS AND AWARDS

The Interior Design Magazine Hall of Fame inducts Pamela Babey, Thierry W. Despont, Jed Johnson (posthumously, after his death in the crash of TWA flight 800), and Peter Shelton and Lee Mindel; special honors go to Karen Fisher of Designer Previews and John L. Dowling of Cushman & Wakefield. For *Interiors* magazine, Designers of the Year are Richard Brayton and Stanford Hughes of Brayton Hughes. For the ASID, the Designer of Distinction is Joseph Minton. The American Society of Furniture Designers institutes its annual Pinnacle Awards.

MAGAZINES

House Beautiful celebrates its one hundredth year of publication. *Wallpaper* begins publication in England.

PROGRESS IN THE PROFESSION

The National Kitchen and Bath Association requires passage of its own exam and NCIDQ certification for membership.

TECHNICAL AND SCIENTIFIC ADVANCES

Digital cameras are developed.

1996

From left to right:

Alexander Gorlin's own house at Seaside, Florida

Naomi Leff

Andrée Putman's redesign of Morgan's hotel, New York

Giorgio Armani shop, San Francisco, by Naomi Leff

Pamela Babey

Carolyn Iu's Bangkok Club, Bangkok, with antique Thai roof finials. The daybed is by Ludwig Mies van der Rohe, the wire-based table by Warren Platner.

The Guggenheim Museum Bilbao by Frank Gehry is completed; the Getty Foundation, Los Angeles, by Richard Meier is being completed in stages; and the Beyeler Foundation Museum in Basel, Switzerland, is designed by Renzo Piano. Sverre Fehn of Norway is the year's Pritzker laureate.

John Stefanidis Living by Design: A Country House and Garden is published. The centenary edition of *The Decoration of Houses* by Edith Wharton and Ogden Codman, Jr., first published in 1897, is released. *Andrée Putman* by Sophie Tasma-Anagyros and *History of Interior Design & Furniture* by Robbie G. Blakemore are published. Mel Byars writes *50 Tables*. The two-volume *Encyclopedia of Interior Design*, edited by Joanna Banham, is published.

The Lion King reopens New York's New Amsterdam Theater, newly renovated by Hardy Holzman Pfeiffer. Mother Teresa and Princess Diana die.

Felderman+Keatinge design West Coast headquarters for MTV in Santa Monica. The Kips Bay Decorator Showhouse presents rooms by Thomas Britt, Mario Buatta, Mark Hampton, McMillen, Parish-Hadley, and Alexandra Stoddard, among others. Adam Tihany designs two New York restaurants in two distinct styles: the handsomely restrained Jean-Georges and the no-holds-barred Le Cirque 2000. Don Brinkmann of Gensler & Associates designs offices for Swiss Re New Markets in New York. Shelton, Mindel designs the Baltimore headquarters for Fila Sportswear and public

EXHIBITIONS

FURNITURE
AND FURNISHINGS

HONORS AND AWARDS

TECHNICAL AND
SCIENTIFIC ADVANCES

spaces on Celebrity Cruises' oceanliner *Mercury.* Brayton and Hughes renovate the Lodge at Pebble Beach, California. Mario Buatta, Geoffrey Bradfield, Juan Montoya, and Mariette Himes Gomez all design New York apartments for themselves. Sarah Tomerlin Lee retires from professional practice at eighty-six. George Beylerian founds Material ConneXion to inform designers of new and innovative materials. It will have offices in New York and Milan.

A Grand Design: The Art of the Victoria & Albert Museum opens in Baltimore and will travel to Boston, Toronto, Houston, and San Francisco. In London, the Victoria & Albert shows the work of Carl Larsson and his wife, calling them "creators of the Swedish style." The Museum of Modern Art, New York, shows the work of Achille Castiglioni. The New York School of Interior Design presents the hospitality design of Sarah Tomerlin Lee in *Hotels without Reservation. A Legacy of Invention: The Work of Charles and Ray Eames* opens at the Vitra Design Museum, Weil-am-Rhein, Germany, and will travel to the Library of Congress, Washington, D.C., and then to New York, St. Louis, Los Angeles, and Seattle; its catalog, edited by Donald Albrecht, will win the Philip Johnson Award of the Society of Architectural Historians. The newly opened Material ConneXion shows the work of Gaetano Pesce in *Is the Future Now?*

Kevin Walz designs a line of lighting fixtures for Baldinger. Vitra introduces the "Meda" chair by Alberto Meda. Haworth introduces the "Flo" workstation. Shelton, Mindel designs a collection for Nessen Lighting and will add further pieces the following year. Vico Magistretti designs the "Maui" chair for Kartell and the "Variantes" sofa for De Padova. Pascal Mourgue designs the "Dune" folding chair for Fermob and the "Tempo" stacking chair for Artelano. Jasper Morrison designs the "Lima" stacking chair for Cappellini. Enzo Mari's "Box" chair-in-a-kit is produced by Driade. Angelo Mangiarotti's "Ipslyon" bookshelf is produced by Baleri Italia. Ingo Maurer produces his own "Pierre ou Paul" pendant light.

Carolyn Iu and Neville Lewis of Iu + Lewis are *Interiors* magazine's Designers of the Year. Phyllis Martin-Vegue is the ASID Designer of Distinction. The Spanish Ministry of Industry honors Barcelona designer Jorge Pensi. New to the Interior Design Magazine Hall of Fame are Richard Meier, Tony Duquette, Lauren Rottet, and Clodagh; special honors go to the Kips Bay Decorator Showhouse and to Dianne Pilgrim of the Cooper-Hewitt, National Design Museum.

Computers operate with voice recognition. Embryologist Ian Wilmut clones a sheep named Dolly.

Carolyn Iu and Neville Lewis designers of the year

1997

From left to right:

The "Zettel'Z" pendant lamps designed by Ingo Maurer

Clodagh

Dining room aboard Celebrity Cruises' oceanliner *Mercury,* designed by Shelton, Mindel

The "Meda" chair designed for Vitra by Alberto Meda

Adam Tihany's Jean-Georges restaurant, New York

Adam Tihany's Le Cirque 2000 restaurant, New York

ARCHITECTURE

Yoshio Taniguchi wins an international competition for the expansion of New York's Museum of Modern Art. Steven Holl designs the Kiasma Museum of Contemporary Art in Helsinki. Alvaro Siza designs the Museu de Serralves in Oporto, Portugal. Herzog & de Meuron design the Dominus Winery near Yountville, California. Cesar Pelli designs the twin Petronas Towers in Kuala Lumpur, Malaysia. Rem Koolhaas designs a house in Bordeaux, France. Renzo Piano designs the Tjibaou Cultural Center in New Caledonia and, in a ceremony hosted by President and Mrs. Clinton at the White House, is awarded the Pritzker prize.

BOOKS

Mayer Rus writes *Loft*. Treena Crochet writes *Designer's Guide to Furniture Styles*. Benjamín Villegas edits *Juan Montoya*. Jack Lenor Larsen writes *Jack Lenor Larsen: A Weaver's Memoir*. Leslie Piña writes *Alexander Girard Designs for Herman Miller*. Mel Byars writes *50 Products*. Peter Thornton writes *Form and Decoration: Innovation in the Decorative Arts, 1470–1870*.

CULTURE AT LARGE

Frank Sinatra dies. The centenary of George Gershwin's birth is celebrated. Monica Lewinsky is on TV, as is *Teletubbies*.

DESIGNERS AND INSTALLATIONS

Mark Hampton dies at fifty-eight; the *New York Times* calls him "a celebrated symbol of gracious living." David Hicks dies at fifty-nine; *Time* calls him "the 1960s avatar of interior design, a sworn enemy of chintz." Don Brinkmann dies at fifty-three; one of his last works with Gensler is the design of New York offices for Baron Capital. Shelton, Mindel, & Associates design a New York apartment with views of the Guggenheim Museum and the Central Park reservoir. Peter Eisenman designs a Los Angeles showroom for Dakota Jackson. Christian Liaigre designs interiors for New York's Mercer Hotel, a remodeling of an 1890 structure. Kips Bay Decorators Showhouse designers include Kitty Hawks, T. Keller Donovan, Bunny Williams, and Anthony Antine.

Aalto remembered in Rotterdam, Los Angeles

EXHIBITIONS

An Alvar Aalto retrospective is designed by Lily Hermans for the Netherlands Architecture Institute, Rotterdam, and the Pacific Design Center, Los Angeles, honors the centennial of Aalto's birth. Musée des Arts Décoratifs, Montreal, shows a retrospective of designs by Gaetano Pesce. Knoll's San Francisco showroom exhibits *Harry Bertoia: A Memorial Exhibition of Sculpture, Furniture and Works on Paper*. Material ConneXion shows *Titanium!* and *Tensions in Architecture*, the latter exploring the use of fabric in buildings and interiors.

FURNITURE AND FURNISHINGS

Ross Lovegrove and Stephen Peart design a translucent office system for Herman Miller, and Herman Miller for the Home reintroduces fabric designs by Alexander Girard. Suzanne Tick designs the "Integrated Interiors" fabric line for Knoll Textiles. Mario Bellini designs the "Bellini" plastic chair for Heller. Shelton, Mindel design for Nessen Lighting. The Archivio Storico Olivetti opens in Ivrea, Italy. Michael McDonough designs bamboo chairs for Summit. Lilia Mélissa designs the "Park" rug for Odegard. David Weeks Lighting presents the "Aluminum Ballet" chandelier. Chris Lehriche designs a lighting collection for Pucci. Verner Panton dies at seventy-two.

HONORS AND AWARDS

Interior Design Magazine Hall of Fame inductees are: Vicente Wolf, Laura Bohn and Joseph Lembo, Eva Jiricna, and Rysia Suchecka. *Interiors* names David Rockwell the 1998 Designer of the Year. The ASID names Janet Schirn the Designer of Distinction. A MacArthur Foundation "genius grant" is given to architects Elizabeth Diller and Ricardo Scofidio.

MAGAZINES

Interior Expressions, *Modernism*, and *Nest* begin publication.

PROGRESS IN THE PROFESSION

NCIDQ conducts an analysis of the interior design profession, updating its analysis of a decade before.

TECHNICAL AND SCIENTIFIC ADVANCES

The U.S. Department of Energy contracts with IBM for a 10-trillion-operations-per-second computer. In China, 570-million-year-old eggs are found. Dolly, the cloned lamb, gives birth to a healthy daughter.

1998

Adam Tihany's King David Hotel, Jerusalem

Vicente Wolf

"Sutil" chair by Jorge Pensi

Textile design by Suzanne Tick for Knoll

"Gimlet" swivel stool by Jorge Pensi

ARCHITECTURE

The Pritzker prize is awarded to England's Sir Norman Foster. The Royal Institute of British Architects' gold medal goes this year not to an architect, but to a city: Barcelona. James Stewart Polshek is selected as the architect of the Clinton presidential library. New buildings include Richard Meier's Siemens headquarters in Munich, Frank Gehry's Vontz Center for Molecular Studies in Cincinnati, Smith-Miller + Hawkinson's addition to the Corning Museum of Glass in Corning, New York, and Arata Isozaki's COSI science museum in Columbus, Ohio.

BOOKS

The IIDA Foundation publishes *A Study of Interior Design: Analysis of the Needs of Practice and Implications for Education*. Mel Byars writes *50 Lights*.

CULTURE AT LARGE

Michael Graves designs toasters and household gadgets for Target Stores. *Shakespeare in Love* is filmed.

DESIGNERS AND INSTALLATIONS

Davis Allen dies at eighty-three, Tony Duquette at eighty-five, and Charlotte Perriand at ninety-six. Philippe Starck moves his practice from Paris to New York. Adam Tihany designs New York's Time Hotel. Naomi Leff designs a prototype retail store and spa for Helena Rubenstein. At the Merchandise Mart, Chicago, Lauren Rottet of DMJM Rottet designs a showroom for Steelcase Wood, and Michael Vanderbyl designs one for Teknion. Carolyn Iu designs New York offices for Bertelsmann Inc. At the Kips Bay Decorator Showhouse are rooms by Thomas Britt, Mariette Himes Gomez, Dakota Jackson, Thomas O'Brien, and (posthumously) Mark Hampton Inc. The Radio City Music Hall reopens after renovation by Hugh Hardy of Hardy Holzman Pfeiffer. The Design Store of the Museum of Modern Art, New York, is redesigned by 1100 Architects. The office of the late Jed Johnson designs the Fressen restaurant in Manhattan's meatpacking district, and Powell/Kleinschmidt designs a restaurant for the Art Institute of Chicago. In San Francisco, Jeffry Weisman and Andrew Fisher of Fisher Weisman redesign a Nob Hill apartment for themselves. Brayton and Hughes are renovating the Hotel Del Coronado, Coronado, California. Albert Hadley, at seventy-eight, closes Parish-Hadley and opens his own firm, Albert Hadley, Inc.

EXHIBITIONS

The National Building Museum in Washington, D.C., presents an exhibition curated by Donald Albrecht on the impact of air-conditioning. The Carnegie Museum of Art, Pittsburgh, shows *Merchant Prince and Master Builder: Edgar J. Kaufmann and Frank Lloyd Wright*. The Museum of Modern Art, New York, shows *The Un-Private House* and *Modern Starts*. The drawings and watercolors of Mark Hampton are shown at the New York School of Interior Design. The work of Richard Meier is shown at the Galerie Nationale de Jeu de Paume, Paris, and at the Museum of Contemporary Art, Los Angeles. Material ConneXion presents *Going Digital* and its own first annual product review.

Diaz-Azcuy, Clodagh, Tick, Pollack, and Bellinger introduce collections

The design of Philippe Starck is the subject of an exhibition at the Lighthouse, Glasgow, and another (with exhibition design by Philip Johnson) at the P.S. 1 Contemporary Art Center, Long Island City, New York. The tapestries of Helena Hernmarck are seen at Prince Eugen's Waldemarsudde, Stockholm, and at the Fashion Institute of Technology, New York.

Orlando Diaz-Azcuy introduces his "Images of Paris" fabric line at Pallas, Clodagh designs the "Celtic Collection" for Lees Carpets, and Diaz-Azcuy and Clodagh both design fixtures for Boyd Lighting. Niels Diffrient's "Freedom" chair for Humanscale is introduced at NEOCON, as is IDEO's "Leap" chair for Steelcase. Gretchen Bellinger introduces "Tale of the Dragon," a jacquard weave, and Suzanne Tick designs fabric for Groundworks/Lee Jofa and wallcoverings for Knoll. Rodolph presents three new fabric collections, "Play It Again," "New Pizzazz," and "Imagination." Maharam revives five textile designs from the '40s by Charles and Ray Eames. Sally Sirkin Lewis designs the "Resort Collection" for J. Robert Scott. Alan Mack designs the "Fast Forward" chair and the "Wedgtable" for Brueton. Herman Miller presents the "Resolve" office system designed by Ayse Birsel. Sherrie Donghia and Stephanie Odegard colloborate on a rug collection. Zanotta introduces the "Centerpiece" glass and aluminum tray by Andrea Branzi.

NATO forces, including the United States, bomb Serbia in response to genocide against Kosovo. The U.S. Senate acquits President Clinton of impeachment charges.

The IIDA institutes an annual Leadership Award; its first recipients are Richard Carlson of Swanke Hayden Connell and Neville Lewis. The *Interiors* magazine Designer of the Year is William McDonough. *Interiors* also institutes the annual George Nelson Design Awards, its first honorees including furniture designers Karim Rashid, Alberto Meda, and Ross Lovegrove. The ASID Designer of Distinction is Gary Wheeler. New members of the Interior Design Magazine Hall of Fame are Celeste Cooper, Peter Gluckman, and Laurinda Spear and Bernardo Fort-Brescia of Arquitectonica; a special award is given to Jack Lenor Larsen.

Princeton biologists develop a genetically smarter strain of mice. Furniture sales are increasingly being conducted online.

1999

From left to right:

IIDA honoree Richard Carlson

Mario Buatta's "Dog Lamp" for Frederick Cooper Lighting

San Francisco living room by Jeffry Weisman and Andrew Fisher of Fisher Weisman

Mark Pollack's "Alpha Workshops" fabric collection for Pollack & Associates

ASID Designer of Distinction Gary Wheeler

Council chamber, Hôtel du Département de la Haute-Garônne, Toulouse, France, by Venturi and Scott Brown

James Stewart Polshek designs the Rose Center for Earth and Space at the American Museum of Natural History, New York; within it, Ralph Appelbaum designs the exhibits. The Tate Modern opens in London in a former power station, its redesign by Herzog & de Meuron. Frank Gehry shows his scheme for a new Guggenheim Museum to be built off the island of Manhattan and designs a company cafeteria for Condé Nast in New York. Christian de Portzamparc designs the LVMH building in New York. The Pritzker prize is awarded to Rem Koolhaas, and the AIA gold medal to Ricardo Legorreta. Prospective commissions for museum design include: Steven Holl

for an addition to the Nelson-Atkins Museum of Art in Kansas City; Renzo Piano for an addition to the Art Institute of Chicago; Frank Gehry for an addition to the Corcoran Gallery of Art in Washington, D.C.; Zaha Hadid for the Contemporary Arts Center in Cincinnati; Rafael Moneo for an addition to the Museum of Fine Arts, Houston; Antoine Predock for a museum at Skidmore College, Saratoga Springs, New York; Santiago Calatrava for an addition to the Milwaukee Art Museum; Tadao Ando for the Modern Art Museum of Fort Worth, Texas; and Tod Williams and Billie Tsien for the new Museum of American Folk Art in New York.

San Francisco designer John Wheatman shares his *Meditations on Design,* featuring designs by Peter Gilliam and others on his staff. Alexander Gorlin presents *The New American Townhouse,* including some of his own designs. Henry A. Millon edits *The Triumph of the Baroque.* A monograph is published on the work of Smith-Miller + Hawkinson. Peter Bradford writes *The Design Art of Nicos Zographos.* John Pile writes *A History of Interior Design.* Mel Byars writes *50 Beds.*

A best-selling book is *Harry Potter and the Goblet of Fire.*

Diller and Scofidio redesign the Brasserie restaurant on the ground floor of the Seagram Building, New York. Gwenael Nicolas designs Issey Miyake Pleats Please in Paris. Powell/Kleinshmidt design the Fixler house in Jupiter, Florida. Carolyn Iu forms a new partnership with Nathan Bibliowicz, and Iu, with John Lijewski of Perkins & Will, designs the Swiss Re American headquarters in New York. Philippe Starck designs the Sanderson and St. Martins Lane hotels in London and the Hudson in New York. Babey Moulton Jue & Booth designs the Matsuri restaurant in Santiago, Chile. Kips Bay Decorator Showhouse designers include Mario Buatta, Charles Spada, David Barrett, and Stewart Manger for David Anthony Easton Inc.

The Cooper-Hewitt, National Design Museum, New York, presents its first National Design Triennial, *Design Culture Now,* and *The Opulent Eye of Alexander Girard.* The Jewish Museum, New York, shows the work of Bauhaus weaver Anni Albers. The Metropolitan Museum of Art, New York, shows *American Modern, 1925–1940: Design for a New Age* and, simultaneously, *A Century of Design, Part II: 1925–1950.* The Carnegie Museum of Art, Pittsburgh, shows *Aluminum by Design: Jewelry to Jets.* The Vitra Design Museum opens a branch in Berlin. The furniture design of Pierre Paulin is seen in Paris. In Washington, D.C., the National Building Museum shows *On the Job: Design and the American Office,* and the National Gallery shows *Art Nouveau 1890–1914.*

IIDA honors the leadership of Margo Grant

FURNITURE
AND FURNISHINGS

GOVERNMENT EVENTS

HONORS AND AWARDS

MAGAZINES

PROGRESS IN
THE PROFESSION

TECHNICAL AND
SCIENTIFIC ADVANCES

John Saladino designs the "Tuscan" sofa. Philippe Starck designs the "Bubble Club" line of chairs and sofas for Kartell and the "Hudson" aluminum chair for Emeco. Karim Rashid designs the polypropylene and steel "Chair, Oh Chair" for the Canadian firm Umbra. Ross Lovegrove designs a polypropylene foam chair for the Italian firm Edra and aluminium and glass tables for the German firm Loom. Antonio Citterio designs the "Freetime" sofa and the "Cross" storage unit for B&B Italia. Rafael Moneo designs the "Estocolmo" bench for Casas, and Michele De Lucchi the "Piazza di Spagna" bench for Poltrona Frau. Emilo Ambasz designs the "Vox" stacking chair for Vitra, and Jasper Morrision the "Tate" stacking chair for Cappellini.

World population exceeds six billion, roughly four times the world population of 1900.

The *Interiors* magazine Designer of the Year is exhibition designer Ralph Appelbaum, and the ASID Designer of Distinction is Paul Vincent Wiseman. The IIDA's second annual Leadership Award goes to Margo Grant of Gensler, and the AIA names Gensler the Firm of the Year. Barbara Barry, Bruce Bierman, and Gary Wheeler are inducted into the Interior Design Magazine Hall of Fame. The Cooper-Hewitt, National Design Museum announces its first annual National Design Awards: Frank Gehry receives the Lifetime Achievement Award, Apple receives the Corporate Achievement Award, and John Hejduk and Morris Lapidus (both of whom die shortly afterward, at age seventy-one and ninety-eight, respectively) are named American Originals.

Dwell magazine begins publication.

At the end of the century, 13,500 interior designers have been certified, and certification laws are in effect in nineteen states plus Puerto Rico and the District of Columbia and in eight provinces of Canada.

The survey of the human genome is completed.

2000

From left to right:

Interior Design Magazine Hall of Fame inductee Barbara Barry

IIDA Leadership Award winner Margo Grant of Gensler

Berman house, near Bowral, Australia, by Harry Seidler

Frank Gehry's company cafeteria for Condé Nast, New York

Powell/Kleinschmidt's Fixler house, Jupiter, Florida

INDEX

Numbers refer to years and categories, not to pages. Year references in italics indicate illustrations, but illustrations that duplicate text entries are not separately indexed. For products, the designers and manufacturers have been indexed, but not the product names themselves. Books are indexed under their authors' names, but not under their titles. Contextual items, such as those in the "Culture at Large" category, have been indexed only when directly relevant to interior design. Mentions in the preface or the summaries preceding each decade are not indexed.

A

Aalto, Alvar, 1928A, 1931, 1931F, 1932,
  1932F, 1933A, 1933E, 1935A, 1935F,
  1936F, 1937A, 1937E, 1938A, 1938E,
  1946F, 1947A, 1949D, 1951A, 1952F,
  1953A, 1955A, 1956F, 1958A, 1960A,
  1962A, 1964A, 1965D, 1970A, 1971A,
  1974A, 1976A, 1978A, 1988E, 1998E
Aarhus town hall, Denmark, 1937A, 1942A
Aarnio, Eero, 1963F, 1967F, 1968F
Aaron, Didier, 1970D
Abercrombie, Sir Patrick, 1939B
Abitare, 1962M
Abitare store, New York, 1978D
Abraham & Strauss, Brooklyn, 1928E
Acconci, Vito, 1993D
Acerbis, 1981F, 1983F, 1985F, 1992F
Acerbis, Ludovico, 1981F, 1983F, 1992F
Ackerman, Phyllis, 1923B
Adams, Maurice, 1930B
Adams, Rayne, 1914B
Adjmi, Morris, 1990D
Adler and Sullivan, 1977E
Adler, David, 1918D, 1931D
Adler, Hazel, 1916B
Adnet, Jacques, 1922D, 1927D, 1928D, 1929F,
  1937E, 1947D, 1953F, 1970P
Adnet, Jean, 1922D
Adrian salon, Beverly Hills, 1951D
A&E Desian, 1968D
AEG (Allgemeine Elektricitäts Gesellschaft),
  1905D, 1907D, 1908A, *1909*
Aeolian Hall, New York, *1912*
Affrime, Marvin, 1958D, 1977D, 1986H
"After All" (de Wolfe house), Beverly Hills, 1940D
Agnelli offices, Paris, 1975D
Ahlstrom, Tom, 1968D
Ahrenten, Sherry, 1989B
AIA *see* American Institute of Architects
AID *see* American Institute of Decorators,
  American Institute of Interior Decorators, and
  American Institute of Interior Designers

Aid Association for the Lutherans, Appleton, WI,
  1975D
Airborne, 1964F
Air-conditioning, *1904*, 1906T, 1929T, 1999E
Air France offices, London, 1957F
Air France offices, Tokyo, 1957F
Akane Shokai, 1955F
Akron Art Institute, 1946E
Alamillo Bridge, Seville, 1992A
Alaton, Kalef, 1988H
Alba apartment, Madrid, 1926D
Albers, Anni, 1949F, 1959F, 1961H, 1978F, 2000E
Albers, Josef, 1919D, 1923F, 1925F, 1929F, 1959F,
  1973
Albini, Franco, 1935D, 1936E, 1938D, 1938F,
  1940F, 1950D, 1950F, 1952D, 1952F, 1954F,
  1957D, 1959F, 1962D, 1963D
Albini, Marco, 1963D
Albinson, Don, 1965F
Albrecht, Donald, 1997E, 1999E
Albright Art Gallery, Buffalo, NY, 1947E
Album, 1986M
Alchimia, 1978F
Alcoa, 1957F
Alcoa showroom, New York, 1936D
Aldo Citterio shop, Milan, 1991D
Aleph, 1993F
Alessi, 1921F, 1983F, 1990F
Alias, 1979F, 1982F, 1987F, 1996F
À l'Innovation store, Brussels, 1901D
Alitalia terminal, Milan, 1960D
Alix, Charlotte, 1935D
Allen, Davis, 1954D, 1961D, 1965A, 1970D, 1975D,
  1982D, 1983F, 1984F, 1985H, 1986D, 1990B,
  1999D
Allen, Gerald, 1974B
Alley Theater, Houston, 1965A
Allied Fibers showroom, Atlanta, 1982D
Allied Fibers showroom, Dallas, 1984D
Allied Furnishing Industries, 1917P
Allom, Charles Carrick, 1901D, 1911D
Alo-Alo restaurant, New York, 1985D

Alpha, 1971F
Aluminum by Design . . ., 2000E
Alumni Memorial Hall, I.I.T., Chicago, 1946A
Ambassador East Hotel, Chicago, 1944D, 1954D
Ambassador Hotel, New York, 1921D
Ambassador West Hotel, Chicago, 1958D
Ambasz, Emilio, 1972E, 1976E, 1977H, 1979D,
  1979F, 1980H, 1981H, 1984F, 1987H, 2000F
America Can't Have Housing, 1934E
America ocean liner, *1940*
American Academy in Rome, 1935M, 1994H
American Academy of Arts and Sciences,
  Cambridge, MA, 1980D
Americana Hotel, Fort Worth, TX, 1981D
American Airlines plane interiors, 1968D
American Bicentennial Commission, 1975E
American Can Co., Greenwich, CT, 1970D
American Can Co., New York, 1986D
American Center, Paris, 1994A
American Crafts Museum, New York, 1991E,
  1993E, 1995E
American Designers' Gallery, 1928P, 1929E
American Designers Institute, 1938P
American Federation of Arts, 1968F
American Furniture, 1993M
American Institute of Architects, 1949A, 1961H,
  1976P, 1978P, 2000H
American Institute of Architects Journal, 1983M
American Institute of Decorators, 1936P, 1941P,
  1948H, 1951P, 1953H, 1953M, 1955P, 1957P,
  1958H, 1959H, 1961B
American Institute of Graphic Arts, 1914P
American Institute of Interior Decorators, 1931P,
  1932P, 1933P, 1936P, 1961P
American Institute of Interior Designers, 1961H,
  1961P, 1964H, 1965H, 1966P, 1968H,1975P
American Institute of Kitchen Dealers, 1963P,
  1969P, 1982P
American Modern, 1925-1940, 2000E
American Museum of Natural History, New York,
  2000A
American National Exhibition, Moscow, 1959E

American National Industrial Design Award,
  1980H
American Originals, 2000H
American Radiator building, New York, 1924A
American Restaurant, Kansas City, MO, 1974D
American Society for Testing Materials, 1902P,
  1914P, 1961P, 1968P, 1971P, 1972P
American Society of Furniture Designers, 1981P,
  1996H
American Society of Interior Designers, 1975P,
  1976H, 1976P, 1977H, 1978E, 1978H, 1978P,
  1979H, 1980H, 1981H, 1982H, 1983H, 1984H,
  1985H, 1986H, 1991P, 1992B
Americans with Disabilities Act, 1991G, 1995B
American Union of Decorative Artists and
  Craftsmen, 1928P, 1930B, 1930E, 1931B
Amsler, James, 1949D, 1954D
Anderson, Harry, 1959H
Anderson, Robert O., 1987H
Ando, Tadao, 1977A, 1981A, 1986A, 1987D, 1989A,
  1991D, 1993A, 1993E, 1995A, 1996A, 2000A
Andrea Doria ocean liner, 1952D
Andrew Belschner Joseph Vincent, 1989D
Andrews, Edward Deming, 1937B
Andrews, Faith, 1937B
Andy Warhol Foundation offices, New York, 1995D
Angelo Pietro restaurant, Kyushu, Japan, 1992D
Anholt apartment, New York, 1962D
Anne Klein Collection boutique, Saks Fifth
  Avenue, New York, *1994*
Anne Klein shops, 1995D
Anns, Kenneth, 1927D
Another Chance for Housing, 1973E
Anscombe, Isabelle, 1984B
Antine, Anthony, 1993D, 1994D, 1998D
Antine house, Ft. Lee, NJ, 1993D
Apollo, 1925M
Appelbaum, Ralph, 1993A, 2000A, 2000H
Apple Computer, 2000H
Applegate, Joseph, 1936B
Arad, Ron, 1985D, 1987D, 1988D, 1989F, 1991D,
  1993D, 1993F, 1994D, 1994F, 1996F

PICTURE CREDITS

Key: l = left, r = right, c = center, t = top, b = bottom.

Alvar Aalto: 76r, 109rb, 127r. Stanley Abercrombie: 35l, 127lt, 132rt, 168c, 179l, 179r, 182r, 189r. Museum of Arts & Design, New York: 18r, 36r. The American Federation of Arts, New York: 23, 29r, 67r, 78, 84ct. Arxiu MAS, Institut Amatller d'Art Hispànic, Barcelona: 27r, 35rb, 11, 45lt. Avery Library, Columbia University: 34l. Babey Moulton Jue & Booth (Phil Toy): 217l. Luis Barragán: 174c. Barbara Barry (Dominique Vorillon): 224lt. Thomas Bartlett: 204l. Bauhaus-Archiv Berlin: 81; (Erich Consemüller) 51. B&B Italia: 156rb, 164c, 178, 186r, 194lt. Barbara Beckmann Studio: 198r, 200r. Gretchen Bellinger: 64c, 192l. Brahl Fotografi, Copenhagen: 105rt, 113r. Marcel Breuer and Associates: 5, 55r, 62l, 66l, 69l, 69rt, 69rb, 79r, 85, 89r, 150l, 157r; (Kurt Blum) 154l; (Carla de Benedetti) 145l; (Yves Guillemaut) 160r; (Shin Koyama) 141l, (Bon Schnall) 121l. British Art Center, New Haven, Connecticut (Tom Brown): 159. British Museum: 15r, 16l, 18ct, 20lb, 25r, 31l, 21r. Mario Buatta: 173r, 198lb; (Ted Hardin) 204r; (Pallas Photo) 222lb. Buch und Tun, Gütersloh: 140r. Cassina USA: 42c, 82c, 130l, 166r, 167c, 171r, 172rt, 173l, 175, 185l, 189lb, 196rb. Chicago Historical Society (Hedrich-Blessing): 25l, 103r, 112l. Chrysler Museum: 20lt. Clodagh Design International: 218lb. Christie's Images: 37r, 162rt. Country Life: 17r, 29l. Cranbrook Archives: 49l. Arthur De Mattos Casas: 215. Design Within Reach: 220rb, 221r. Elsie De Wolfe: 49r. Orlando Diaz-Azcuy: 196c. Donghia (E. Addeo): 200l, 214c. Dover Pictorial Archive: 20r. Dorothy Draper & Co. Inc.: 70l, 88l, 88r, 98rt; (Phil Fein) 04r; (Hedrich-Blessing) 96lb. © ESTO: (Peter Aaron) 36l, 77r, 170r, 196l, 213, 216lt; (Scott Frances) 206l; (Guggenheim Museum, New York) 200r; (Wolfgang Hoyt) 177r, 186l, 194r; (Peter Mauss) 205r; (Roberto Schezen) 24, 71r; (Ezra Stoller) 61r, 89l, 90r, 92c, 107r, 117r, 124l, 126, 129, 131, 132l, 146r, 152r, 153l, 157l, 162rb, 166c, 172l, 177r, 186l, 194r. Anna Castelli Ferrieri: 179c. Fisher Weisman (Paul Margolies): 222c. Fondation Le Corbusier, Paris: 68l. Samuel T. Freeman & Co., Philadelphia: 33, 13l. Barry Friedman Ltd.: 22lt. Fundació Mies van der Rohe: 58rt, 71l. © Galerie de Beyrie, New York: 122c. Gensler: 193lb, 224lb. Alexander Girard: 130l. The Glasgow Picture Library (Eric Thorburn): 19r. Glasgow School of Art: 47l. Walter Gropius: 34rt, 42l. Solomon R. Guggenheim Museum, New York: (Robert E. Mates) 115. Cedric Hartman: 151r, 160l. © Hedrich-Blessing: 142c, 184r, 206c, 206r, 208l; (Christopher Barrett) 201lt, 201lb, 225r; (Jim Hedrich) 166l; (Elbert Hubbard) 36c; (Marco Lorenzetti) 2, 74lt; (Nick Merrick) 199r; (Jon Miller) 192r, 201r, 209l, 214r. ICF, New York: 22lb, 34rb, 41ll, 84l, 86r, 87rt, 107l, 122r, 187r. Instituto Italiano di Cultura: 140l. *Interior Design* magazine: 61l, 80r, 106rt, 133l, 142l, 155l, 174l; (Kenn Duncan Ltd.) 191rt. Carolyn Iu: 212ct. Iu + Bibliowicz (Prasert Panyuenyong P. N. Studio): 217r. Arne Jacobsen: 163. Louis Kahn: 164l. Knoll: 90lt, 90lb, 98l, 101rt, 106l, 111r, 116rt, 120rt, 128cb, 130r, 148l, 191rb, 207, 221l; (Earl Woods) 124rt. Naomi Leff & Associates Inc.: 216lb; (Michael Mundy) 216r. Library of Congress, Gottscho-Schleisner Archives: 74r, 82r, 86lb, 97, 100, 101rb, 109l, 110rb, 119lt, 119r, 122l, 125r, 128l, 135r, 138c. Alen MacWeeney, Lester Dundes: 193lt. Maison Gerard, New York: 54r, 56lt, 56lb, 60rt, 63, 68r, 79lt; (David Zadeh) 64rb, 74lb. Ingo Maurer: 150c, 218lt. Bernard Maybeck: 37l. Norman McGrath: 40, 154c. Metropolitan History, New York: 16r. Metropolitan Museum of Art: 82lt; (Purchase, bequest of Emily Crane Chadbourne, 1972) 42r; (Gift of the estate of Ogden Codman, Jr., 1951) 18cb; (Gift in honor of his mother, Mrs. Theodore Robert Gamble and Lita Annenberg Hazen Charitable Trust Gifts, 1983) 56c; (Purchase, Theodore R. Gamble, Jr., gift in honor of his mother, Mrs. Theodore Robert Gamble, 1982) 66c. Herman Miller: 80l, 101c, 104, 110rt, 112r, 113l, 116l, 120rb, 121r, 123lb, 124rb, 125lt, 128rb, 134l, 135l, 141rt, 145r, 147, 151l, 154r, 149, 190l, 203; (Michael Booth) 108r; (Charles Eames) 116rb, 118r, 143r; (Effective Images) 105l; (Baltazar Korab) 143; (Olivier Mourgue) 156l; (Ezra Stoller) 106rb; (Phil Schaafsman) 118lt, 183rb; (Earl Woods) 105rb, 128rt. Michael Moran: 225l. Musée des Arts Décoratifs, Paris: 38l, 54l, 58rb. The Museum of Finnish Architecture, Helsinki: 149r; (Ezra Stoller) 92r; (Hayas) 91. Museum of the City of New York (Byron Collection): 17l, 22r, 35rt, 38r, 39l, 41r; (McKim, Mead & White Collection) 13r, 18l, 26r, 30l. Museum of Modern Art, New York: 53l, 64l, 75, 83, 98rb, 99r, 117l, 119lb, 182l; (Alexander Georges) 127c; (Gift of Edgar Kaufmann, jr.) 20c, 102; (Gift of Philip Johnson) 46l; (The Mies van der Rohe Archive): 67l. National Academy of Design: 44. National Monuments Record: (Millar & Harris) 92l. National Trust for Scotland, reproduced by kind permission: 28r. Netherlands Architecture Institute, Rotterdam: (J. Oosterhuis): 12l. Collection of The New-York Historical Society: 19l, 26l. Verner Panton: 177l. Parsons School of Design, The Anna-Maria and Stephen Kellen Archives: 76l, 79lb. I. M. Pei: 176r. Gaetano Pesce: 161, 165l. Peter Paige: 185r, 191l, 195l, 196rt, 197r, 205l, 210l, 210r, 211l, 214l, 219r, 220l. Mary Petty: 125lb. PF-Studio, Helsinki: 170l. Photo Pascal Perquis: 39r. Photofest, New York: 70r. Leslie Piña: 39c. Pollack (Maryanne Solensky): 209r, 222r. John Portman & Associates (Alexandre Georges): 153r. Louis Poulsen: 103l, 109rt, 112c, 123r, 146l, 149l, 183rt, 195r. Harvey Probber: 156rt, 171lb, 187l. © Pucci International Photo: 49rt, 60rb, 63r, 64rt, 65, 82lb, 84cb, 99l. Andrée Putman: (Todd Eberle) 216c; (Deidi von Schaewen) 66r, 181, 188l, 189lt, 190rb, 212r. George Ranalli (Catherine Bogert): 212cb. Gerrit Rietveld: 60l, 144l. Willy Ronis, MBA: 139. Jacques-Emile Ruhlmann: 56r. Eliel Saarinen: 31r, 48l. John Saladino: 164r, 197l. F. Schumacher: 27l, 45r, 77l, 118lb, 123lt, 128rt, 171lt. Kurt Schwitters: 59l. Harry Seidler & Associates: 167r, 174r, 193r, 224r; (Max Dupain) 111l. Shelton Mindel: (Dan Cornish) 212l; (Michael Moran) 218c. Gwathmey Siegel: 172rb. Silz, Günter: 162lt. Skidmore, Owings, & Merrill: 87l. The Society for the Preservation of New England Antiquities, Boston: 14c, 151. SOM: 148c, 148r, 188rt; (Alexandre Georges) 141rb; (Joseph Molitor) 138r; (Dan Morgan) 120l; (Lawrence Williams) 144rb. Ettore Sottsass: 156c, 184l. Philippe Starck: 199l. Steelcase: 46rt, 55l, 142r, 144rt. Tim Street-Porter: 176l. Strong Museum, Rochester, New York © 2002: 25c, 43l. Swanke Hayden Connell: 222lt. Tecno: 194lb. TLCR Associates: (Jaime Ardiles-Arce) 188rb; (Alexandre Georges) 183l; (Todd Lee) 167l, 194c. University of Glasgow, Mackintosh Collection, Hunterian Art Gallery: 12r, 14r, 22c, 46rb. University of Rochester Libraries, Department of Rare Books, Special Collections and Preservation: 45lb. Venturi Scott Brown and Associates: (Matt Wargo) 223r. Virginia Museum of Fine Arts: 41lb, 49lb, 30l. Vitra Design Museum, Birsfelden, Germany: 110l, 134r, 137, 165r, 218r; (Barragán Archives) 108l; (Richard Bryant) 211r; (Nelson Archives) 95; (Terragni Archives): 73, 86lt. Voysey, C.F.A.: 14l. VSBA: (Tom Bernard) 168l; (Drawing by Robert Venturi and Gared Clark) 152l; (Cervin Robinson) 168r. Fisher Weisman (Bard Martin): 184c. Gary Wheeler: 223l. Wilsonart Decorative Metals: 198lt. Vicente Wolf: 220rt. Frank Lloyd Wright Home and Studio Foundation: 28l, 87rb; (Hedrich-Blessing) 30r. Frank Lloyd Wright Preservation Trust, Oak Park, Illinois: 21l, 43r, 52, 57. Russel Wright: 93. Zanotta: 162lb, 162c; (Masera) 96r; (Marino Ramazzotti) 152c, 155r; (Ramazzotti & Stucchi) 190rt. Zographos, Nicos (George Papantonlun): 150r.